THE CAPTAIN'S BEST MATE

Journal of
Whaling voyage of
Ship Addison of
New Bedford. Mass.
Captain Samuel Lawrence.

Written by Mrs. Samuel Lawrence
(The Captain's best "mate".)
Vol 1.

The Captain's Best Mate

THE JOURNAL OF
Mary Chipman Lawrence
ON THE WHALER
Addison
1856–1860

EDITED BY STANTON GARNER

PUBLISHED FOR BROWN UNIVERSITY PRESS
BY UNIVERSITY PRESS OF NEW ENGLAND
HANOVER AND LONDON

University Press of New England
Brandeis University
Brown University
Clark University
University of Connecticut
Dartmouth College
University of New Hampshire
University of Rhode Island
Tufts University
University of Vermont

© 1966 by Brown University
Second printing, University Press of New England, 1986

Printed in the United States of America

LIBRARY OF CONGRESS CATALOGING-IN-PUBLICATION DATA

Lawrence, Mary Chipman, 1827–
    The captain's best mate.

    Includes index.
    1. Lawrence, Samuel.   2. Whalers (Persons)—
Massachusetts—Biography.   3. Lawrence, Mary Chipman,
1827–   .   4. Whalers' wives—Massachusetts—
Biography.   I. Garner, Stanton.   II. Title.
SH20.L38L38   1986   639'.28'0922 [B]   83–40018
ISBN 0–87451–366–9

Maps in this book were drawn by Sam H. Bryant, Marblehead, Massachusetts

This edition is dedicated to
FRANCIS FREEMAN JONES
whose dignity, integrity, and
irrepressible good humor keep alive
the spirit of Mary Lawrence's
New England

Preface

Mary Chipman Lawrence wrote her journal during a three and one-half year whaling voyage, and it is in her narrative that this book's interest lies. However, in the Introduction, Epilogue, Appendixes, and Notes I have attempted to add as much circumstantial information about her experience as is practicable and relevant, for the purpose of placing this single whaling voyage in the larger context of the busy Pacific Ocean of the 1850's. For this information I am indebted to a number of sources besides such standard works as Alexander Starbuck's *History of the American Whale Fishery*.

The most remarkable and unexpected source is a rare tract by Mrs. Helen E. Brown, *A Good Catch; or, Mrs. Emerson's Whaling-Cruise*, published in Philadelphia in 1884 by the Presbyterian Board of Publication. This Christian tale was inspired by letters and a visit to Mrs. Lawrence from one of the *Addison*'s crew many years after the Civil War, when the voyage itself was a dimming memory. The crewman was Edward Leighton, a runaway English boy from London, who had given his address in the *Addison*'s shipping articles as St. Johnsbury, Vermont. Leighton credited the Lawrences with reconciling him with his family, claiming that the presence of the mother and daughter on the ship had set him once again to thinking of his loved ones at home. As a result, he had returned to England and made peace with his parents, and by the time of his visit to the Lawrences' Brooklyn home he had become a respected merchant ship officer. Mrs. Brown, a minor but prolific author of inspirational tracts with whom Mrs. Lawrence had become acquainted, was so captivated by the adventurous voyage and its evangelical outcome that, with some advice and guidance from Mrs. Lawrence, she constructed the plot of *A Good Catch* on the framework of the journal and the Leighton incident. It was perhaps inevitable that in the process the genuine, dependable Leighton, who had on more than one occasion during the voyage rendered indispensable services to Captain Lawrence, was transmuted into a ne'er-do-well lad named Aleck Fielding who, prior to his reclamation, was perpetually in trouble aboard ship and ashore. Many of the passages of the book are direct quotations from the journal; others seem to be based on Mary Lawrence's own recollections and are included in the Notes and Appendixes. *A Good Catch* was discovered almost by accident in the valuable Morse Whaling Collection of the Brown University Library.

A journal kept by George L. Bowman during the last cruise of the voyage has also been used to amplify Mrs. Lawrence's journal. Bowman, a native of Falmouth, had by coincidence sailed from Fairhaven as a boatsteerer aboard the *Sharon* on the day of the *Addison's* departure from New Bedford, across the Acushnet River. Captain Lawrence shipped him for "a cruise and home" during the *Addison's* last stop at the Sandwich Islands, promoting him to third mate in the process (apparently as a favor, since he could then sign on his next whaler as an officer). His journal (and another journal he kept aboard the *Sharon*) is now in the Nicholson Whaling Collection of the Providence (Rhode Island) Public Library.

Mrs. Lawrence's journal was written on the tall blue pages (8 by 13 5/16 inches) of two otherwise blank books of the sturdy type used for whaling logs. Writing in a neat but compact hand, with the elaborate capital letters of her era, she filled 160 pages of the first volume and 60 pages of the second. She was an educated, naturally gifted stylist. It has therefore seemed appropriate to normalize her few departures from modern usage in spelling, capitalization, and punctuation (but not in grammar) and to correct silently her rare slips of the pen. These principles have also been followed in transcribing all other manuscript materials which appear in the Appendixes and Notes. However, modern equivalents have not been substituted for archaic geographical terms. (See the Glossary of Obscure Geographical Terms, Appendix F.)

Mr. Francis F. Jones, of Palto Alto, California, first brought the manuscript to my attention. It had reached Mr. Jones, grandson of Mrs. Lawrence's brother Charles Chipman, through his family and is now on deposit in the Nicholson Collection. Mr. Jones, through whose courtesy the journal has been published, also provided me with a great deal of background material, a letter from Charles Chipman to Mrs. Lawrence, and two photographs of Mrs. Lawrence and Minnie.

Two other persons have been of particular assistance. Mrs. Ruth W. Sterling, the gracious and resourceful secretary of the Falmouth Historical Society, has been a steady source of information and encouragement throughout the preparation of this edition. She was able to provide me with the private account or "slop" book of Samuel Lawrence (also used on other voyages by his brothers, paper being scarce) and other papers in the archives of the Society, and with two photographs of the Lawrences, which she located after all hope of finding them had been abandoned. In addition to her time and materials, Mrs. Sterling also contributed recollections of Mrs. Lawrence, Minnie, and the last of the aging Falmouth whaling captains. Mr. Carleton R. Richmond, of Little Compton, Rhode Island, grandson of the *Addison*'s agent, generously allowed me to inspect and use the marvelously detailed records of the voyage and provided certain facts about his grandfather, Deacon Isaac Bailey Richmond.

Mr. Reginald B. Hegarty, curator of the Melville Whaling Room of the New Bedford Free Public Library and the major source of first-hand whaling information in the country, has rendered invaluable assistance with his knowledge and memories of whaling and with his remarkable records of the industry. Mr. Grant Dugdale, director of the Brown University Press, and Professor Robert C. Kenny of Brown University have been most helpful with their counsel about various aspects of this edition, as has Mr. Stuart C. Sherman, librarian of the Providence Public Library, through whose courtesy portions of the journal of George L. Bowman are included here. The scrupulous eye and lively imagination of Mrs. Sandra Magrath of the Brown University Press have been indispensable.

I would like to acknowledge the research assistance of Mr. James Patrick Dillon; Mr. Lewis Lawrence, grandson of Captain Lewis H. Lawrence; Mr. Milford Lawrence, trustee of the Oak Grove Cemetery in Falmouth; Messrs. Philip F. Purrington, George Bowditch, and Howard P. Nash, Jr., of the Old Dartmouth Historical Society whaling museum, New Bedford, Massachusetts; Mr. Edouard A. Stackpole of the Mystic Seaport, Mystic, Connecticut; Mr. David Jonah, director of libraries of

PREFACE

Brown University; Mr. Gerald W. Gillette, research historian of the Presbyterian Historical Society, Philadelphia, Pennsylvania; Mr. Charles S. Cantwell of the Herkimer (New York) *Evening Telegram*; the staffs of the New York Public Library, the Brooklyn Public Library, the Sturgis Library, Barnstable, Massachusetts, and the Library of Congress; and especially Mrs. Hazel C. Atwood and her energetic colleagues of the Falmouth Public Library. I would like to acknowledge also the valuable assistance in preparing the text rendered by Mrs. Harriet Mayerson and Mr. J. Courtney Sheehan. Many others too numerous to acknowledge by name have given incidental aid along the way. The assistance of these generous people is greatly appreciated. They are responsible for most of the excellence of this book and none of its blemishes.

S. G.

Contents

ILLUSTRATIONS AND MAPS

ILLUSTRATIONS

Frontispiece
From the Title Page of Mary Lawrence's Journal

Following page xvi
Mary and Minnie Lawrence

Minnie Lawrence in the Sandwich Islands

Captain Samuel Lawrence

Mary Lawrence in Later Years

MAPS

[*Geographical names are in the form given in the text. See Appendix F for modern equivalents.*]

Introduction

New England sailing ships of the eighteenth and nineteenth centuries sought out and killed giant whales in the farthest and most inaccessible seas. The courage and determination of the men who sailed them and the privation and isolation which they voluntarily endured are unparalleled in American history, even in the better publicized exploits of the frontier scouts and pioneer settlers. The impunity of the whalemen's challenge to the forces of nature was astounding: they sailed often uncharted waters aboard fragile wooden ships, from islands inhabited by unfriendly natives to the Arctic ice pack, weathering deafening gales to pursue the mightiest animal which has ever inhabited the earth. Nor were the whalemen's profits commensurately great: the most difficult and dangerous voyage was often a financial failure.

The vicissitudes of whaling were well known to Captain Samuel Lawrence and his wife Mary, for his only previous command had ended in disaster. He had returned from his earliest known voyage, as mate of the *Magnolia,* at the beginning of 1845 and had remained ashore at Falmouth, Massachusetts, for the next two and a half years, building a home and courting and marrying Miss Mary Chipman. At the end of 1847 he returned to the sea as master of the sperm whaler *Lafayette,* of New Bedford. He cruised off the west coast of South America until 1850, when, while approaching an anchorage off the Galápagos Islands, the *Lafayette* struck a rock and sank.[1]

This accident temporarily ended Samuel Lawrence's career as a whaling captain, for in 1851 he could find no berth higher than mate of the *Eliza Adams.* When he was later hired to command the *Addison,* it was only after the contracted captain had defaulted. She was a typical middle-sized whaler. One hundred and eight feet long, with two decks, three square-rigged masts, a square stern, and the figurehead of a woman, the Philadelphia-built ship had sailed both as a merchantman and as a whaler, and had sperm whaled in 1848 under the command of Samuel's brother Thomas Lawrence. Thomas had retained a two thirty-seconds share in the ship, and it may have been through his influence that Samuel was given this second chance as a master, making it possible for his wife and daughter to accompany him.[2]

The decision to sail or not to sail with her husband must have been a difficult one for a wife to make, for the dangers and discomforts of a whaling voyage were great. But wives who stayed at home suffered severely, both from the ever-present specter of widowhood and from the daily fact of prolonged separation. During the "golden age"[3] of adventure and discovery before 1835 whaling wives had waited more or less patiently at home while their husbands engaged in their dangerous occupation half a world away.

Just two years before Mary Lawrence's departure another Falmouth whaling wife had complained to her diary, "We have been married five years and lived together ten months. It is *too bad, too bad*."[4] But in the "age of gold" after 1835 women and children were seen more and more frequently on the decks of whalers by passing merchantmen. Resident families, as well as wives put ashore to wait out the last days of pregnancy, formed New England communities in the kingdom of Hawaii and in the South American ports of Talcahuano, Callao, and Valparaiso. American Protestant missionaries, long outraged by the licentious conduct of carousing whalemen in port, welcomed the ladies as a civilizing influence. According to the Reverend Samuel C. Damon, of Honolulu, in 1858, "A few years ago it was exceedingly rare for a Whaling Captain to be accompanied by his wife and children, but it is now very common. An examination of the list of whalers shows that no less than 42 are now in the Pacific. Just one half of that number are now in Honolulu. The happy influence of this goodly number of ladies is apparent to the most careless observer."[5]

There were precedents within the Lawrence family for Mary Lawrence's decision to be one of the "goodly number of ladies" who accompanied their husbands on whaling voyages. The six sons of Thomas Lawrence, a substantial Falmouth contractor, were all whalemen. The oldest, Joseph, had made only one voyage before joining the gold rush to California, and George, the youngest, never rose higher than mate until after he had abandoned whaling for the merchant trade. But Captain Thomas

Mary and Minnie Lawrence. A daguerreotype taken in 1851 when Minnie was three months old. (Courtesy of Francis Freeman Jones.)

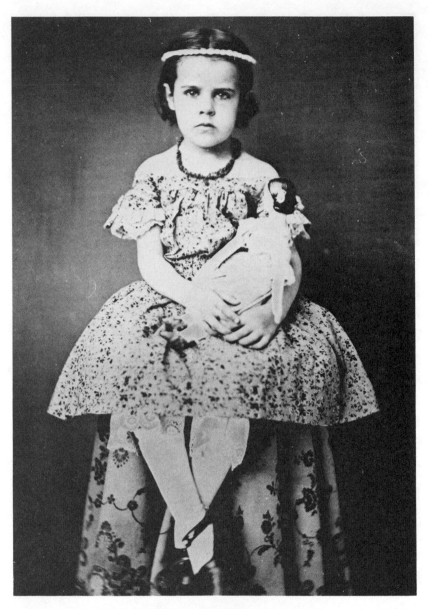

Minnie Lawrence in the Sandwich Islands. Mary Lawrence arranged the
"wreath" in her hair so that she would look like a Kanaka. The picture is
an ambrotype, probably taken by "Mr. Howland, over the *Advertiser*
printing office" in Honolulu. (Courtesy of Francis Freeman Jones.)

Captain Samuel Lawrence, taken while he was in the employ of the Old Dominion Steamship Line, New York City, *ca.* 1885. (Courtesy of the Falmouth Historical Society.)

Mary Lawrence in her last years, probably in Falmouth *ca.* 1900. (Courtesy of the Falmouth Historical Society.)

Lawrence took his wife Mercy to the Pacific in the *Anaconda* and the *Alto;* one daughter was born to them on Pitcairn Island and another at Fayal, the Azores. And Captain Lewis Lawrence's wife Eunice accompanied him on several voyages on the *Commodore Morris,* presenting him with children at Tahiti, Norfolk Island, and Honolulu.[6]

But the fate of the sixth Lawrence brother, Captain Augustus, may well have been the most immediate cause of Mary Lawrence's determination not to be separated from her husband. Five months after Augustus had sailed from New Bedford in the *Java,* leaving behind his wife Sarah and a new baby, he was dead of "lung fever" in Valparaiso. His body was brought home to Falmouth for burial in the family plot just three and a half months before the departure of the *Addison.* It was a grim reminder of the dangers which awaited whalemen. Not that Mary Lawrence was faint of heart. She was resigned to the fact that death was an ever-present shipmate aboard a whaler. But the thought of a lonely death among strangers and burial in an unmarked grave on foreign soil oppressed her, as her journal amply demonstrates. She decided to keep her small family together by sailing on the *Addison.*[7]

We know comparatively few biographical facts about this remarkable woman who with her five-year-old daughter boarded a whaleship in November, 1856. She was nine years younger than her husband, having been born in Sandwich, Massachusetts, in 1827, one of the many children of Jonathan and Celia Chipman. She married Samuel Lawrence in 1847 and bore him their only child Minnie in an interval between his voyages. In appearance she was a small, bright person, not glamorous by modern standards. Like other New England women of Puritan ancestry, she valued ornament of character and spirit rather than of person, and her hair and attire, though not unfashionable, were plain.[8]

However, her journal entries tell us much more about her. They reveal her New England piety, in which there was an occasional dissonant note of pride, her feminine warmth, her wifely subordination, and her deep resources of courage. Her remarks are spiced occasionally by a puckish wit and a sense of the absurd which could enliven the commonest occurrence and restore the daily irritations of life on a whaler to their proper perspective. But they also reveal another facet of her personality, a constant, almost morbid, awareness of the transitory nature of life. In every letter from home she was prepared to receive news of the death of a loved one and, like Emmeline Grangerford in *Huckleberry Finn*, greeted each bereavement with a conventionally facile eulogy. Yet this concern with death was tempered by an awareness, inherited from her Calvinist forebears, of the constant presence and perfect justice of the First Cause who ordered all human events, whose mortal command she was nearly always prepared to accept.

The tension between the demands of the spirit and those of the flesh, the paradoxical longing for the other world of the soul and the commitment to the present material world, which had long been central to the New England experience, was strong in Mary Lawrence. During the early phases of the voyage she was filled with missionary fervor and seemed to have been little concerned with the commercial purpose of the voyage. Believing in the imminent world-wide triumph of Christianity, she carried on board the *Addison* a small spiritual arsenal of books, money, and intentions with which she expected to participate in the final skirmish against beleaguered sin, idolatry, and atheism.

But her hopes were badly treated by the realities she found at her first port of call, Lahaina. There she was forced to admit that the Kanakas, who had long been under missionary influence, were far less "civilized" than she had been led to believe. Nor did her evangelism fare better with the *Addison* crew, for she found that, in spite of their willingness to accept Testaments, several of the crewmen had been locked up in the fort for unrestrained carousing. But nineteenth-century ladylike delicacy was a perishable commodity aboard a Pacific whaler, and during a subsequent visit to the islands she merely commented, "Have had several men in the fort as before." [9] And toward the end of the voyage she could describe with sophisticated objectivity polygamous white men who had gone native on remote islands.

As her initial expectations were disappointed, the practical aspect of her New England character asserted itself in a deep concern for the commercial outcome of the voyage. And with this concern her relation to the mechanics of shipboard life changed. At first a delighted and dignified stranger to housekeeping aboard a ship where female work was not part of the economy, she was restricted in her chores to laundering and mending her own and Minnie's garments and to preparing an occasional table delicacy, which she was not even allowed to put into the oven herself. But in the later stages of the voyage she cooked and served meals while the men were off whaling and cleaned her own quarters. And as the ship approached New Bedford she joined the crew in preparing the ship for entering port.

She had not been long at sea before she began to see her husband in a new light, as the master of a ship. Early in the voyage she wrote, "We are . . . in a little kingdom of our own of which Samuel is prime ruler. I should never have known what a great man he was if I had not accompanied him." [10] Only once, en route from New Bedford to the Pacific whaling grounds, was she tempted to assert wifely authority. On this occasion Captain Lawrence decided to bypass Paita, Peru, where their correspondents had been instructed to address mail. Letters were of first importance during a voyage of this great length, and she confided petulantly to her journal that "it will be a great disappointment to me, but of course I have nothing to say about it. But our letters that were to be sent to Paita will remain there, I suppose, and much good will they do us. I want oil as much as any of them, but it is hard telling just what to do." [11] Mary Lawrence spoke consistently in a public voice, despite the protest in her initial entry that she had no intention of interesting anyone outside of her own private family, and this near mutiny was one of her few lapses into a personal voice.

The journal reveals surprisingly little of the child Minnie. She appears to us through those occasional engaging remarks and activities her mother thought worth recording, but these tell us less about the girl than about the constant companionship and influence of her mother. Minnie's mission to the forecastle, her hopeful attempt to speak the word which would calm the waters, her desire to exhume the body of Moses, and her belief that it could not be corrupted suggest the pervasively religious atmosphere of the women's quarters. Yet their devout lives were not gloomy. Mother and daughter washed and sewed together, played together, and watched the various occupations of the seamen. They observed the holidays, and though the *Addison*'s fortunes did not always flourish, Minnie's Christmas stocking was always filled. And on All Fools' Day the crew conspired to enjoy Minnie's pranks. Yet behind these vignettes there is another Minnie, a silent spectator in the background of events, an often lonely little stoic asked too early to join an adult world in which she was necessarily an afterthought, a grave witness to the grim combat between man and leviathan.

Mary Lawrence does not give detailed descriptions of the routine of a whaler and the mechanics of whale killing and processing so faithfully recorded in Eliza Williams' contemporary journal.[12] Nor does she communicate girlish experiences with the semiliterate directness of Annie Ricketson's diary.[13] She gives instead an overview of the whaling armada and sees its pursuit of leviathan as the great epic it was.

Perhaps more than any document of its kind, her journal recreates for us the people and places of the Pacific in the mid-nineteenth century. In it she captures the whalemen's hopes and despair, their piety and Yankee shrewdness, describes their business and social lives, and, most of all, conveys a sense of the great community which transcended their competitive individualism, binding them together in an alliance against ever-threatening disaster. She sketches nineteenth-century Hawaii, Siberia, Cape Horn, the Arctic, New Zealand, and the Marquesas. She introduces us to scores of captains and occasionally to cabin boys, mates, and boatsteerers. She gives us glimpses of the royal family of the Hawaiian kingdom, the Kanaka missionaries on their remote island stations, and even some of the whalemen from Europe.

But most memorable in the cast of characters are the tall ships, whose recurring names help to give an epic dimension to her journal. There are ships with patriotic names (*Congress, America, General Scott, Dr. Franklin, Massachusetts*), wives' and children's names (*George and Susan, Martha, Mary Frazier*), the names of famous whaling families (*Jireh Swift, Levi Starbuck, William C. Nye*), heroic and mythological names (*Young Hero, Black Warrior, Tamerlane, Hercules, Marengo*), exotic names (*Arab, Euphrates, Rajah*), and literary names (*Addison, Rousseau, Goethe*). Most amusing are the ship names which express the commercial hopes of their sponsors, sometimes in puns (*Kingfisher, Midas, Enterprise, Fortune, Good Return, Harvest, Lancer, Speedwell, Nimrod*). Ships appear, disappear, and reappear, sometimes after a return to New England and a change of masters. Occasionally a ship develops a peculiar character of its own. Its share of the catch is usually noted, often by the exact number of whales and barrels of oil it has taken. The captains also have their individuality: old and greedy, young and sociable, convinced that they are bewitched, or overdependent on the "intoxicating cup."

In Mary Lawrence's own epic the great battle—the Cape Thaddeus cut of June, 1859—took place at a distance from the *Addison*. Of this cut, which yielded half a normal voyage's supply of oil to the ships lucky enough to have participated, she wrote, "I have never felt so heartsick in my life . . ." [14] The Cape Thaddeus cut assumed such great proportions in her imagination that thereafter she divided whalers into two classes: those which had shared in the windfall and those which had not. For the former she had no pity, no matter how poor their subsequent luck. The latter she believed deserved every whale they could bring alongside. Because the *Addison* missed this great good fortune, it was necessary to extend the voyage for an additional southern cruise, which was ironically unsuccessful. Like Ulysses, the Lawrences were condemned to a season of fruitless wandering before they were permitted to return to their native land.

The voyage of the *Addison*, begun on a rising note of optimism, thus ended on a minor chord of disappointment. [15] But the fortunes of the Lawrences were symbolic of the larger course of the industry, for the watershed of American whaling occurred during the *Addison's* voyage. All before had been expansion and development of new weapons, new whaling grounds, and new tactics for finding and attacking whales. All afterward was decline, retrenchment, a waiting for the end. The gallant whaling fleet and the heroic whalemen, captured at the moment of their greatest success, give the pages of Mary Lawrence's journal epic character. Among the thousands of whaling logs and journals which have survived, few are as distinctive, articulate, perceptive, and engaging as the narrative Mary Lawrence began to write not long after the *Addison* cast off from the steam tug *Spray* and headed out to sea from New Bedford on the morning of November 25, 1856.

"Samuel is all the world to me, and why should we live with half the globe between us? We have been married ten years, and for two-thirds of that time oceans and continents have separated us, and we have both decided that it shall be so no longer. From this time, where he goes I shall go; and my happiness will be in making him a home wherever business calls him."

—MRS. HELEN E. BROWN, *A Good Catch,* p. 12

FIRST CRUISE

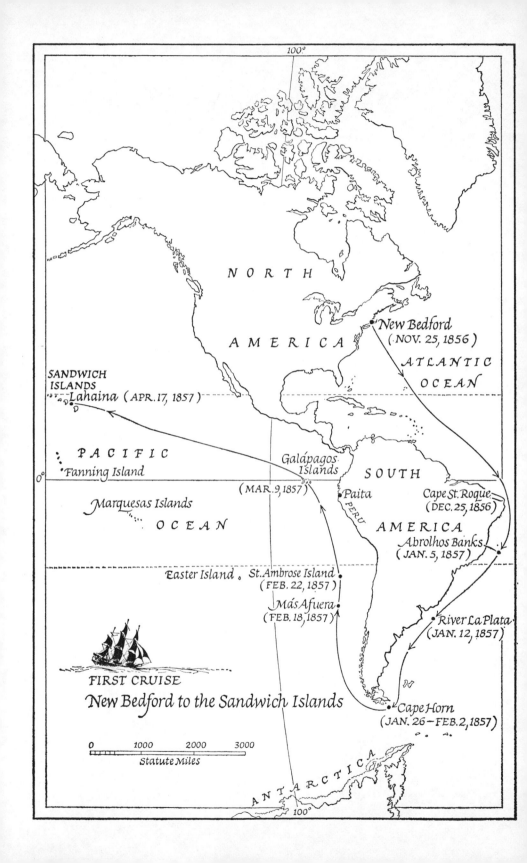

NORTH

AMERICA

New Bedford
(NOV. 25, 1856)

ATLANTIC

OCEAN

SANDWICH
ISLANDS
Lahaina (APR. 17, 1857)

PACIFIC

Fanning Island

Galápagos
Islands
(MAR. 9, 1857)

SOUTH

Paita

PERU

Cape St. Roque
(DEC. 25, 1856)

Marquesas Islands

OCEAN

AMERICA

Abrolhos Banks
(JAN. 5, 1857)

Easter Island St. Ambrose Island
(FEB. 22, 1857)

Más Afuera
(FEB. 18, 1857)

River La Plata
(JAN. 12, 1857)

FIRST CRUISE
New Bedford to the Sandwich Islands

Cape Horn
(JAN. 26 – FEB. 2, 1857)

0   1000   2000   3000
Statute Miles

ANTARCTICA

New Bedford to the Sandwich Islands

NOVEMBER 1856 – APRIL 1857

———————◆·◄◆►·◆———————

NOVEMBER 25 [AND 26]. As this is my first experience in seafaring life, I have thought it advisable to attempt keeping a journal, not for the purpose of interesting anyone out of my own private family, but thinking it might be useful to myself or my child for future reference. We left New Bedford on the morning of the twenty-fifth of November, 1856, with a sad heart, knowing not whether we should ever behold the faces of friends near and dear to us again on earth. God grant we may all meet in that better land where the parting tear is never shed, the word good-by never spoken. We had a good wind from the eastward and a fine sail down the bay, out into the wide ocean which is to be my home for months and years to come. Went on deck before dark to take my last look at my native land. With what different feelings shall I behold it should I be permitted to return.

The next day was sick more or less throughout the day. Got over it before night, but Minnie's seasickness lasted throughout the next day. We were very fortunate in getting over it as we did, for we had exceedingly rough weather for ten days, a constant gale from the west. Not much transpired during that time except the ordinary duty on board ship. Each one had as much as he could do to look out for himself. As for Minnie and myself, we were obliged to sit in our bed the whole time, except as we went on deck. It was of no use for us to attempt to sit up in the cabin, for we were tossed from one side to the other without the least mercy.

NOVEMBER 27. Thanksgiving at home. What a pity we could not have remained at home until after that event. We all thought we

[3]

should relish a plate of Grandma's[1] nice turkey for dinner as we were sitting on deck but had no appetite for anything they had here. I delight to be on deck and watch the ocean in its varying moods. Truly, "they that go down to the sea in ships, that do business in great waters, see the works of the Lord and his wonders in the deep. For he commandeth and raiseth the stormy wind, which lifteth up the waves thereof. They mount up to the heaven and go down again into the depths." [2] It sometimes seems impossible that we can live through it, but our gallant ship rides along fearlessly. It is grand beyond anything I ever witnessed, sublimity itself.

DECEMBER 1. The first day of winter seems not much like it with us. How I should enjoy a calm day. Think I shall get accustomed to gales if this continues much longer.

DECEMBER 5. One year today since dear brother Augustus left home and friends to embark on the ocean. In five short months he found a stranger's grave, far away from wife, children, and friends; stranger hands bathed his brow and cooled his parched tongue. It is a satisfaction to surviving friends that his remains could be brought home and placed in a spot of his own selection.[3]

DECEMBER 7. Another Sabbath has dawned upon us. It seems somewhat different from the other days, even here. No one unnecessarily employed, most of the company engaged in reading, it *seems* like a day of rest. But no Sabbath bell greets our ear, no holy man of God proclaims to us the glad tidings of the Gospel. They may be found when diligently sought for, and a Sabbath well spent at sea, in communing with our own hearts and reading God's holy Word, may be productive of much good.[4]

DECEMBER 8. Moderates a little. Well, that is enough to be thankful for. We have had a long gale and been tossed about enough to appreciate good weather when it does make its appearance. Saw two birds flying about the ship, which seemed much like home. They were tropic birds.

DECEMBER 10. Had a very still night, and today it is delightful—a pleasant breeze and just warm enough for comfort. Went on deck immediately after breakfast to view old Ocean in another aspect. Everything is smiling and serene; one would never suspect the treachery that lurks in his bosom. Everything seems changed. This is one of the most delightful moments of my life. I do not wonder that so many choose a sailor's life. It is a life of hardship, but it is a life full of romance and interest. As I went on deck, the first sight that greeted my eyes was the pigs and chickens running about at large on deck. Altogether they made an appearance so homelike that I could hardly realize that I was thousands of miles away from home.

DECEMBER 21. For the last ten days nothing of interest has transpired. During the most of our passage the sea has been rather rough and the wind not very favorable. Occasionally we catch a glimpse of a distant vessel, and as we are going different directions, they soon vanish, and we are left alone, a solitary speck on the ocean. Several days ago several dolphins were following the ship for some time, but they did not succeed in catching any of them, to my disappointment. Flying fish are very plenty. One flew over the side of the ship one day, and the steward cooked him for my breakfast. Was very nice; tasted some like a fresh herring. Have seen none of those monsters of the deep yet, although occasionally we hear from the masthead the cry of "There blows!"

DECEMBER 22. We are now nearly to the line. It is very warm indeed, not much, I imagine, like the weather at home. Minnie enjoys herself very much, running about on deck and making new acquaintances. Her little heart swells sometimes when she thinks of her dear friends she left behind. Yesterday I broke a wishbone with her; she wished that she could see Aunt Susan.[5]

DECEMBER 23. Nothing of interest occurred except catching a few fish of the kind called skipjack, not the nicest that ever were caught, but very good in the absence of better. We live very well. Many on the land would be glad to have the luxuries which we enjoy. There is one luxury which I will note in my journal, for fear that I may forget it when I get home and provide for the table myself: a pumpkin with a round piece cut out at the top to take the seeds and inside out, then filled up with stuffing and the little cap put on again, and stewed. It comes on the table whole with the stem in the center of the cap.

DECEMBER 24. A very pleasant day, but we are not going as we would wish. Are too near Cape St. Roque; expect to have to beat in order to get by. We have a very good steward but are not as fortunate with our cooks. Are trying the fourth now (five weeks out). The first was good for nothing; the second did not like being in the galley—it made his head ache; the third had sore hands, so that he could not perform duty; and I cannot say what will befall the fourth.

DECEMBER 25. Christmas. It seems to me very much as if it had come in July, instead of December. We generally associate Christmas with cold weather. Minnie hung up her stocking last night. She was fearful that she should get nothing in it, as we could not go to the store, but she succeeded as well for eatables as if she had been at home. We had quite a Christmas dinner: roast chickens, stuffed, potatoes, turnips, onions, stewed cranberries, pickled beets and cucumbers, and a plum duff.[6] For tea I had a tin of preserved grape opened and cut a loaf of fruitcake. The twenty-fifth of November I went on deck before dark to take my last look at my native land (for the present) and tonight (just a month) went to take my first look at a foreign land. Cape St. Roque is in sight, so we shall have to beat tonight.

DECEMBER 26. A ship in sight at a distance in the same predicament that we are. Misery loves company. Minnie is very happy. I think she enjoys herself as well as if she were at home. She came to me the other day to know if, when she got old enough to read writing, I would write on a piece of paper what things she must not do, because she was afraid she would forget; and then she could look at her paper and read, "Minnie must not do so, for it is not right." I hope she will always be as conscientious as she is. I feel that if she is not brought up aright, the sin will be my own. She has a mind capable of receiving good impressions, and it can be very easily molded. What a responsibility rests upon a mother:

Yet could a mother's prayer of love,
Thy destiny control,
Those boasted gifts that often prove
The ruin of the Soul:
Beauty and fortune, wit and fame,
For *thee* she would not crave,
But tearful, urge a fervent claim
To joys beyond the grave.

DECEMBER 28. This morning caught a porpoise. The meat looks very much like beef. The oil is contained in the skin, which they will boil out tomorrow. Had some of the meat fried for dinner and some made into sausage cakes for supper. They are as nice as pork sausages. We spoke the ship today, which proved to be the *Grey Eagle* from Philadelphia bound to Buenos Aires. She was thirty-two days from Philadelphia and we thirty-four from New Bedford. She has not beat us much, if she is a clipper.

1857

JANUARY 1. The old year has departed and the new year advances fresh and bright, laden with blessings for all. To many the cup of happiness will be filled to overflowing; to others it will be mixed with sorrow even to the dregs. We may not know what is for us; none but the Unseen can look into futurity, but happy will it be for us if, with every sorrow that is borne to us on the wings of almighty faith and love, we can look up with a sweet and submissive trust and say, "Father, not my will, but thine be done." [7]

The past has been an eventful year to us. A father, brother, and niece have been called to the world of spirits: Infancy, Manhood, and Old Age.[8] We mourn that they have left us, and those far away will mourn when they have heard the sad tidings. Dear sister Sarah and her fatherless children have been called to drink deep of the cup of affliction. May He who is the God of the widow and the Father of the fatherless be very near to them.

We have passed the cape now and go along smoothly. We saw several catamarans out today, fishing, from off the coast. They are small boats made of logs with a sail. We passed one very near with the ship in the evening. We obtained about two gallons of oil from one porpoise. That will be enough to keep us from darkness for a season, perhaps, until we can get some more.

JANUARY 2. I have been writing letters today to have on hand in case we should see an opportunity to send home. I have three on hand now, one for my mother, one for Thomas and Mercy, and one for James and Anna.⁹ I hope they may depart speedily. We see vessels at a distance every day. I delight to watch them as they gallantly pursue their way over the boundless ocean. We are now enjoying moonlight evenings, and there never were any more lovely, I think. There are several very fine voices forward,¹⁰ and they now improve them. "Home Sweet Home" and "Do They Miss Me at Home?" ¹¹ I can appreciate. I have yet to find out that sailors belong to another class than that of human beings. I hope I may be fortunate enough to remain in ignorance of the fact by my own experience. I tell Samuel that I shall not think they are entirely depraved as long as I hear them singing their Psalms tunes.

JANUARY 4. Another Sabbath, mild and lovely. I think of friends at home wending their way to the house of God and wish I could bear them company. After breakfast I generally dress up a little more than on ordinary days and take a book and go on deck; sit there the most of the day. Has been five sail in sight today, one ahead that appears to be a whaler laying to. Think we shall get up to her about sunset; then perhaps we may have company. How I should enjoy it, but I will not make too much dependence.

JANUARY 5. The ship we saw last night was the *Dr. Franklin,* of Westport, Captain Russell, about two months out, clean, an Atlantic whaler. He came on board and passed the evening with us. Mr. Nickerson went on board his ship. When he went back, he sent me about two dozen nice oranges. They were very acceptable. He procured them at Brava.

Samuel talks very strong this morning of proceeding immediately to the Okhotsk Sea instead of sperm whaling a year as he intended. If he does, it will be a great disappointment to me, but of course I have nothing to say about it. But our letters that were to be sent to Paita will remain there, I suppose, and much good will they do us. I want oil as much as any of them, but it is hard telling just what to do. We are now on the Abrolhos Banks. If we should happen to get a whale, think very likely it would change the whole course of proceedings.

Yesterday morning we found one of our hens dead. Minnie said her papa told her it died for "want of breath." I suppose that was the case. Old Mother Grey Neck was her name. Hannah Butler commenced laying Saturday, and two others lay beside. Besides the hens for pets we have two pigs; one we call Juba and the other Wiggie. They are very tame; will let Minnie go up to them and play. There is another whaler in sight; perhaps we may have more company tonight. We treated our captain last night to fruitcake and wine.

JANUARY 12. Have seen no vessel since Monday until yesterday, when we saw one at a distance, and another this morning which was a French ship. Not much of interest transpired during the week with the exception of a change of weather. We have had some rain and considerable rough weather during the time, and it is much cooler, thermometer at 70 degrees. It has been for several weeks back extremely warm and uncomfortable. Yesterday they saw whales from the masthead, but they soon disappeared. I must confess that I was glad; I did not care about their going after their first whales on the Sabbath. I believe it is decided now that we shall make a straight course for the Islands and proceed to the Okhotsk. I hope we may be successful in obtaining what we diligently seek after. My plants that I brought from home, I think, are all dead. I am watching a geranium very narrowly, hoping it may spring up from the root, but I think it very doubtful. I have planted some orange seeds so that I may have something growing. We are now off the River La Plata, which is good whaling ground. It would help along very much if we could get a few barrels.

JANUARY 13. Saw whales this morning. I heard the sound and thought I would go on deck; if there was a whale to be seen, thought I would like to see it. I went, and very soon I saw him blow and then saw the monster turn flukes. He was a formidable creature indeed. The three mates went off in their boats. Samuel remained on board, as there was a squall coming up. How thankful I felt. I almost dreaded seeing whales, as I feared I should feel badly having him go off for the first time before I became accustomed to it. They stayed out until about noon; the whales got out of their way, so they returned to the ship.

Just as we had seated ourselves at the dinner table, the cry of "There blows!" was heard again. They all left the table with a rush. I thought I might as well finish my dinner as I could do no good, so Minnie and myself remained at the table. The three mates went first; then soon after Samuel went with his boat's crew. I saw him go off without fear and wished him good luck. Presently they told me that one of the boats had fastened. We watched them long, but the whale continued to spout.

After a while one of the boats started for the ship. When he arrived, we found it was Mr. Baxter with his boat stoven. Just as they had got on board, I heard the cry of "Another boat stove!" I looked and saw an empty boat. I had not the heart to ask whose boat it was but went down into the cabin. I could stand it no longer. I comforted myself some by thinking if anyone was hurt, they would proceed immediately to the ship. I never was more rejoiced than when I heard Samuel's voice again as he came near the ship with some of Mr. St. John's crew. His boat was stoven, and they were all thrown into the water; the other two boats picked them up. (How it must have dampened the ardor of the new beginners.) Samuel came back to alter the course of the ship, hoping he might recover the stoven boat, in which he was successful. As soon as he arrived, he sent Mr. Baxter off again in his boat.

They all remained off as long as they could see, then were reluctantly obliged to cut from the whale, though not until another boat had been stove. Thus ended our first day's experience. They are some in hopes of getting him yet. (They think with so many irons in him he must die.) I hope they will. We ought to have him to pay for our stoven boats.

JANUARY 14. We kept round in nearly the same place all night and today but have seen nothing of the whale. They think he would have made about 60 barrels. I am told it is very seldom you see such a whale as that; it is a chance if we see another during the voyage.

JANUARY 15. Have made sail again and give up, though very unwillingly, all chance of the whale. We see plenty of birds flying around us, gonies (mallemucks) and Mother Carey's chickens. I like very much to see them as they skim over the water and suddenly disappear beneath the waves.

JANUARY 16. This morning before we were up, the steward came to our door and told us there was a sail near us. Samuel went on deck, came down in a few minutes, and told me to get my letters all ready, for there was a chance of getting near enough to speak her. I needed not to be told twice, so I added a little to my three letters, got them all ready, looked out the cabin window, and saw that she had passed us. She was a Spanish brig. I was exceedingly disappointed. We have had no opportunity as yet of sending letters, and I know my mother, at least, feels very anxious.

JANUARY 17. Nothing of importance occurred today. A school of porpoises came near the ship, but did not succeed in taking any. We need the oil from one very much if we cannot get any whale. We are saving all our oil that we have left now for the binnacle and burning sperm candles now in the cabin that were put on board for trade. I suppose Deacon Richmond[12] thought if we could get no oil before going round the Horn, we might go in darkness. Minnie took her doll this afternoon to look out the cabin window, as she said, to look at the whitecapped billows. "Sarah," says she, "shouldn't you think I would be afraid of those deep, deep billows? Well, I *ain't*, for I know there's Somebody up in heaven that will take care of me."

JANUARY 18. It is the Sabbath again. I miss the privileges I was accustomed to enjoy at home. How little we appreciate the blessings we enjoy until deprived of them. It is cold and rainy today. After tea it cleared away so that we went on deck for a while.

JANUARY 26. Nothing of interest has occurred for the last week, except that we have had cold, stormy, and rough weather; for the last three days I have kept my bed most of the time. Nothing in the cabin has been safe. We are in the vicinity of Cape Horn and have a very unfavorable time to get round. Last night we caught another porpoise, which was very acceptable just now for something fresh as well as the oil.

FEBRUARY 2. We have had a continuation of rough weather all the week. Are about where we were a week ago. The wind is very variable; have been obliged to lay to in a gale several times. I do not like Cape Horn weather at all. It is midsummer here now. We have it very cold with snow and hail. What must their winters be! The long days are something new to me. I can see to read distinctly in my stateroom at bedtime. The sun does not set until after eight o'clock, and when the nights are clear, daylight does not go out at all. We are as comfortable in the cabin as can be expected; have a good fire in the stove. The captain and officers have rather long faces at the prospect of another week here, but perhaps all will come out right in the end.

FEBRUARY 5. We have not made much headway for several days, although today we have entered the broad Pacific. We have head winds and calms besides a great deal of rough weather. I shall be quite glad to leave this country. Today we killed Juba; fresh pork, I think, will taste nice at this time.

FEBRUARY 6. This morning caught two porpoises and fresh meat abounds. There were tears in Minnie's eyes this morning, when we went to the breakfast table, to see her Juba on the dish. I comforted her with the assurance that she should have another one when we arrived in port. She thinks Wiggie must be very lonely. We have had cook number three back again for some time. After his hands got better, they decided that it was all he was good for, as he was so nearsighted he could not steer, neither could he look out for whales. He does not make a first-rate cook. Saw a brig this morning bound in the same direction with us. Probably they have had such a time as we have in getting round.

FEBRUARY 7. Saw a ship today which we passed; but did not speak her. Have had a very rough day; the ship pitched badly. I sat in my bed all day, except as I went out to my meals, preferring that to being moved about in my chair. Minnie does not appear to notice the rough weather at all. She sat in the bed with me a part of the time, hemming a handkerchief for Mr. St. John, and occasionally she would say, "Oh, Mother! Ain't we taking comfort!"

FEBRUARY 8. The ship is much stiller today than she was yesterday, but it is quite rainy. The wind is fair, but it is almost a calm. It has been so these two weeks; when it is fair, there is a calm. We make our way along slowly, but we are advancing. It makes the ship's company feel worse because they are aware that they have no time to lose.

FEBRUARY 9. The weather is cold and rainy. The wind has been fair for a short time. I believe it was only an aggravation to the captain and officers. Two ships are in sight, one astern and one ahead, quite a distance from us.

FEBRUARY 10. It is with a great degree of pleasure that we depart from the rough and storm-beaten shores of Cape Horn, a fitting country for the rude and savage inhabitants who dwell there.[13] A fair wind. Two ships in sight.

FEBRUARY 12. Saw a school of porpoises this afternoon. As the men were hurrying forward preparing to strike them, one of them frightened Hannah Butler, and she flew overboard. As soon as she touched the water, the birds (gonies and mallemucks) dove down in pursuit of her. I felt very sorry, for I have a sort of affection for everything that has life on board, and she had become quite tame. Did not succeed in taking a porpoise.

FEBRUARY 13. Lost sight of the ships that have been near us for several days. Passed an English brig, not near enough to speak. We have had a fair wind for several days and plenty of it, and our gallant *Addison* makes her obeisance to the god of the waters as she plies majestically along. Made 225 miles the last twenty-four hours.

FEBRUARY 14. Caught a porpoise this morning. Have been running with a large clipper ship today. She had a much greater amount of sail out than we, but she did not advance upon us at all. The weather grows warmer now. Soon we shall have the thermometer at 90 degrees again, I suppose. I am making preparations now for going in port. Minnie grows so that I shall be obliged to let down all her clothes that she wore at home last summer. Made 200 miles the last twenty-four hours.

FEBRUARY 15. Another Sabbath of rest, rest for the body and rest for the soul. Let us so live that we may enter into that rest which is prepared for the people of God. Saw another school of porpoises this afternoon. It is a beautiful sight to see the water full of them, jumping about in all directions. They are very pretty fish, especially the right whale porpoise. Went 180 miles today.

FEBRUARY 16. The weather is quite warm today. We have had a regular washing day, the first one for several weeks. I have a small tub which fits in my sink, in which I can wash my small pieces.[14] It is rather cool for me in the house on deck. When it is warmer, I shall go there and assist Samuel in washing. He has a large tub there and a pounding barrel. Saw a school of blackfish this morning about a mile off. Did not lower for them. There is one man sick (John Gadson). I suppose he is in a consumption. He raises a great deal of blood, has a pain in his chest, etc. If he does not get better, shall be obliged to leave him at the Islands. He was a very smart fellow. I pity him. There are but few conveniences in the forecastle of a ship for sickness. Perhaps there are as many as he has been accustomed to in port. He says he was sick all last winter. We set Pinkey today on five eggs. We may have a chicken or two in three weeks.

FEBRUARY 17. Nothing of interest occurred today. Saw a ship in the afternoon. Went on deck in the evening to witness the creative power of our Heavenly Father, and nowhere more than on the ocean can it be displayed—the sky above and the water beneath, "a plank between us and eternity." I never saw the sky so brilliantly bestudded with stars as it is here in this latitude. The Magellan Clouds are also to be seen, two white clouds and a small black one. We are enjoying fine weather now.

FEBRUARY 18. Saw Más Afuera this morning and intended to

touch but, the wind not being fair, decided that it would take more time than we could afford to lose. How welcome the sight of land to a wanderer on the ocean. I longed to climb those cliffs, and Minnie enjoyed it as well. "Why, Mother," said she, "is that ground, really?" The island is very high and presented a fine appearance from the ship with the clouds playing around the heights. Should like very much to have had some of the fish and goats with which the island abounds. Saw one ship near which had sent boats in fishing and another at a distance.

FEBRUARY 19. One ship in sight which we saw yesterday. We are hoping every day to fall in with brother George,[15] as he may be in this vicinity. How pleasant it would be to fall in with friends. We are, as it were, shut out from our friends in a little kingdom of our own of which Samuel is prime ruler. I never should have known what a great man he was if I had not accompanied him. I might never have found it out at home. I think if they do their duty on shipboard, they will have no reason to complain of him. He is the same affectionate husband to me that he has always been. Hope I may continue worthy of his love.

FEBRUARY 20. We are still pursuing the even tenor of our way;[16] nothing occurs to disturb or molest us. The sailors have cheerfully performed their duties thus far, and all has gone on smoothly. I enjoy myself here more and more every day. I never weary of watching old Ocean in his many varying aspects. At one time, it is as still and placid as a lake; scarcely a ripple disturbs the surface of its water. We would never dream of the treachery that lurks in his bosom. Again, the waves rise mountain-high and dash against our noble ship with redoubled fury. Yet still we pursue our way. The mandate has gone forth: "So far shalt thou go and no farther. Here shall thy proud waves be stayed."[17] It is this that I enjoy most to witness; it is sublime beyond conception.

FEBRUARY 21. A ship in sight at a distance. No whales or fish of any kind to be seen. We are on good whale ground now, and I wish we might be so fortunate as to capture one, at least.

FEBRUARY 22. The glorious birthday of our immortal Washington.

Saw the island of St. Ambrose this morning at a distance. A fine wind and a pleasant day, the Sabbath day. In imagination I wend my way to the house of God with friends near and dear. I hope we may pass a Sabbath at the Islands.

FEBRUARY 23. A general washing day again. Minnie has had a little tub made, and she is busily engaged in washing clothes for Sarah Price and Billy. Saw a finback quite near the ship.

FEBRUARY 24. This is the anniversary of my dear brother Walter's birth. Oh, that we knew his fate—of a whole vessel's crew, probably not one was left to tell the sad tale.[18] How little we thought when he left home on that memorable morning, buoyant with youth and exultant with hope, that he never would return. It is hard to give him up, but month after month has elapsed and still no tidings, and it is hoping against hope to indulge a thought that he might have been saved. Poor, dear brother, many loved ones you have left behind who would fain have watched around your bedside and planted blossoms around your grave. Your last sad requiem has been sung by the moaning wind and the murmuring ocean wave:

> The sea, the deep blue sea, has one,
> He lies, where pearls lie, deep.
> He was the loved of all, yet none
> O'er his low bed may weep.

FEBRUARY 25. Three months today since we left home and friends for a "home on the ocean wave." [19] I flatter myself that I have become quite a sailor. Saw a ship this afternoon, at a distance, of course. There are a plenty of birds flying about: Mother Carey's chickens and a kind called boobies.

FEBRUARY 26. It is very still today, almost calm. Her sails flutter loosely about, and the good ship moves on her way very lazily. It is exceedingly warm; the sun beats down upon us, in the absence of the wind, without any mercy.

FEBRUARY 27. Just such a day as we had yesterday, like one of our July days at home. I imagine that our friends at home are rejoicing in a February thaw. What delightful walking. They might, were they to see me, envy my ship's deck. I always have good walking, no great extent of territory, 'tis true, but what I have is always clean and dry. Plank sidewalks are very nice. Saw a school of killers today and killed a couple of skipjacks.

FEBRUARY 28. Saw finbacks and blackfish today; did not go after them. Samuel made a nice chowder of those skipjacks that were caught yesterday. It tasted very nice to me, nicer, I imagine, than if anyone else had cooked it. I knew that it was clean. If I had not eaten my peck of dirt before I came to sea, I am very sure that it will be filled good measure, pressed down and running over, before I return.

MARCH 1. Quite a rainstorm this morning, but cleared away pleasant in the forenoon. Saw a whale of the kind called sulphur-bottom. They are very wild; do not go after them often. There are a great many birds flying around the ship. It seems strange to me not to hear a note from them, but they are silent, all.

MARCH 2. A fine breeze today which wafts us along towards our destined haven. Saw tropic birds today of the kind called mar-linespikes, from the striking resemblance of their tails to that article.

MARCH 3. Saw a school of blackfish this afternoon. Three boats went in pursuit of them. Mr. Nickerson's boat took one. The sun is directly overhead now; it is very warm.

MARCH 4. Today the newly elected President takes his seat in the presidential chair.[20] Hope he may fill it with honor to himself and the nation. Lowered for blackfish this morning. Took three before breakfast. Lowered again in the afternoon but without success.

MARCH 5. Very calm. Lowered again for blackfish; took two. They are very large. I have not much idea of what a whale can be that will make a hundred barrels, when these six blackfish only made about four barrels.

MARCH 7. This is the anniversary of my little sister Annie's death.[21] Four years today since she left us for a happier clime in the arms of Jesus. There rest, loved one, forever. It is very calm, scarcely a breath of air. We have made no headway for several days. We are trying to make the Galápagos Islands; but as there is no wind, it is uncertain whether we shall fetch, as there is a strong westerly current.

MARCH 8. Calm as usual. Saw a great many crabs around the ship, and one or two swordfish were seen. Lowered a boat to see how strong the current was, and I accompanied them, the first time I have had a chance to see the ship.

MARCH 9. Saw a strange-looking fish in the water this morning. Mr. Nickerson lowered his boat and captured it. It proved to be a diamond fish. They are seldom taken. It was considered a great curiosity, none on board having seen one dead before. I witness some delightful sunsets in this region. I often wish that I were a painter, that I might sketch some of these splendid scenes for the benefit of my friends. We are in sight of Albemarle Island (one of the Galápagos).[22] Hoped to go in and get some terrapin and some fish, but we do not get along any at all.

MARCH 10. Saw a ship in the morning off the weather beam. Lowered for blackfish without success. In the afternoon saw another ship. We hauled up our mainsail for them to come down to us. They started and, by taking their boats, succeeded in reaching us about eight o'clock. It proved to be the *Golconda*, Captain Howland, and the bark *Ohio*, Captain Baker. They stopped on board until about one o'clock. We were very happy to receive visitors, as doubtless anyone would imagine. Pinkey's time was up for setting yesterday, so we broke up her nest today, and no chickens were to be found.

MARCH 11. This morning Captains Howland and Baker came on board again and passed the day with us. Captain Howland brought a small pet terrapin for Minnie and a large one to be killed for me. I am assured they are very nice eating. He also gave Minnie a little basket of feather flowers, with which she was very much pleased. Saw another ship about noon which gradually drew near, and just before tea Captain Daggett of the

General Scott came on board. He is sixty years of age and is taxed for $70,000. I told him I thought he was a very foolish man for leaving his family at that age, when he could live comfortably at home; but from what he says I should judge that he likes for his family to make a good appearance. We procured some sweet potatoes of Captain Baker, which are very nice. They left us about twelve o'clock, and I decided that I had enjoyed gamming enough for once.

MARCH 12. The *Golconda* is near us, the *Ohio* at a distance, and the *General Scott* out of sight. In the afternoon Samuel took Minnie and went on board the *Golconda* for a short time. While there they made the discovery that the *Ohio*'s boats were after a whale. Afterwards they saw it alongside. Minnie came home much pleased with her visit. The captain and officers felt rather badly that one ship had taken a whale when they had seen none, but it cannot be helped, and we must make the best of it.

MARCH 13. No ships in sight. Samuel changed the ship's course last night. Thought he would try no longer to make the island, but there is but very little wind, and how long we shall be obliged to remain in this vicinity we cannot say. Soon after breakfast raised a school of whales. Lowered our boats and were so fortunate as to take two. It was so calm that it was nearly night before we got them to the ship. They were considered small whales, but they looked formidable to me.

MARCH 14. Commenced cutting in; all hands busily employed except Minnie and myself. We are supernumeraries; nothing for us to do but look on, and we avail ourselves of that privilege. I want to see everything that is going on. I may never have another opportunity.

MARCH 15. Employed in boiling yet. Sabbath day, but it seems not much like it. I do not see how it could be avoided very well without much loss. They work day and night. Minnie and I have amused ourselves by watching the fish from the cabin window that follow our ship for the refuse of the whale that is thrown overboard. We saw at one time six sharks following the ship, with the pilot fish ahead of them and no end to the skipjack and albacore, while on the surface of the water and flying around are hundreds of Mother Carey's chickens. The air is almost black with them. Minnie says, "How many pretty things we see on the ocean, don't we?"

MARCH 16. Have finished boiling and are busily engaged in cleaning up. Shall stow down 60 barrels, quite a good beginning. We had some albacore for breakfast this morning, and Minnie saved one of the bones to dry and carry home that they might know what an albacore was. She is much engaged in collecting curiosities. I have a crab's leg in my workbox now to be sent to Cynthia[23] the first opportunity.

MARCH 17. The ship's company have been engaged some parts of the day in catching albacore to salt down for trade at the Islands. It is said they always command a good price there. Put up several barrels. They are very plenty and look beautifully, especially in the night; the water is illuminated with them.

MARCH 18. Stowed down 60 barrels oil today; have a clean ship again. Have been catching more fish today. Caught some pilot fish. They are very pretty fish about the size of a trout, blue, striped around with black, and are considered very nice eating.

MARCH 19. Had some of those fish fried for supper last night and the rest for breakfast this morning. They tasted very nice, nicer than they ever will again to us, I fancy. About ten minutes after I had finished my breakfast my face began to burn and my head to ache badly. I looked in the glass and my face was a sight to behold, just as red as it could be all over, chin, forehead, ears, and neck. I lay down upon the sofa, and my head ached so that I could not get up to ring the bell for Samuel. Presently he came down, and of all the looking creatures that I ever saw—his face was fairly purple. Said I, "What is the matter?" He replied, "I did not know what was the matter with me until I saw you. Now I know that we are poisoned by eating those fish after they had been kept overnight." At that time Mr. Nickerson came down; he was aloft. He did not know what was the matter with him, but he felt so badly he did not dare to stay any longer. So it went on, one came down after another, until all who had eaten them felt the consequences. Some were fortunate enough to throw them off their stomachs without any help; others were obliged to resort to emetics. We all felt poorly enough for the remainder of the day. Now the very sight of a pilot fish is enough to make us sick.

MARCH 20. Caught some more albacore today; some very large ones measure four feet around them. I caught about a dozen; some of them I could pull up myself and others I required some assistance.

MARCH 21. Killed my terrapin today. We are going on a little faster than we have been, but at a slow rate, still only three or four knots an hour.[24] It will take us some time to get to the Islands at this rate.

MARCH 22. We are having the weather a little cooler now than we have done, but it is very warm. I think I never knew what warm weather was at home, but in a calm around the Galápagos Islands we have the full benefit of it. When there is a breeze, we can manage to keep comfortable anywhere out of the sun.

MARCH 23. We are moving along at about the same pace as we have done for several days. I have caught about twenty large fish today. It is grand sport for me, although I cannot pull them all up. We have a piece of white cloth put onto the hook and keep bobbing it up and down to make it look like a flying fish. Nothing in sight that will make oil.

MARCH 25. Four months out today. Time passes rapidly, even here. One-tenth part of our voyage has probably passed. Have had no wind yesterday or today. At this rate it will be some time before we reach the Islands.

MARCH 30. For several days nothing has occurred of interest, except we are favored with a fine breeze, and the good ship *Addison* seems endowed with life as well as motion as she leaps from wave to wave.

MARCH 31. A fine breeze which is wafting us on speedily toward our destined haven. We are about two weeks' sail from the Islands. I think I shall hardly know how to speak to a lady. It is now over four months since I have spoken a word to one of my own sex (except Minnie). There is one comfort in it, at least: I have not been guilty of the sin of scandal. This afternoon we killed two hens, Cynthia and Coopie. It made Minnie feel very sad to have Cynthia killed. I must not allow her to name her chickens for her friends; it makes her feel so badly when they are killed.

APRIL 1. All Fools' Day. Minnie has enjoyed herself very much, telling us to look at whales, blackfish, porpoises, and flying fish. She was very sorry when the day was past. I made our chickens into a pie today. The officers said it seemed like home. It was not baked well; the crust was not done. I should have more courage to make knickknacks if I could attend to the baking of them, but of course it would not do for me to go into the galley. Today one of the birds called boobies flew on board. Samuel wrote our report on a piece of kid and tied it around his neck and sent him away. It would be very funny, I think, to be reported by a bird.

APRIL 2. I cannot decide in my mind whether fast was appointed for today or next Thursday. I am inclined to think that this is the day. Our breeze still continues. We have been 200 miles every twenty-four hours for five days. Last Sabbath I gave Minnie some Bibles and Testaments that were put on board for distribution to carry forward to the men if they liked to have them. So she filled her little carriage and went forward. She came back very quick with an empty carriage, had it reloaded, and went again until she gave away every one that we had. She said they all wanted one, even the Portuguese, that could read. I could but think they were taken far more readily from her than they would have been from anyone else. It may be we can do some good through her.

APRIL 12. Since my last date nothing of interest has occurred. We are quietly pursuing the even tenor of our way,[25] steadily advancing to our desired haven. Are within three days sail of the Islands. With what feelings shall I first step my foot upon a foreign soil.

APRIL 15. Saw the land today for the first time, the island of Hawaii. It delighted me very much to take a view of land, when for days and weeks nothing was to be seen from the east, west, north, or south except the boundless ocean.

APRIL 16. Land in sight today, but we are having quite a storm and very rough, are making but little headway.

APRIL 17. Samuel deemed it prudent to keep off last night, as it was very rough, dark, and stormy. This morning we are rapidly approaching our resting place.

P.M. Maui is in sight, the town of Lahaina exposed to our delighted gaze. I looked in vain for a resemblance to my own dear native land. The mountains looming up in the distance with the clouds playing below their summits, their gloomy and barren sides with here and there a spot green and fresh like an oasis in the desert, the trees and houses—all seemed different from anything I had ever witnessed. As soon as we anchored, the customhouse officer came on board with a boat's crew of natives; and when he returned, my husband accompanied him for the purpose of obtaining a boarding place for us while on-shore. I remained on board, busily engaged in preparing Minnie and myself for the shore in case he should be successful. In the course of an hour we were in the boat on our way to the house of a Mr. Gilman,[26] and very happy were we to step our feet upon the land once more.

APRIL 18.[27] We are very pleasantly situated in a straw cottage on the shore, surrounded by trees, with walks laid out bordered with flowers. It is a bachelor's establishment but looks very much as if it had a presiding genius. He has a native cook and native women to take care of the house. The house contains four rooms, a sitting room, two bedrooms, and a dining room.[28] The sitting room extends the whole length of the house (as indeed do most of the sitting or bedrooms on the island), with a door opening at either end, four windows with crimson and white drapery, straw matting upon the floor, Chinese chairs and lounges, sofa, a whatnot filled with Japanese curiosities, a secretary and library, center and side tables, and the walls hung around with paintings and engravings. It altogether presents a very picturesque appearance. My idea of straw houses were small huts with no windows and holes made for doors, of which I saw many specimens. As I am sitting here by the table writing I can look out the door and view my ocean home, also the breakers as they rise and break with fury upon the shore. Everything is new and strange. There are two boarders at the house beside ourselves, Judge Chandler, of Maine, the American consul, and his secretary, Mr. Pike.

A little girl (Lizzie Bigelow) called this morning to see Minnie, and Mrs. Bigelow and Mrs. Brayton[29] called this P.M. We were delighted to enjoy female society once more. In the evening received a call from Mr. Bishop, the "Seamen's Chaplain," and lady.

APRIL 19. Once more have we been permitted to wend our way to the house of God. How thankful should we be that we may worship the God of our fathers in a strange land. I felt that it was good to be there. Mr. Bishop preached to a very small congregation from the words, "And they left their nets and followed him." [30] The number of foreign residents is very small, so that his hearers are generally very few except during the shipping season. There were but two ships in port when we arrived, the *Cincinnati*, Captain Williams, and the *Enterprise*, Captain Brown. Services at the Bethel are held only in the morning.

In the P.M. we attended the native church. Was much interested in the services there; had very excellent singing. Of course we could understand nothing that was said, but from the gestures of the preacher we could imagine something of the tenor of his discourse. I was much amused at the appearance of the natives. Their dresses of whatever material, from coarse calico to the richest silk, are made like a nightgown—a skirt gathered into a yoke and mutton-leg sleeves. A shawl or handkerchief [is] put on—not cornerwise as we wear them, but square —and the two corners tied around the neck. And what shall I say of their bonnets? I should think every fashion from the days of Methuselah until the present time had centered in that church. They do not tie them but set them on the top of their heads. They are only worn at church, neither do they wear shoes at any other time, and I noticed at church when they got ready to settle down to hear the sermon, they took off their shoes. They are much pleased to see strangers at their church. They all turned and gazed upon me to their hearts' content. I bore their scrutiny, I flatter myself, with a very good grace. Some appeared quite interested in the remarks of the preacher; others were not very attentive.

In the evening we received a call from Dr. Dow, physician at the hospital. He thinks John, the man that we leave there, will live but a very short time. I wanted to call and see him before leaving the Islands, but my husband thought it too far for me to walk. I have never accustomed myself to riding on horseback, and there is but one carriage owned on the island. I hope his last days will be made comfortable. He has a mother residing in New York.

APRIL 20. I confess that I am disappointed in the appearance of the natives. They are not nearly so far advanced in civilization as I had supposed. Why, the good folks at home pretend to hold them up as a model from which we would do well to copy. I do not doubt but that there has been a great deal done for them, but there is a vast deal more to be done to raise them very high in the scale of morals. From what I saw and heard of them (and I made many enquiries) they are a low, degraded, indolent set. They have no apartments in their houses; all huddle in together. Many of them go without clothing; both sexes bathe in the water entirely naked, unabashed. As I am writing, two men are close by my door without an article of clothing. Minnie says, "I have to turn my head the other way." There are but very few that can be depended upon, even members of the church. They will lie and steal whenever an opportunity offers. I am aware that the foreign influence, especially of sailors, has been very bad, but they are very far from what I expected to find them.

Passed the afternoon at Mrs. Bishop's. Had a pleasant time. They have three interesting children, the eldest four years and the youngest six months.

One of our men went to the consul today, stating that a man shipped to go in the *Addison,* but he got sick of his bargain; and so he stepped in his place, took his shipping papers, name, and everything and ran away from his parents. Now he has repented and wants his discharge, but the consul can do nothing for him, as no one knows that it is the truth. He is known by that name to the whole ship's crew and has always answered to it. So he has written home, and if it is as he says, probably his parents will send a statement of affairs and request his discharge. I am sorry for him. Probably he finds a seafaring life not as pleasant as he anticipated. I was always interested in him. He seemed to have been brought up somewhat delicately. He appears to make the best of it, however, and seems cheerful and happy.[31]

APRIL 21. Passed the day with Mrs. Bigelow. After dinner we took a very pleasant walk. Had an opportunity of seeing many of the tropical fruits, the breadfruit, banana, fig, coconut, pineapple, etc. The foliage of the breadfruit is beautiful.

APRIL 22. Passed the day with Mrs. Brayton. Most of the foreign residents, I notice, have Chinese cooks in preference to the natives. They are bound for five years and are more to be depended on. Saw several of our sailors pass, who told me that one of our number had been taken to the fort for drinking and being unruly in the street.[32] It made me feel badly; I had hoped there would be no such doings among our crew. I thought better things of them, but my husband has always told me that sailors would be sailors and that after we had been in port, my eyes would be opened. I am fearful that it is so.

APRIL 23. I enjoy being here very much. There is much that is new and interesting all around us. This is one of the prettiest residences which I have seen, but there are many things too which puts one to the blush who is not accustomed to such scenes. It struck me very forcibly hearing little fellows not more than knee-high swear in English; not a word of our language beside did they know. It is very humiliating, I confess.

APRIL 25. We intended to leave here for Oahu today, but the vessel that was to bring our potatoes has not arrived. Consequently we shall be detained here until Monday. We have a little rain occasionally. The rainy season is not quite over yet. I think the climate delightful; in the sun it is very warm, but away from the sun it is very comfortable. Have a fine sea breeze, and the nights are cool and invigorating. The town is situated at the foot of the mountains and at the edge of the water. About two miles up the mountain is the village of Lahainaluna, where the mission schools are located. The *Pelican*, Captain Cleaveland, touched here today;[33] no oil since leaving here in the fall. He is bound for Kodiak; thinks he shall gam with us once a week throughout the season. Captains are delighted to go on board a ship where there is a lady; it reminds them so forcibly of home. Five months today since, leaving home and friends, we commenced our wanderings upon the deep. Within that time how many mercies have we experienced, how many blessings enjoyed. May we realize how much cause we have for thankfulness, and may we look to the Source from whence all our blessings flow.[34]

APRIL 26. Attended divine service at the Bethel again in the morning. Heard a discourse from the parable of the house with a true and false foundation.[35]

P.M. Attended the native church. They were very happy to see us again. As fast as they came in, they looked around at me and bowed. I never received so many bows from strangers in my life, especially at church. I did not return them as I was not sure that it would be etiquette to return them in church. It amused me very much to see their spittoons. They would have one for about every three pews, a small calabash with a hole made in the side, and when anyone coughed or wished to spit, which I thought was very often, they were passed around. Our potato schooner has arrived, so there will be no excuse for our stopping after tomorrow. I could content myself very well to pass a few weeks here, but that is not what we came for, and my husband is in haste to be about his business.[36]

APRIL 27. Quite rainy this morning, but about nine o'clock the sun came out, and we had a fine day. All the foreign residents came to see me before we left, and I felt as if I were leaving near and dear friends again. I shall look forward with pleasure to the time when we shall again visit these islands of the sea. I received a number of little presents, most of which will be a luxury on shipboard—crackers, turkeys, coconuts, walnuts, tamarinds, chocolate, also a parasolette and a box of cologne—and Minnie received several baskets, toys, and books.

We went on board and left for Oahu about five o'clock. Found a state of affairs on board which made my heart ache: four men were in irons. One was fighting with a sailor, and when reproved by the officer, attacked him; a second jumped overboard and attempted to swim ashore. (One has deserted before and nothing has been heard from him.) [37] The remaining two refused duty. This is the beginning of trouble to me. I was foolish enough to believe that everyone would stay by us, not one leave voluntarily. We discharged the blacksmith; he was no workman and had a bad leg so that he was not of much use about deck. Have shipped two Kanakas forward and a cook.

APRIL 28. We are laying off and on at Honolulu. My husband, Minnie, and myself went onshore. As soon as we touched, found a horse and carriage in readiness for us, although no one knew who we were. Captain Spencer came forward and carried us to the house of a Captain Dudoit, where we were very cordially received. They sent out for a carriage and took us up in Nuuanu Valley, where we enjoyed a delightful ride. I saw the house where the queen was visiting. If we had had time, the lady would have taken us to see her, but our time was very limited. On account of affairs on shipboard, my husband was in haste to get away from the land.

On our way to the valley we stopped at the residence of a Mr. Bates. His wife is a sister of Dr. Judd, and his mother resided there. Their residence answered to my ideas of a happy home: a beautiful house, a group of young and happy children. Mrs. Bates was engaged in her garden when we arrived, and we begged to accompany her about her grounds. In front of the house was a little pond filled with beautiful goldfish, a miniature canoe in the center and marble statues about the margin. On one side of the pond was a house made of wire with plants all around it, filled with canaries; a little streamlet ran from the pond to a little distance where it descended in a beautiful little waterfall to another pond, which was well stocked with goldfish, trout, and mullet. Several geese were swimming in the pond, and turkeys, ducks, and chickens were wandering around the yard. In one corner of the yard a cow was daintily chewing her cud with her calf lying down beside her. In another was a horse and her colt, while a flock of sheep were at a distance. Another swampy place was filled with a lily patch, while every tree and flower and shrub, it seemed to me, were centered there. In one of their flower beds I noticed a dandelion. She told me that she had the seed sent her from the States last summer, the only one that the Islands produced. She presented me with [a] beautiful bouquet, which I prized very highly, especially the roses; they breathed such a homelike air.

We procured some delicious oranges and sweet potatoes at the market and left our kind entertainers at about 3 P.M. There was a Mrs. Stivers boarding there from Stonington. Her husband is mate of the *Baltic*. I suppose he felt as if he would like to see her and sent for her to come out this spring. She started with her child, an entire stranger, and after reaching the Islands, heard the tidings that her husband had been gone a week, so she will be obliged to stop there without seeing him until fall. She did not intend going north with him. I think board at the Islands for a season must be quite expensive. I have a letter to carry to him from her and trust we shall see him. We returned again to our ocean home where we shall probably remain for months to come.

The missionary packet *Morning Star* was in port. It pleased Minnie very much to see her, as she owns stock in her. She was purchased wholly by children. She is designed for carrying supplies to the missions. She is now bound to the Marquesas Islands, from thence back to the Sandwich Islands, and then to Micronesia. I would like to have gone on board with Minnie very much but had not the time. The *Tybee*, of Stonington, Captain Freeman, was laying off and on. He took his wife out with him. She was very seasick all the time, and her seasickness brought on other complaints, so that he was obliged to send her home from Valparaiso. He says it seems very lonely on board now, more so than if he had not attempted to take her. I am sorry for him. We deposited six single letters and four double ones in the office today. May they speedily wing their way to their destination bearing the tidings of health and prosperity.[38]

SECOND CRUISE

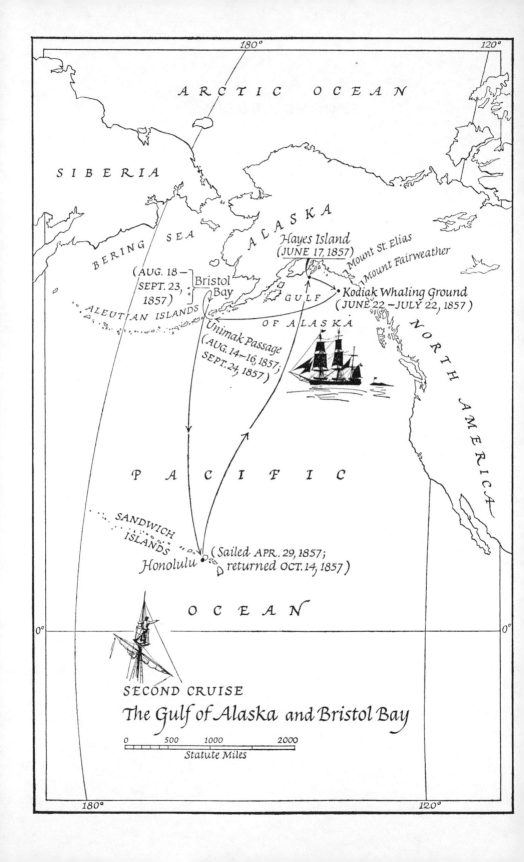

ARCTIC OCEAN

SIBERIA

BERING SEA

ALASKA

Hayes Island
(JUNE 17, 1857)

Mount St. Elias

Mount Fairweather

(AUG. 18 –
SEPT. 23,
1857)

Bristol
Bay

ALEUTIAN ISLANDS

GULF

Kodiak Whaling Ground
(JUNE 22 – JULY 22, 1857)

OF ALASKA

NORTH AMERICA

Unimak Passage
(AUG. 14–16, 1857;
SEPT. 24, 1857)

PACIFIC

SANDWICH
ISLANDS

Honolulu

(Sailed APR. 29, 1857;
returned OCT. 14, 1857)

OCEAN

SECOND CRUISE
The Gulf of Alaska and Bristol Bay

0   500   1000   2000
Statute Miles

The Gulf of Alaska
and Bristol Bay

APRIL 29. We are now making our way toward Kodiak, where I hope we may be successful in obtaining that for which we shall diligently seek. We have everything nice to eat, sweet and Irish potatoes, cabbages, onions, cucumbers, string beans, bananas, coconuts, melons, pumpkins, preserved meats, vegetables, oysters and lobster, sausage meat, etc., butter and soda crackers, tamarinds, preserves, arrowroot, pigs, turkeys, ducks, and chickens, a goat, and kid for a pet, also a terrapin, and a little dog named Pincher, a very pretty dog notwithstanding his name.

Mr. Nickerson received one letter from his wife, the only one received on board while we were on Lahaina. I sent to see what the news was, for I thought if anything had occurred to any of our family, she would be likely to mention it. Tonight he read me the sad tidings of the death of little Grace Walter, brother Charles's little child. I did not think she could live long when we left her. Still it made me feel very sad to hear it. I sympathize deeply with the bereaved parents. May they remember that they now have a treasure in heaven, that they have added one star to the Saviour's diadem. Minnie says, "Don't feel sad, Mamma, for little Grace has gone to live with Jesus, and if we are good, perhaps we shall go and see her sometime."

MAY 1. May comes in with sad recollections of the past, the commencement of our father's final sickness and of brother Augustus' death.

MAY 2. The men are all free again, sorry for what they have done and glad enough to perform their several duties once more. I hope it may be a warning to the rest. I cannot think the same ones will get caught so again.

MAY 3. The Sabbath is to be spent at home again. A sail in sight, supposed to be a whaler. As we are steadily gaining upon her, we may find out who she is before night.

MAY 4. After tea last night we spoke the ship, which proved to be the *Julian,* Captain Cleaveland. He came on board for a short time, but as it was rough and blowing a strong breeze, did not like to stop.

MAY 5. We have had quite rough weather since leaving the Islands, cloudy, damp, and cold. Shall be obliged to put up the stove in the cabin in the course of a day or two. Opened a slop cask today, and quite a brisk trade was carried on for a little while.

MAY 6. Think we have a cook worth having now, after taking up with all sorts. He is quite an old man, fat, and black as ebony. He made me some very nice starch the other day, the first good that I have had yet. I cannot go to the galley. He said he knew how to make starch, and I found that he did. Minnie was playing tea party yesterday with her dishes; she wondered how the little girls at home would like to play tea party with orange, banana, and coconut for the treat.

MAY 8. Saw a couple of sulphur-bottoms; two boats went in pursuit of them but without success. Had our stove put up yesterday in the cabin. It is quite sunny today. For a number of days back have had much fog.

MAY 11. Has been very rough today. This afternoon the ship made a sudden lurch which threw me with such force from my chair as to overthrow the melodeon from its standard to the floor, where we all fell together. The melodeon was not so much injured as we feared, although there is a large hole made in the bellows and the frame is somewhat marred. Shall put it away for the present. I tell my husband, so much for having the "old woman" with him, but he seems to think he can get along better without that than he could without me.

MAY 18. Have had a succession of damp, foggy, windy, cold, dreary days, very far from pleasant on deck. I get along very comfortably with it, however. Have a nice little stove, a good cozy fire, a kind husband, and a dear little daughter. How ungrateful should I be to complain. I also have plenty of books and an abundance of work.[1] It would be delightful indeed to see friends near and dear, but uninterrupted happiness is not for mortals to enjoy.

MAY 20. Have had a very pleasant day, clear, bright, and sunny. Have seen no right whales as yet. Almost every day we hear the sound of "There blows!" but they all prove to be finbacks or humpbacks. I hope we may commence our labors before long. Have been obliged to kill Minnie's terrapin and the little kid to save their lives, as the weather was much too cold for them. Pincher gets along very prosperously.

MAY 24. Saw two ships this P.M. Went down to them and spoke them. They proved to be the *Benjamin Rush,* of Warren, Captain Wyatt, clean, and the *William and Henry,* Captain Grinnell, no oil since leaving the Islands. Heard of the *Enterprise* with one whale. They had all experienced very rough weather. Samuel went on board the *Benjamin Rush* for a few minutes, but as it was rough, did not like to stop.

MAY 25. Saw two right whales this morning, being the first we have seen, but it is of not much use to see them such rough weather as this. Two boats lowered in pursuit of them, but they soon came back to the ship. Had a very rough day. At sunset saw another whale.

Six months today since we have been in our floating home. They have passed very rapidly and pleasantly to me. What the next six months may have in store for us, the All-Wise only knows. But we have the assurance that "as our day is, so shall our strength be."[2] It is so rough that I make sorry work at writing.

MAY 27. Spoke the *Cincinnati* this morning, Captain Williams, clean, of Stonington. Captain Williams came on board and passed the day with us. In the afternoon spoke the *Contest,* of New Bedford, Captain Ludlow, seven months out, 430 [barrels] whale, 20 sperm; nothing this season. Have experienced much bad weather and seen but few whales. We had a very pleasant visit from them. Captain Ludlow has a farm on Long Island, has three children, has been a voyage for each of the two elder children, and is now on his last voyage for the youngest. It is a question in my mind whether it is advisable to do so, whether the children would not be as well off without it.

Heard of the death of Captain Cushman and his wife of the *Lancer*. She sailed a short time before we did for the same owners. He died five days from port, and she, poor woman, took passage in a merchant ship home but died on her passage. I have not heard the particulars, but it may be from the effects of grief. We had two letters on board for the *Contest*. Heard of the *Huntsville*, Captain Grant, having taken one whale, being the second only we have heard of. The captains seem all undecided as to where to go or what to do. The season seems different from what it has in general before; where they have formerly found good whaling, there are no whales to be seen. Perhaps it will all come out right in the end. Captain Ludlow has not been in port since he left home. We gave him a couple of barrels of potatoes, which were very acceptable.

MAY 28. Spoke the *William and Henry* again tonight. Had seen one whale since we last saw him. The weather was so rough he did not come on board.

MAY 30. Lowered twice today for whales without success. Two ships in sight doing the same with like result. Think one is the *Contest*.

MAY 31. Chased whales most of the afternoon. About teatime spoke the *Gay Head;* Captain Lowen came on board. Seven months out, one whale this season. Soon after spoke the *Contest*, and Captain Ludlow came on board again. He brought the daguerreotypes of his wife and children for us to look at, which I liked well to do.

JUNE 1. Comes in at home with flowers and sweet singing birds, very different from what we are now experiencing. I have prophesied that we should get a whale today, but we have lowered our boats twice in vain. The whales are exceedingly shy. They will see the boats before they get near enough to strike them, and surely they cannot be blamed for getting out of harm's way.

JUNE 2. Lowered twice again this afternoon; came back again as poor as they went. Saw three ships today. Spoke, or rather signalized, the *General Pike*, Captain Russell.

JUNE 3. Spoke the *Sarah Sheafe* this morning, of New Bedford, Captain Loper, twenty months out, 800 barrels. He came on board and stopped until after dinner, when we raised whales, and he was off in an instant. Boats were lowered from both ships in pursuit of them, to no purpose. Captain Loper has been on the ground since the last of March and has taken but two whales. He was away from home on his last voyage (a whaling and trading voyage) sixty-six months. When he returned, he purchased himself a farm in the vicinity of Buffalo and has taken this voyage for the purpose of obtaining a little more money so that he may not be obliged to work himself. Caught a fur seal today. Its head resembles the head of a dog; its tail and fins are fish.

JUNE 5. Saw no whales yesterday and have seen none today. The weather is very thick and foggy.

JUNE 6. Nothing of importance happened until about four o'clock we saw a whale and got too near him with the ship, wore round, and presently saw him again. After supper lowered the boats, and about seven o'clock had the good fortune to have a large whale alongside the ship. We are all delighted and hope this is only the commencement of our good fortune.   135 barrels.

JUNE 7. We have been busily employed in cutting in today. I have had a severe pain in my head and face for the last week which has made me sick for three days.[3] I could not sit up at all. The motion of the ship and the noise overhead was very trying to me, but I have nearly recovered now. I was disappointed that I could not go on deck to see the whale. Hope I may have another opportunity very soon.

JUNE 8. Another gale today so that they have been obliged to put out the fires and stop the tryworks.

JUNE 9. The gale has abated, but it is quite foggy. Have commenced boiling again.

JUNE 13. Have been out of the way of whales and ships for the last few days. Finished stowing down our oil today. The whale made us 135 barrels. We have had a very pleasant day, almost calm. I went on deck at noon and passed an hour very pleasantly. While there I had my first good sight at a live whale. A large sulphur-bottom came up close by the ship and performed several revolutions around it, very majestically. A boat was lowered, but he was too quick for them. We are now proceeding north in the direction of Rose Island. What we shall find in that vicinity remains to be seen.

JUNE 17. Saw Hayes Island at a distance this morning. Have had a very rugged day. No whales to be seen. Spoke the *Charles Caroll*, of New London, Captain Parsons; two whales this season. He says there are no whales here, so we are now to proceed to the southeast to see what can be found there. Another ship in sight.

JUNE 19. Fired at a finback from the ship and think it must have killed him, as he went immediately down. Two ships and a bark in sight, the latter chasing whales. In the afternoon saw two whales, lowered the boats, but they were very smart fish and were off in an instant.

JUNE 20. Spoke the bark *Dartmouth* this morning, of New Bedford, Captain Heath; two whales this season. Samuel went on board for a short time and brought back some late papers and some figs for Minnie from Margarita Bay. Lowered in the forenoon for whales; came back minus. Ditto in the afternoon. Saw seven whales today; that looks encouraging.

JUNE 21. Lowered for a whale before breakfast but could not get near him. Shot at a finback from off deck at noon. He turned up dead about half a mile from the ship, but before they could get a boat to him, he had sunk to rise no more. In the afternoon lowered for whales and got one. Got him to the ship about six o'clock and commenced cutting in. One may read every description of a whale that ever was given, but he can form no idea of one until he has seen it with his own eyes. Imagine a whale's head to contain fifteen hundred pounds of bone and a tongue [which yields] ten barrels of oil. I think a right whale is more wonderful than a sperm. Everything seems adapted to the purpose for which it was designed. Two ships in sight, gamming. We happen to be better employed just now.

JUNE 22. Employed in cutting and boiling. Saw Mount St. Elias, lofty and grand, with its summit far above the clouds, covered in snow.

JUNE 23. A perfect calm, not a ripple on the waters. Quite a contrast to some of the weather we have had, warm and pleasant. Two ships in sight, one the *Dartmouth* cutting in a whale. Lowered for whales, but it was too calm to be successful. The whales seemed to be lying upon the water, basking in the sunshine. I have never seen them so still before.

JUNE 24. Samuel went on board the *Dartmouth* this morning to do a little trading.[4] Captain Heath returned with him and stopped until after dinner. Four ships in sight, two chasing whales. We are very near the land. It presents a fine appearance to our gaze: "height above height in grand succession rise." Some of them bare and others covered in snow, Mount [St.] Elias rising majestically in the distance. When I was a schoolgirl studying geography,[5] how strange it would have seemed had anyone told me that I should view these places with my own eyes. We have very pleasant weather now, and I enjoy sitting on the house very much, watching the ships and whales. I am perfectly contented, and so is Minnie. Occasionally a tear dims our eyes when we think of home and friends, but we know they are in the hands of an all-wise Father, and to his care we commit them.

JUNE 25. Have seen no whales today. We are very near the land. Two ships and two barks in sight. Captain Parsons of the *Charles*

Caroll came down in the afternoon and took tea with us; has taken a large whale, since we saw him, that made 240 barrels.

JUNE 27. Stowed down our oil today, about 158 barrels. Saw whales in the afternoon. About half-past seven lowered for them and took one; got him to the ship about ten o'clock. Where we now are, the sun sets about nine o'clock and rises about three. It is daylight nearly all night.   113 barrels.

JUNE 28. Cut in our whale in the forenoon. In the afternoon saw whales again and lowered the boats about half-past three. Got fast to a whale which acted very badly. They were fast to him, all three of the boats, about five hours, when, as they were much fatigued and it was about ten o'clock, they were obliged to cut from him.

JUNE 29. Lowered for whales again this P.M. Took one, and after killing him, had the gratification of seeing him go down to rise no more. We all felt much disappointed, but it could not be helped. Better luck next time—perhaps.

JUNE 30. Saw whales again this P.M. Lowered about six o'clock, got fast to a whale, and—the iron broke. We had hoped there was one more for us in June, but we were mistaken. Saw Mount St. Elias today, 130 miles distant. Suppose our friends at home have received our letters ere this. I am thankful they can hear good news from us, for once at least.

JULY 1. Saw no whales today. Spoke the *Cleone*, of New Bedford, Captain Simmons, about sunset; has taken six whales this season. Samuel went on board of him. He sent me a nice piece of fresh pork, which was very acceptable.

JULY 2. A rough, stormy day; wind blowing a gale.

FOURTH OF JULY. How different from any which I ever passed before, cold, rainy, and disagreeable. A few guns were fired by way of amusement, which was all the celebration we could get up except an extra dinner. We had for dinner a pair of ducks, stuffed and roasted, cranberry sauce, potatoes, pumpkin, and a

boiled pudding, or duff as we call it. Saw whales in the forenoon; lowered and got fast to one. After getting him about half
killed, he took a fancy to run and consequently took the whole
of the line and made tracks for somewhere, leaving a wake of
blood. What better celebration could we have wished for than
a whale alongside. But perhaps it was all for the best as it was,
for the wind blew up a gale, and we must have been obliged to
cut from him alongside, which would have been still worse.

JULY 5. Rainy and blowing a gale. Nothing in sight.

JULY 6. Pleasant. Saw no whales. A ship in sight. Spoke her after
tea. She proved to be the *Tamerlane,* of New Bedford, Captain
Winslow; seven whales this season. Has taken most of them
around here. Heard from Lewis and Eunice by him.[6] He saw
them last winter, all well, 800 [barrels] sperm. He came on
board and passed the evening with us. Procured as many bomb
lances of him as we wished.[7]

JULY 7. Finished stowing down our oil today. The whale made
us 113 barrels.

JULY 9. A gale of wind for two days. Saw a number of whales
yesterday and today. Chased whales towards night and got
fast to one, but it was so rough and growing dark that they were
obliged to cut. Our fourth whale seems very hard to take.

JULY 10. A dead calm. Saw whales, but it was too still to get near
them. Miserable whaling weather, say they. A ship and a bark
in sight. Brought home a curiosity in one of the boats, a piece
of kelp or seaweed (called here a sea serpent) very much the
shape of a serpent, forty-six feet in length. Samuel has had it put
up to preserve today to carry home as a curiosity.

JULY 11. Rainy and blowing a gale of wind. Samuel had hard
thoughts of starting for Bristol Bay today, as there is no weather
for whaling here, although there are whales. He has decided to
wait a few days longer, hoping to get one whale more before
he leaves.

JULY 12. Lowered for whales once but could not get up to them. They were going quick. In the afternoon spoke the *Good Return*, of New Bedford, Captain Wing; 1,300 [barrels] this season. Has cruised around here for the last month. Captain Wing took tea on board.[8] At sunset there were six ships in sight.

JULY 13. The anniversary of our marriage. Ten years today we were united until death us do part:

> Yes, ten most blessed years have passed
> Since Heaven pronounced me thine,
> Each still more happy than the last
> Since first I knew thee mine.
>
> Yes, mine! My precious husband, thou
> More than when first thy bride,
> Full well I know thou lov'st me now;
> My warmth thou wilt not chide.
>
> Stoics have smiled and poets talked
> Of love's first fitful boons;
> But we in heightening bliss have walked
> 'Neath scores of "honey moons."

May the day that shall separate us be far distant.

JULY 14. Saw Mount Fairweather in the distance with its hoary summit clothed in snow. Passed a ship but did not speak her; saw four at a distance.

JULY 15. The boats went after whales and had the good fortune to capture a mother and child, or cow and calf as they are called. The little one will not make much oil. A little shore bird flew on board yesterday from the vicinity of Mount Fairweather, which they caught for me. It is brown and yellow, quite a pretty bird. I have turned my workbasket over for a cage, given him flaxseed and rice to eat and water to drink, so that he seems quite at home. If he will only sing, I shall feel so happy. I long to hear the notes of a bird again. I was exceedingly disappointed at the absence of birds at the Islands. We have enjoyed a warm, pleasant day.

JULY 17. Lowered for whales in the morning, but it was so calm could not get near enough to dart. About noon, as good luck would have it for once, picked up a dead whale. It had been dead too long for the body to be of any use. Saved the two lips and throat, which made us 25 barrels. We put that with the calf and call it five whales.

JULY 18. Minnie's birthday, to which she has been looking forward with much pleasure. She thinks now that she is quite old, six years. She has received from one and another on board as presents a little breastpin and three dollars and ninepence in money. Spoke the *John Howland* at night; six whales this season. My little bird died about sunset.

JULY 19. Spoke the *Contest,* Captain Ludlow, this morning, cutting in a whale. Has taken five this season and picked up one of ours, the one that we cut from the twenty-eighth June. He gave us back our irons. Samuel and Minnie went on board. She brought back a bowl of nice honey in the comb that he gave her.

JULY 21. Spoke the *Enterprise,* of Nantucket, Captain Brown, this morning; taken one whale this season and picked up three dead ones. Captain Brown came on board and stayed to dinner with us. He has lost one man this season by getting a boat stoven.

JULY 22. Start this morning for Bristol Bay direct, unless we see whales by the way. After dinner spoke the *William and Henry,* of Fairhaven, Captain Grinnell; three whales this season. Will cruise up here a while longer before going into the bay. Finished stowing down our oil today: 155 barrels. Have 600 now, all told.

JULY 23. A rough, rainy day with a high wind.

JULY 24. Pleasant and sunny with a head wind.

JULY 25. Cloudy with a good breeze; going six knots. Eight months from home today.

AUGUST 13. For the past three weeks have been making passage to Bristol Bay with head winds and light during most of the time. Have met with nothing of interest. Have seen neither whales nor ships but have been wending our way, solitary and alone, through the trackless deep.

AUGUST 14. Made Unimak Island and the Ugamak group. We are to pass through Unimak strait, a passage ten miles wide. I shall be glad when we get safely through. I do not like such near proximity to land, especially where we are not acquainted. Raised two ships this afternoon, a welcome sight, to me at least.

AUGUST 15. We were nearly through the passage (or I suppose we were through the passage but nearby the land) when it became calm, so much so that we could not steer, with a strong current drifting us directly into the land, which made our situation anything but pleasant, and some part of the time a thick fog. In the course of the night we let go the small anchor. We passed quite near one of the ships this morning, which we found to be the *Benjamin Tucker*. The other has made his escape.

This afternoon, while we were at anchor, the mate, third mate, and boat's crew went onshore. They had just landed when a slight breeze sprang up, and they were obliged to return after just taking a look around. They saw about a dozen underground huts, a hole dug in the ground with a door just large enough to crawl in on all fours. The inhabitants probably had seen them coming and made their escape, as the huts were all desolate but looked as if they had just been deserted. Saw the tracks of bears and foxes. Procured a large bunch of flowers for Minnie and myself, which delighted us very much, also about a dozen strawberries, blackberries, and huckleberries.

We have a fine view of the land here, mountain rising above mountain, their snowy tops peering far above the clouds. Minnie thinks if we were to get on the top of one of those mountains we should be very near to heaven. We also saw the smoke issuing from two volcanoes. Last year several of the ships, as they passed out, got well sprinkled with ashes from one of them. I forgot to mention that the cross was erected on the island. Is it not strange, however degraded, you will always find some system of religion? Probably they have been visited by Russians.

AUGUST 16. Not much short of a calm today. We are not out of the way of land yet. This P.M. there is [a] little more of a breeze, and we may get out. My little cabin is fragrant with flowers today, some of them very pretty indeed. "Oh," said Minnie, "when they gave them to me, I was so delighted I fairly danced with joy." She is very fond of flowers, and they make her think of home. She is well, contented, and happy. Nothing troubles her so much as the want of an apple. She says sometimes she would eat the peelings and core that children at home throw away, even if they were all covered in "antimires."

AUGUST 18. We are now in the bay, clear of all land. This morning picked up a carcass. It had been dead too long to be of much use. We saved about 18 barrels from it and 100 pounds of bone —not much, but worth saving. Spoke the *Benjamin Tucker* in the forenoon. We were both going the same way, so Captain Barber came on board and passed the day with us. He had been in the passage seven days when he first saw us. At sunset saw a right whale.

AUGUST 19. Lowered for whales this morning, but immediately after a thick fog set in so that nothing could be seen. We fired guns and blew horns so that the boats might find their way to the ship, until Minnie thought it surely must be Fourth of July or some other great day; and then I recollected that it was Uncle James's birthday. In the afternoon the fog cleared away and the weather was delightful, but no whales were to be seen. I enjoyed an hour on deck very much. We have lost sight of our consort, and now we are again alone.

AUGUST 22. A thick fog for several days. Today a gale of wind. About sunset the fog has cleared when the weather has been delightful. We are now living on fresh fish, which are very nice. Codfish and flatfish are quite plenty. Caught about forty cod from the ship this morning.

AUGUST 23. A calm again. Lowered for whales this morning, but they very mysteriously disappeared; were not seen after the boats went down. Caught another supply of codfish.

AUGUST 24. Saw a ship at a distance; did not speak her. Saw no whales.

AUGUST 25. A gale of wind. Laying to part of the time. Two-thirds of a year has elapsed since we launched in our little bark upon the ocean wave. God in his goodness has mercifully shielded us thus far from all dangers. May we still trust in him.

AUGUST 26. Nothing in sight that lives. Our company were beginning to feel rather down again, when the cry of right whales resounded from the masthead. The boats were lowered and about eight o'clock P.M. got a whale alongside. Commenced cutting him in immediately, as the barometer gave indications of another gale.

AUGUST 28. Arose this morning and found ourselves in a city of ships. Could count fifteen from off deck. Some were boiling, some cutting in, and others chasing whales. It seems very lively and pleasant. Our boats lowered for a whale in the forenoon; killed a very large one which sunk, but, three boats being fast to him, they succeeded after some time in pulling him up again, much to our satisfaction. Got him alongside about two o'clock. The *Onward* passed us, whaling, but we did not speak her. All seem employed.

AUGUST 29. All hands were up through the night cutting in the whale. The wind blew quite fresh, and the whale inclining to sink, they had rather a hard time; but they accomplished it at length, and our ship presents a very greasy appearance. The blubber room is filled and the rest laying on deck. Saw whales today, but it was very rugged. Six ships in sight today.

AUGUST 30. Rugged still. Have seen several whales today. One ship has been near us, which we think the *Huntsville*. If so, there is a lady on board, but it is so rugged that we could not meet, probably, should they speak.

SEPTEMBER 1. Plenty of whales in sight today; the sea appears to be full of them. Our boats were out the most of the day but did not succeed in getting fast to one. Several ships in sight, trying like ourselves.

SEPTEMBER 2. Whales in abundance. It is a grand sight to see them ploughing through the sea, rising to breathe. If they were aware of their strength, how few would be safe. Our boats went off in the morning for whales. About 10 A.M. fastened to one which knew how to use his flukes very scientifically. At dark they were compelled to cut from him, which they did with a very bad grace. Ten ships in sight. We saw two take a whale, a black ship and a bark. Perhaps we may have a chance to try our luck again tomorrow. There will probably be a dead whale for some lucky one to pick up soon. We are now enjoying pleasant weather, except it is rather cool. It is getting late in the season now, and that must be expected.

SEPTEMBER 3. Nothing to be seen except a few ships. Not a whale left. Fine weather for whaling.

SEPTEMBER 4. Several ships in sight. Passed four carcasses.

SEPTEMBER 5. Finished stowing our oil today, 300 barrels; have 850 of whale now. Lowered for whales in the afternoon but got none. Kept off about sunset for several ships that were together, for a little information in regard to the whales' movements. Samuel went on board the *Benjamin Morgan,* of New London, Captain Sisson, and found Captain Ryan of the *Olympia,* New Bedford, and Captain Comstock of the *Neptune,* New London, there. The *Benjamin Morgan* had taken 700 barrels and the others, two whales each. They say we have done better than an average. The *Good Return* has left the ground with flying colors, full.

SEPTEMBER 8. Passed the *General Teste* and spoke the *General De Hautpoul,* French ships.

SEPTEMBER 11. Spoke the *De Hautpoul* again. The captain came on board and passed the evening. When our boat's crew returned, they brought Minnie a paper of almonds and raisins, which were quite a treat. He has taken 1,240 barrels this season. He informed us that Captain Lowen of the *Gay Head* had lost his mate; was killed by a whale.

SEPTEMBER 12. Saw whales today, but they were going very fast, and a very heavy sea. Lowered the boats but without success.

SEPTEMBER 20. We have had a succession of very heavy gales, the line gale, I suppose, for the last six days. Today we have settled weather again. Spoke the *General Teste* after tea. The captain came on board a short time. I cannot recollect his name. He spoke very good English, much better than the captain of the *De Hautpoul.* He has taken 450 [barrels] this season.

SEPTEMBER 21. Picked up a dead whale this morning, which proves to be about like those we have before taken. A strong breeze in the afternoon.

SEPTEMBER 22. Another gale of wind. It is getting late in the season, and the sooner we are out of this bay the better. The first fair wind probably we shall make our departure.

SEPTEMBER 23. A fair wind, and we bid farewell to Bristol Bay as speedily as possible. Our whale yielded us 33 barrels. We intended passing through Umnak Passage instead of Unimak Passage, but the wind has hauled, so we are to proceed the same way as we came in. I hope we may have a good time.

SEPTEMBER 24. Passed through the straits. Had a fine view of the land. Considerable snow, I should judge, had fallen since we entered. Saw a volcano entirely covered with snow, the smoke issuing from its top.

SEPTEMBER 25. Ten months from home today, and we are ploughing our way through the trackless deep with all sail set, bound for the Hawaiian kingdom, where I anticipate with fear and trembling not unmixed with pleasure the reception of letters. Oh, may they be the bearers of love and gladness and nought of sorrow or trouble be recorded on a single page.

SEPTEMBER 27. We have a fair wind, and the good ship *Addison* bears us on right merrily. A ship in sight also bound for the kingdom. I feel that we have much to be thankful for the past season. Our good Father has kindly watched over us to shield us from all harm. No sickness or accident has befallen us, while, alas, many who left their homes buoyant and exulting with hope have found a watery grave.

OCTOBER 4. For the last week we have been making rapid progress in our passage. Have had a fair wind and for the most part plenty of it. We have plenty to do getting ready for port, and I find my share to perform. What would my friends at home say were I to tell them that I am as much hurried in preparing clothes for port as if I were engaged in the duties of housekeeping. But it is even so. I put off Minnie's clothing as long as possible because she is growing so fast. For the last week I have been making a doll and dressing it for her to carry in port, as Sarah Price seems to have seen her best days. She calls this one Mary Stuart. We are now in warm weather, and it seems delightful once more. Last night we caught a porpoise, so sausage meat is on our bill of fare once more after a long season.

[OCTOBER 14.] Arrived [the] fourteenth just before sunset off Diamond Head, when we signalized for a pilot, who soon made his appearance; also the steam tug *Pele*,[9] which towed us safely in Honolulu harbor. Our good ship was almost filled with visitors, much to my surprise, for I had not arranged my toilet, as I intended to remain on board until morning. Immediately after our arrival my husband went onshore to get our letters, and in the meantime I tried to compose myself against his return. I could only hope for the best, which truly was granted me, as I received the welcome intelligence of the well-being of all my friends. No sickness or death had occurred in either family of loved ones except little Grace Walter, of whose death I heard last spring. How truly welcome were those inky messengers of love from friends near and dear. I received two letters from Mother, one from Cynthia, and one from Sarah. The remainder were at Maui.

OCTOBER 15. I went onshore in the morning and procured a boarding place for us at C. H. Butler's private boardinghouse at $25 per week.[10] Captain Spencer was on the wharf with his carriage and waited on us with his customary politeness. Honolulu does not present so pretty an appearance from the harbor as Lahaina. The latter is situated on the [shore] with a street running the whole length of the village, thickly ornamented with trees. Honolulu covers a much larger space of territory, and it extends farther back. It appears to be made up of mountains and valleys. Considerable attention, I should judge, has been paid to improvements, and there are some very fine residences.

OCTOBER 16. We have a very pleasant boarding place. There are about thirty boarders, two ladies beside myself. [One is] Mrs. Slocum and son, whose husband is in the *Saratoga.* She is an invalid; her husband brought her to the Islands hoping a residence there would prove beneficial to her health, but I fear he is destined to disappointment. The other is Captain Scofield's lady and child of the *Cynthia.* This P.M. received a call from Mrs. Grant of the *Huntsville,* who has been in such close proximity to us all the season. There were four ladies on the ground all the season, but we never met at all. We would often hear from each other. Captain Coggeshall's lady of the *Silver Cloud* (who left New Bedford about the time that we did) has been stopping at the Islands the past season. She is very feeble with a cancer on her tongue and will perhaps never be any better. She was well when her husband left for the north, and what was his surprise to find her in such a situation.

OCTOBER 17. Took a fine ride this P.M. out on the plains. It being Saturday, the natives, both male and female, were enjoying a horse race, which is their usual pastime on Saturday, their holiday. The wahines, or females, sit on their horses the same as the men. They have a piece of gay calico five or six yards in length, which they wrap around their bodies some mysterious way and let it drop down in graceful folds on each side. They present quite a gay appearance with this fanciful dress, and they are really beautiful riders.

OCTOBER 18. Captain Slocum arrived this morning, much to the joy of his good lady, at least. Attended church this morning once more. It seems good to enter the sanctuary again after being deprived of that privilege for six long months. Attended divine service again in the evening; after services received an introduction to Mr. Damon. I have heard so much of him that he already seemed like an old acquaintance.[11]

OCTOBER 19. Received this morning one letter from S. P. Bourne, one from Celia,[12] and one from Sarah, from Maui. It being the Sabbath, they could not get them from the office; consequently we must wait another day for the remainder. Mr. Fish of the *Good Return* called to see us this evening, and we had a nice talk about Falmouth, the first person I have met with since leaving home that I ever saw before. We have decided to send a box home by him, as he leaves Wednesday. We have discharged Dermont and Beecher on account of ill health, and Maxon (the one who shipped under an assumed name) goes home in the *John Land.*[13]

OCTOBER 20. Received another package of letters today, one from my dear mother, two from Cynthia, one from James, one from Charles,[14] and one from George,[15] a note from C. S. Heywood, also a letter from S. P. Bourne. Minnie received a letter from her Aunt Cynthia, one from Aunt Lizzie Robinson,[16] one from Lizzie Whittens, and one from her dear cousin Willie. The mail is expected daily from the coast, when I hope to have later news from home. My latest dates are to the eighteenth of August.

OCTOBER 21. The mail arrived today, but no letters did it bring for us. Consequently we must wait until spring for the remainder. I know that we have more on their way. Passed the day at Mrs. Cartwright's (Mrs. Grant's boarding place). Met with Mrs. Edwards there, who arrived from San Francisco this morning. Came from the States to meet her husband, who is north in the *Black Eagle.* There are quite a number of captains' ladies here at this time: Mrs. Skinner of the *Marengo,* Mrs. Stranburg of the *Congress,* Mrs. Cox of the *Magnolia,* Mrs. Fisher of the *Barnstable,* Mrs. Diman of the *Japan,* and Mrs. Palmer of the *Kingfisher,* besides those I have before mentioned.

OCTOBER 22. Was made very happy this morning by the very unexpected arrival of our dear brother George in the *Harvest,* the very last one I expected to see here. I waited several hours for him to arrive at my boarding place, when Mr. Damon called and invited me to ride with him. I accepted his invitation and had a very delightful ride. He requested the guards to throw open the gates that we might have an opportunity of viewing the king's palace, which they did. It is a very pretty building, and the grounds are well laid out. Have had the pleasure of seeing His Majesty several times.[17] He is a fine-looking young man; has been dressed very plainly when I have seen him. Have seen the queen once only. She is a half-white and very pretty. They are very well educated, and the king has traveled quite extensively. On arriving home, I found brother George waiting to receive us. He is looking very well and is more fleshy than I ever saw him.[18]

OCTOBER 23. Captain Winslow (George's captain) takes his meals at the house. He is looking very thin and feeble, not much as he did when he left home. At night George came up to see us again, and we had a good talk of home and friends. We were spared the pain of telling him what a breach death had made in our family, as he heard it from Captain Jones about two months previous.

OCTOBER 24. Received a call from Captain Cleaveland, who has just arrived. He is bound home now. Probably we may see him again out here with his lady before we leave for home.

OCTOBER 25. The Sabbath, and as we are wending our way to the sanctuary, my husband, George, Minnie, and myself, it seems so much like home that I can hardly realize that we are thousands of miles from home.

OCTOBER 26. Have discharged Mr. Baxter, our second officer, promoted Mr. St. John, the third officer, and shipped a new one by the name of Chappell. Have had several men in the fort as before.[19]

OCTOBER 27. Visited the Sailor's Home. I received many thanks for the society in Falmouth, of which I am a member, for furnishing the room which goes by that name, being the first which was furnished by people at a distance.[20] Mrs. Thrum, the lady of the house, thanked me, while tears were streaming down her cheeks to think that ladies so far off across the wide ocean should sit and sew for them that they might be enabled to make a comfortable home for the sailor. I was much pleased with what I saw there, and it appeared to be as its name would indicate, a home for the sailor.

OCTOBER 28. Visited the clipper ship *John Gilpin* in company with my husband [and] Mr. and Mrs. Butler. I wished very much for a small piece of her spacious cabin to enlarge mine a little. Mrs. Butler (as Miss Howland) came out from the States in this ship about two years since and immediately on her arrival was married to Mr. Butler before going onshore. Consequently the *John Gilpin* seems very near to her.[21]

OCTOBER 30. Enjoyed a morning ride with Mrs. Slocum up the valley. She rides every morning for her health; brought a nice carriage out with her. I have taken several delightful rides with her on the plains, up the valley, and along the seashore.

NOVEMBER 1. This afternoon, in company with Captain Spencer, Mr. Chestnut, Samuel, Mrs. Butler, Mrs. Scofield, Mrs. Stranburg, and Mrs. Palmer, visited the American sloop of war *St. Mary's*. It was my first visit on board a man-of-war, and it was attended with some curiosity. The officers were very gentlemanly and polite in showing us round, etc. After a very pleasant visit they took us onshore in their boat.[22]

NOVEMBER 4. The remainder of the time was spent very pleasantly in visiting and receiving visits, with a call every day from George, until the afternoon of this day when we left our good friends. I become so attached to those I am with onshore that it seems like breaking away again from near and dear friends to leave them. Mr. and Mrs. Butler were very kind to us while we were with them. Yesterday Captain and Mrs. Phillips with three children arrived in the *Syren Queen* and have taken up their residence here. They have a pair of twin daughters nine years of age. Minnie felt very sorry to leave them so soon. As soon as we left, Captain and Mrs. Homer of the merchant ship *Messenger-Bird* were to occupy our room with two children, one little boy four years of age who swears equal to any man that I ever heard in my life. He made nothing of repeating an oath to his mother.

How she could bear it I cannot tell, but it made the tears start to my eyes.

George brought us out to the ship in his boat, which was lying off and on. We were late, and the ship had given us up for that night, so kept off. Consequently we had to go about six miles in the boat when it was almost dark and very rough. I will say that I was very thankful to step my foot once more on the deck of the old *Addison*. George and his crew stopped all night with us, and early in the morning we were forced to bid him good-by. Probably we shall not meet again during the voyage.

NOVEMBER 5. Just after the *Harvest's* boat left us, it was discovered that there were two men on board who had secreted themselves. As we had lost five by desertion, we had no desire to keep the deserters of other ships. One belonged to the *Harvest* and the other to the *Janet*. As the ship *Black Eagle* was just going in, we sent them by her to their respective owners, and we then made sail for the New Zealand cruising ground.

THIRD CRUISE

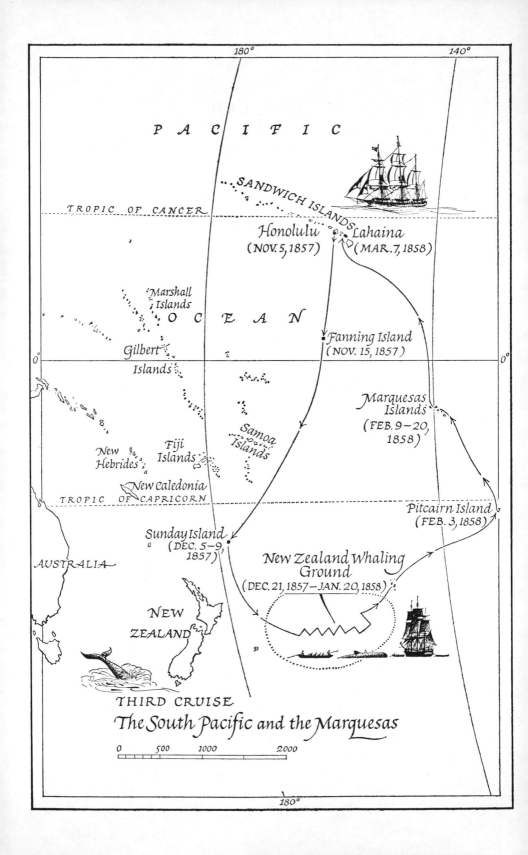

PACIFIC

SANDWICH ISLANDS

TROPIC OF CANCER

Honolulu
(NOV. 5, 1857)

Lahaina
(MAR. 7, 1858)

Marshall
Islands

OCEAN

Fanning Island
(NOV. 15, 1857)

Gilbert

Islands

Marquesas
Islands
(FEB. 9–20,
1858)

Samoa
Islands

New
Hebrides

Fiji
Islands

New Caledonia

TROPIC OF CAPRICORN

Pitcairn Island
(FEB. 3, 1858)

Sunday Island
(DEC. 5–9,
1857)

AUSTRALIA

New Zealand Whaling
Ground
(DEC. 21, 1857 – JAN. 20, 1858)

NEW

ZEALAND

THIRD CRUISE
The South Pacific and the Marquesas

0   500   1000   2000

The South Pacific and the Marquesas

NOVEMBER 1857—MARCH 1858

NOVEMBER 13. It being rainy and rough, had no lookout at the masthead. Soon after breakfast we were startled by the cry, "A school of sperm whales close to the ship!" They got the boats down immediately, but it was so rough that they soon lost sight of them.

NOVEMBER 15. Saw Fanning Island; went quite near it. It appeared to be very low land covered with coconut trees. It is said to be inhabited. This is the first low land we have seen on the voyage; all other islands have been very mountainous.

NOVEMBER 18. We are having very warm weather, but as there is quite a breeze, we manage to keep comfortable. While we were in port, my bedroom was enlarged, and now I do not think there is a lady on this cruising ground who has a larger and better room than I have. Crossed the line today for the third time in my voyage.

NOVEMBER 21. Samuel sat up most of the night last night to look out for a small island called Bennets Island that was in our immediate vicinity. Passed to the westward of it, however, and did not see it.

NOVEMBER 22. Last night there were several islands on each side of us, and Samuel deemed it prudent to be up again a part of the night. These islands are very low sand islands, and they can be seen but a short distance in the daytime. Probably we passed directly between them as he hoped, but it will not answer to place too much confidence on observations, as an error of the chronometer or a false position on the chart might prove very disastrous.

NOVEMBER 25. One year of our voyage has passed, and we are now commencing the second year of our pilgrimage. May it prove as pleasant to us as the past has been.

NOVEMBER 26. Probably this is Thanksgiving at home, and as Father, Mother, brothers, and sisters gather around the festive board, may they bestow one thought on their children who are wanderers on the sea. As it was blowing quite fresh and a heavy sea, we made no preparation for a special dinner. We were intending to be at Rarotonga about that time, but the wind changed so that we could not fetch. After that we hoped to fetch Aitutaki, but it was of no use. I am much disappointed, for I depended upon the nice fruit we could get there for trade, also pork and fowls. We were in want of wood from the island, but we shall be obliged to wait until the cruise is up and touch somewhere on our way to the Islands.

NOVEMBER 27. I have kept an account of the miles we have sailed since we left home. Up to the twenty-fifth November, one year out, we have sailed 36,985 miles. For the last twenty-four hours we have had a fine breeze, which has borne us 200 miles. We are now in cooler weather again, which I like much better than the warm weather we have on the line.

DECEMBER 5. Made Sunday Island just before sunset.

DECEMBER 6. Went around to the other side of the island, and as it was the Sabbath, we only sent a boat in to see if wood might be obtained there. Had no further communication with the shore during the day. As there is an abundance of wood to be procured there, we shall probably lay off for several days.

DECEMBER 7. A hard rainstorm, so that we kept off from the island until afternoon, when we wore ship and stood in for the land. The ship *Ocean* was in here the day before we arrived, out thirteen and a half months with 950 barrels sperm oil.

DECEMBER 8. In the afternoon three boats went onshore for

wood. Returned about sunset with three boatloads of wood and some strawberry tomatoes, which they sent off to me. There are two families there occupying one house. One man, the proprietor of the establishment, has two wives and quite a number of children. The other works for him and has taken a sister of the other man's wives for his wife. The females are natives of New Zealand. The males are Americans. Within a short time another family has arrived, but as they are rather destitute of provisions, the probability is they will not take up their abode there. Mr. Nickerson brought us a letter from Lewis and Eunice written two years ago and left there for Samuel or Augustus. They had strong hopes of seeing one or both of us.

DECEMBER 9. The boats went off again this morning. I wanted very much to go onshore, but as it was rough and bad landing, owing to the surf, Samuel thought it not best. So I put up a bundle of needles, cotton thread, wax, a few yards of calico, and a piece of flannel, with some toys, books, and papers from Minnie, and a bag of crackers for the children, and sent ashore with a letter I had previously written for Lewis and Eunice, should they touch there. Boats returned about three o'clock. It was so rough they could not bring off any wood. They obtained some bananas, bird's eggs, a goose, some turkeys, a bag of tomatoes which the women sent me, and three little pigeons which were sent to Minnie.[1] As we were having bad weather and it was such bad landing, Samuel thought it best to leave the island without attempting to get more wood; so we stood off immediately after. They brought me a few leaves and flowers to press and a few shells and stones, but nothing choice. Pumice stone is found in abundance on the shore.

DECEMBER 10. Have been making pies and preserves of my strawberry tomatoes today, which we found very nice. They grow wild and in great abundance here. They are called cape gooseberries here, strawberry tomatoes at home, and *powhas* at the Sandwich Islands. I think these are much larger and nicer than those at the Sandwich Islands. Sunday Island in sight at sunset, as we have had a calm day.

DECEMBER 11. Saved our goat's milk last night, and this morning took some of our bird's eggs which we procured from shore and made a real homelike Indian pudding. Those eggs, I think, are nearly equal to hen's eggs. They are speckled; the yolks are about the size but are much higher colored. About teatime a sail was raised from the masthead, the first we have seen since leaving the Islands.

DECEMBER 12. As we were both under short sail during the night, the ship was just about the same distance from us this morning. We hoped it was the *Commodore Morris,* and Samuel would have tried to speak her, but she seemed inclined to avoid us. We hoisted our colors, but she took no notice of it. In the afternoon she went on one tack, and we another, so that we soon lost sight of each other. Today we find ourselves in east longitude.[2]

DECEMBER 13. Spoke the ship that we saw yesterday, which proved to be the *Amethyst,* of New Bedford, Captain Jones. He came on board about six o'clock and stayed until one o'clock. We had a very pleasant gam; had much to tell him that had transpired within the last three years. He gave me a few pine-apples, the first I have seen for the voyage.

DECEMBER 14. Saw Macauley or Goat Island in the morning.
   P.M.   Two boats went in fishing. Failing to get fish, they went onshore and killed two wild hogs. Came back to the ship about sunset. The *Amethyst* in sight all day.

DECEMBER 15. Two boats went ashore today. Came back in the afternoon with a few fish, two wild goats which they had killed, and a kid which they succeeded in taking alive. The island is very small, uninhabited, nearly destitute of vegetation; no water to be found on the island. An abundance of goats, hogs, and parakeets to be found. They caught one of the latter to bring to Minnie, but it got drowned on their way to the ship. We had some of our pork cooked for dinner today that they killed ashore yesterday. I made great dependence upon my dinner, but when it was brought upon the table, the flavor thereof was sufficient. We were obliged to have it removed before we could eat our dinner. Hope the goats may prove more palatable. Saw a ship at a distance about sunset. We hoped to see a whale off this island but have been disappointed.

DECEMBER 18. As the wind was fair this morning and Samuel had become nearly discouraged looking for sperm whales and finding none, we started for the south, right whaling. I was disappointed, for I wanted to get in with the sperm whale fleet, hoping that we might see the *Commodore Morris*. We may perhaps see sperm whalers on our way south. The goats we procured at the islands are very good eating. The taste resembles very much that of mutton. Had it stewed, boiled, and fried, and a very nice hash made, as we have of sheep's heads, of the head and haslet. For the last few days have had very pleasant weather; shall have it more rugged as we proceed south.

DECEMBER 21. Saw a finback very near the ship about sunset, the first whale of any kind we have seen since we crossed the line. The weather is now quite cool but pleasant.

DECEMBER 22. Weather much cooler today. Have had the stove put up in the house on deck instead of the cabin for the present.

DECEMBER 25. Christmas Day reminds us of home and friends. Minnie wished to hang up her stocking as usual, and as I had a tin of candies which her grandpa put up for her, Santa Claus managed to fill it very well. We sat down to a Christmas dinner of two roast turkeys, sweet and Irish potatoes, boiled onions, stewed pumpkin, and cranberries, pickles, and a nice Indian pudding made of milk and eggs. Had a goat killed for the benefit of those living in the forecastle, to which, I should think, they did ample justice, as there are but two legs remaining. In the afternoon they were cheered by the sight of a right whale; lowered the boats, but it was rough and a heavy sea so that their efforts were without success, as he kept under water most of the time. About sunset again we heard the welcome sound of "There blows!" but it was too late to send the boats out in pursuit of them.

DECEMBER 26. Spoke the ship *Falcon* in the morning, of New Bedford, Captain Norton, twenty-eight months out, 700 barrels. The captain came on board and passed the day with us. I sent a letter to Thomas and Mercy by him, as he was confident that he should see them at Talcahuano.[3] About 5 P.M. saw another ship but did not get near enough to speak.

DECEMBER 27. A thick fog in the morning, regular right whale weather or "hoggy," as the French captain of the *De Hautpoul* called it. In the forenoon had a hard shower, so that we soon caught water enough for our next washing day.

DECEMBER 28. Saw whales just before breakfast; immediately after breakfast lowered the boats. Mr. Nickerson's boat soon got fast to one, when he capsized the boat and precipitated them all in the water. Mr. St. John with the waist boat immediately went to their rescue, but before he reached them, one poor fellow had found a watery grave. He said he could not swim, so Mr. Nickerson gave him an oar that he might keep himself up, but we think he must have had the cramp and let go his hold on the oar.

Poor Antone! He came out as one of the cabin boys and had lived in the cabin for a year and then at his own request went to live in the forecastle. He was so anxious to go out in a boat after whales. He was a smart, active boy of eighteen years, and I had become quite attached to him. Only the week before I had proposed to Samuel that we should take him home with us and give him the benefit of a little education. That was a sad day for us, Antone, when thou wast summoned into the mysteries of the unseen world without a moment's warning. May God in his infinite goodness have mercy on thy soul.[4]

In the afternoon saw whales again, lowered the boats, and Mr. Chappell struck one which they soon killed. Commenced cutting in about half-past three; finished at 11 P.M. The sad events of the day had made me almost sick, so I took a cup of tea by myself and went early to bed.

DECEMBER 29. A high wind and so rugged that it was not fit to commence boiling. Saw five ships today.

DECEMBER 30. Commenced boiling this morning. We had one black pig killed yesterday afternoon; have one small one left yet. As it was getting to be quite cool in the cabin, we had our stove put up, a nice little stove that was purchased at Honolulu.

Minnie says, "Mamma, I think I was something like a missionary the other day." Said I, "Why?" "When I was helping the steward pick over some dried apples, I talked to him about God." She has been much engaged lately in reading *The Peep of Day, Line upon Line,* and *Precept upon Precept,* three books which I purchased of Mr. Damon.⁵ She was interested especially in the account of the storm at sea where He rebuked the wind and said unto the sea, "Peace, be still." ⁶ A few days after she had been reading that passage, we had a gale of wind and a heavy sea; and when I was putting her to bed, she told me that she got up to the cabin window and said "Peace, be still" to the sea, but it did not obey her as it did Jesus.

1858

JANUARY 1. Another new year has opened upon us. The old year which opened upon us so fresh and smiling departed in sadness, for a cloud was hung around our pathway; even at the very threshold of the new year one of our number left us, never again to return. May not the sad news come to us from across the sea that any of our loved home faces have passed to the spirit land during the past year. As far as we have heard from, they have been mercifully preserved. God grant that it may not be otherwise. Saw four ships during the day. In the afternoon a high wind prevailed with rain.

JANUARY 2. Nothing in sight, neither ships nor whales. We are going back to where we saw the whales before. If we are not successful in finding them there again, shall look up another cruising ground. We had a gony, or albatross, killed yesterday, and I am going to try to save the feathers, as they are very soft and nice.

JANUARY 3. The holy Sabbath, first Sabbath of the new year. I should much like to attend church today to hear the new year's sermon. May it be a profitable and well-spent year to us all. In the evening commenced blowing a heavy gale. The barometer had been indicating it for several days.

JANUARY 4. Still blowing a gale. Had the deadlights shut to the cabin windows, and I was obliged to take my work onto the bed. In the afternoon the gale abated. It was a famous day among the officers and crew for sewing. I imagine all the old clothes got a good mending on this day.

JANUARY 5. A ship in sight in the afternoon but no whales.

JANUARY 6. Saw four whales in the morning before breakfast. Soon after breakfast the boats went in pursuit of them. They fastened to two, but the iron from the second mate's boat came out, so that we were successful in taking but one, which we were very happy to have. They were employed until dark in cutting him in. Saw a ship at a distance. Commenced blowing hard before they finished cutting in the whale.

JANUARY 8. Commenced boiling this forenoon. Saw a ship which we thought to be the *Japan,* but as soon as we commenced boiling, he started off. Quite rugged in the morning, but about noon it cleared away, and we had fine weather for the remainder of the day.

JANUARY 9. Fine weather in the forenoon. In the afternoon were obliged to lay to in a gale. Saw a ship after tea which we judge to be the same one that we have seen at times for several days.

JANUARY 10. The wind died away during the night to nearly a calm. Fine weather this morning. The ship still in sight. Fine weather during the day. Spoke the ship after tea, which proved to be the *Japan,* Captain Diman. Did not gam. He had been chasing the whales this afternoon without success. Has taken two whales since leaving the Islands. About sunset commenced raining and blowing a gale.

JANUARY 11. Weather rainy and thick in the forenoon; in the afternoon pleasant. All hands employed in stowing down oil. Stowed down 140 barrels from the two whales.

JANUARY 12. Fine weather during the day with the exception of one or two squalls. After dinner spoke the ship *Splendid,* of

Edgartown. Captain Smith came on board and passed the afternoon with us. As he was bound for Talcahuano very soon, I sent some letters in by him that he might mail them home. I sent two sheets to Falmouth, one to S. P. Bourne and one to Sarah, one to New Bedford to George, one to Father and Mother, one to Charles and Lizzie,⁷ and one to Cynthia to Sandwich, and one to be left at Talcahuano to Thomas and Mercy. Hope they may reach their destination before letters that we shall send from the Islands. Captain Smith has not taken a drop of oil for eleven months; has 250 [barrels] sperm and 1,400 whale. In the afternoon there was another ship in sight.

JANUARY 13. Pleasant weather with quite a strong breeze. The ship *Splendid* in sight astern of us. After tea our goose flew overboard, and we were obliged to send two boats out after her. They finally succeeded in catching her after injuring her with the boat hook. Consequently we were under the necessity of killing her. About dark the wind increased.

JANUARY 14. Pleasant weather with a strong breeze. The ship still in sight. In the afternoon the gale increased and blew with great violence during the night. About one o'clock I was awakened by a sound as of the rushing of many waters. My first thought was that the ship was going down, but my fears were entirely groundless, as we only shipped a heavy sea which broke one of the skylights and sent the water into the after cabin. The steward was called up to bail it out, which he soon did; but almost everything was wet through.

JANUARY 15. The gale continued unabated until about eleven o'clock, when it rapidly increased. About twelve o'clock shipped another heavy sea which went across the ship with such force as to carry away the bow boat, davits, etc., from the other side. The gale was much harder than any we have experienced since leaving home. In the afternoon the gale rather abated, and the sea went down.

JANUARY 16. Quite a strong breeze, but the gale has left us. Minnie says she wishes that Papa would "luff up his helm" and start for the Islands; she is quite tired of this weather, "for we came here for whales and can find nothing but gales"—and I think it is even so. Saw a ship today quite near us; probably she was not far distant during the gale. Had a severe pain in my face today, which I suppose proceeds from a defective tooth.

JANUARY 17.[8] Another strong breeze with some rain, and very thick. Saw some indications of whales, so Samuel thought it best to lay to and not go over the ground in a fog. Have been confined to my bed for two days with the pain in my head and face. The sore broke this afternoon, so that I think I shall soon get over it.

JANUARY 18. A thick fog again this morning. Had some trouble with one of the forward hands, which ended in confining him in the run. Such things are very unpleasant to me. He has been down there once before during the voyage, and I hoped that would be sufficient for him, but it seems that it has proved otherwise. In the afternoon a hard rainstorm.

JANUARY 21. A gale came on the night of the seventeenth which has continued without abatement ever since, and last night Samuel resolved to go before the wind and leave this region as quick as possible. It is useless to stop here; for if we should see whales, which we do not, it would be of no use with the wind blowing a gale. Have had no one looking out at the mastheads for a week. Saw a ship bound in the same direction with ourselves.

JANUARY 23. We are now in fine weather, considerably warmer than it has been. In a few days shall be in warm weather again. We shall probably cruise now around some of the islands near the line,[9] hoping we may see sperm whales. For the last week I have been confined to my bed with my face. It did not get better as I expected, and I could get no rest either day or night. Night before last Samuel opened the gathering, which relieved me very much. I am now nearly well again.

JANUARY 26. Raised a ship a long way ahead. We gain upon her considerably. Perhaps we may be up with her tomorrow morning. We are enjoying delightful weather now, which we fully appreciate after the southern gales and storms we have experienced.

JANUARY 27. Just after breakfast we spoke the ship that we saw yesterday. She proved to be the *James Maury*, of New Bedford. Captain Curry came on board and passed the day with us, as it was nearly calm. He boarded at Mr. Butler's with us at Honolulu, so that he seemed like an old acquaintance. He has taken one whale this season; has experienced very rough weather like ourselves. There were other boats lost, I conclude, beside ours, as he had seen the wrecks of two and had heard of another. Captain Curry sent me, when he returned to his ship, *The History of Pitcairn Island,*[10] some yams, and some dried bananas put up at Rarotonga. I gave him several books.

JANUARY 28. We have not beat the ship much today, as they are mending the mainsail. She is in sight a short distance from us. Captain Curry told us of the still further rise of whalebone, which is a matter of rejoicing to us. An unheard-of event in the annals of history for whalebone to be $1.50 per pound. The ladies are to be thanked for that, and I presume all interested in right whaling are truly thankful for this skirt movement. May the fashion long continue. One month today since Antone was swallowed up in the relentless waters.

JANUARY 30. It has been a dead calm for two days. Consequently the ship moves on very lazily. Saw something that looked like land today. Probably it was Michell's group of islands, as we supposed ourselves to be in their vicinity. The weather is getting to be uncomfortably warm. Still we shall have it very much warmer than it is now.

JANUARY 31. We are favored today with a nice little breeze, supposed to be the trade winds. Have put up the studding sails this morning, and we are now making our way finely to Pitcairn Island, where we hope to get a sperm whale.

FEBRUARY 1. A strong breeze today which wafts us along right merrily. The *James Maury* still in sight every day for a short time and then disappears. We do not beat her as we did the first time we saw her.

FEBRUARY 3. Pitcairn Island in sight. We sailed around the island and very near it so that we had a full view. It is famous as being the home of the mutineers of the ship *Bounty,* and it seems almost incredible that so small an island could have been the scene of such awful tragedies as have there been enacted. Old John Adams,[11] the last survivor of the mutineers, had two dreams which caused him to repent of his sins and turn from his evil ways. Since that time their descendants have been brought up in a simple Christian-like manner and have won the respect of all who have visited them. As the island was too small for their subsistence with their increasing population, Norfolk Island was presented them by the English government, and to that place they have since removed. Consequently Pitcairn is now deserted. We could see their houses and their little church, with holes all around it resembling the portholes of a ship instead of windows.

It is a very pleasant, fresh-looking isle, rising abruptly from the sea, well stocked with trees of various kinds. The highest point rises one thousand feet above the level of the sea. It is interesting to us, especially, as being the birthplace of our little niece Mary Stuart, and it reminded us of how much we want to see her. The *James Maury* was around the island also, and in the afternoon we set a signal for him to come on board, which he did. I wanted some of the fruit that we suppose to be on the island, oranges, plantains, bananas, etc., but it is a very bad landing place without a pilot; and as the wind was the wrong way, Samuel thought it not advisable to attempt to send in a boat. We found our chronometer to be about thirty miles out of the way by the latitude and longitude of the island. I like to see land occasionally so that her rate may be corrected, if wrong.

FEBRUARY 4. Have been trimming ship today so that we may sail faster; had not enough in her, so they have been filling casks with salt water. About sunset was near enough to the *James Maury* to speak her. After that we passed her.

FEBRUARY 5. A strong breeze which carries us speedily on our way. The *James Maury* beat us a little last night. We have seen nothing as yet to indicate whales, not even a blackfish, porpoise, or finback. Now we are proceeding on our way to the Marquesas Islands, where we shall touch for wood. At sunset the *James Maury* was as far astern as she could be seen from aloft.

FEBRUARY 6. A strong breeze. Made 200 miles the last twenty-four hours. Our consort is not to be seen.

FEBRUARY 7. A strong breeze, fine and pleasant. Made 228 miles the last twenty-four hours.

FEBRUARY 8. Made 200 miles the last twenty-four hours. Expect to see the island of Magdalena, or Fatu Hiva, in the morning.

FEBRUARY 9. In the morning arrived in sight of the island; a ship in sight appearing to be bound in, which we took to be a merchantman. As we approached the land, we saw a ship in the harbor, a sight that was pleasing to me, as I felt somewhat anxious in regard to going among those wild savages.[12] As we drew near, a boat came off to us, filled with frightfully tattooed naked men. One who said he was chief could talk a little broken English. He is to stay on board while we are procuring wood to look out for the natives as, he says, "They sava plenty steal." One of our boats went ashore, and another went on board the merchant ship to see if we could obtain late papers and to carry letters in case she should be bound to California, which proved to be the case. She was the bark *Glimpse*, Captain Dayton, bound to California from Sydney with forty passengers. The ship in the harbor was the *Japan*, Captain Diman; no oil since we last saw him. When the boat returned, she brought off some bananas, coconuts, and some fowl as a present to me from John's (the chief) wife.

FEBRUARY 10. Samuel decided to anchor here instead of laying off and on as he at first intended, which we did about noon. The ship was filled with native men through the day. The women are not allowed to go in a canoe; it is "taboo" to them. If they wish to go to another bay, they are compelled to go over rocks and ridges while their husbands go in their canoes. They may

go in a whaleboat, however, when opportunity offers. We have
had pigs, fowls, coconuts, breadfruit, bananas, and pineapples
brought off today, and I have had sufficient employment in
watching them as they came off in their canoes.[13] Everything
is new and strange to me. What would my friends at home say
to see such frightful-looking creatures? They appear delighted
to see Minnie and myself. I believe there never was but one
white woman here before we came. They come up to us and
put their hands on us and say, "Verry goot here, verry goot
here," etc., pointing about us.

This afternoon the Kanaka missionary and native teacher
came on board. The missionary, Mr. Kaivi, is from Oahu; came
here with his wife in the *Morning Star,* the children's ship. They
took tea with us, and the native teacher, Abraham Natua, asked
a blessing at the table in his native language. I think it is a
glorious era in the history of our world for those who once were
heathen and have embraced the Gospel to come to these other
islands of the sea and proclaim the glad tidings to their brethren
who are still in darkness. I sympathize with them in their labors
and have assisted and will do all in my power for them.

Old John, the chief, brought his wife off in our boat to see me.
Her clothing consisted of a piece of red flannel tied around her,
earrings of porpoise teeth, and an abundance of beads around
her neck. She is my friend—everyone has a friend here. That
means among them, "Me give you, you give me." She brought
me some sugar cane, fowl, and pineapples. I gave her a few
yards of cloth and some beads.

FEBRUARY 11. The ship has been filled with natives, the same as
yesterday. Natua came on board to dinner, and he attempted
to ask a blessing in English. I will put it down as near as I can
recollect: "O great Fader, got no moder, got no broder, got no
sister. Make fust de sea, make fust de dry land, make fust de
moon and de stars, make fust de trees, den he make man; and
now great Fader, give man he belly full. Amen." He is the first
convert among them, and I am much pleased with him. He
certainly seems much better than many of them or, I might say,
than most of them. He says, "Me throw my taboo all away. Me
throw my Kanaka god all away. My God, Jehovah," and as he
spoke the name, he looked up very reverently. He says again,

"Before missionary come, me no good. Me sava plenty lie, me sava plenty steal, me sava plenty fight, me sava plenty kill Kanaka. Now me no sava. Missionary God no like." The missionary has but few followers. They think too much of their taboos to give them up readily. They are a very superstitious people. No woman is allowed to touch a man's head or anything that touches a man's head, and anything they put over their head is taboo to anyone. I noticed several with little bags around their necks. I inquired what it was for; they told me it was powder. They wanted to keep it for themselves, and so they put it over their heads and made taboo of it.

In the afternoon Samuel, Minnie, and myself went onshore. They made a great deal of us, examined our clothes, and thought everything in any way appertaining to us was "verry goot." Their houses are built of bamboos and leaves platted together for the roof, and the floor is made of little stones something like our gravel walks, only the stones are larger. They have nothing in their houses but mats to sleep on; and if anything gets under these mats, let it be ever so valuable, it is taboo and they must go and bury it on taboo ground. They do not bury their dead but put them in houses up in the mountain. If a woman loses a husband, she scratches her face all over with the bark of coconut and lets the blood dry on. We saw two mourning in that way. They have a number of gods, but the greatest among them is what they call the Sea God; that is, the white man's God, who makes all the powder muskets and ships and cloth. They also have god-men, who talk with the gods and tell the people what to do. When they kill an enemy, they take his body up to a taboo house, and the god-men go there and eat it.

The people of the other two bays on this side of the island are at war constantly with the people of this tribe, in the Oomoa Bay as it is called. There are not as many killed, they say, now, since they have commenced using firearms, as when they went to war with clubs and spears. They are great cowards. John, the chief, says, "Me no like fight. Me afraid." Sometimes he says they say, "Come, John, you go fight. Me say me no go. Me sick, me too much sick. They go off. Me no sava sick. No more me sick. All go off."

FEBRUARY 12. Captain Diman came on board and dined with us.

We are engaged in getting wood, buying hogs and fowls, etc.

FEBRUARY 13. Natua and his wife came off to see us, also the missionary Kaivi, his wife, and two children. I gave each of the women some calico for a dress and made a little dress for each of the two children. At night another chief's wife came off in our boat to see me. I gave her one of my old dresses and put it on her, with which she was much pleased. The king came on board today and wanted to know if Samuel had not got a friend for him. So he gave him a shirt, and I assisted him in putting it on, the first time I ever had the honor of putting on a garment for a king. He is a great beggar, and I dislike him more than any that I have seen. They are all great thieves; nothing can be left within their reach that they will not take.

Today a ship touched here. A boat went out to it and found it to be the *James Maury*. Had taken 80 barrels sperm oil since we left her. The *Japan* took up her anchor today; will lay off and on until tomorrow. He has had three men to run away here.

FEBRUARY 14. Most of our ship's company went onshore today to church. We—Samuel, Minnie, and myself—did not go as we knew we should attract the attention of the people from the minister and thought we might do more good by staying away. In the afternoon John brought his wife (my friend, as he calls her) to see me again.[14]

FEBRUARY 15. We are getting the last of the wood today and shall probably leave tonight. I went ashore in the afternoon and went to the missionary house. Both times when I have been ashore, I have been surrounded by a crowd of people, and they all followed me to the house. They appeared to feel badly to have us to leave. They say, "Plenty ships come here, but you more better; plenty ship come here, no have wahine, no have daughter." Natua says, "When you go, me cry. Captain all same my fader, you all same my moder." About sunset we took the missionary on board to carry to Dominica and bade the people of Fatu Hiva farewell.

FEBRUARY 16. Passed the island of St. Pedro and in the afternoon lay off Puamau Bay, Hiva Oa, or Dominica, which is the Rev.

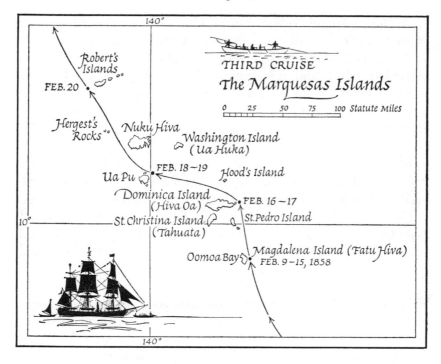

THIRD CRUISE
The Marquesas Islands

0   25   50   75   100 Statute Miles

Robert's Islands
FEB. 20
Hergest's Rocks
Nuku Hiva
Washington Island (Ua Huka)
FEB. 18–19
Ua Pu
Hood's Island
Dominica Island (Hiva Oa)
FEB. 16–17
St. Christina Island (Tahuata)
St. Pedro Island
Oomoa Bay
Magdalena Island (Fatu Hiva)
FEB. 9–15, 1858

140°
10°
140°

Mr. Kekela's station. He came off to us in his boat and another boat filled with Kanakas. Mr. Nickerson went ashore to see what he could find fresh, and when Kekela decided to dig a few potatoes that afternoon, Samuel took the missionaries and went after them. The missionary has a plenty of potatoes, but Samuel does not like to stay here long. He wishes to go tomorrow, and they are not dug yet. About sunset the boats came off with a few barrels of potatoes and an abundance of bananas. The missionaries are to come off in the morning to trade. The *Nassau* is laying off here also; has taken 100 barrels sperm this season.

FEBRUARY 17. Rev. Mr. Kekela and Kaivi came off this morning with a few more potatoes and bought goods to quite an amount.[15] They gave Samuel an order on the treasurer of the Hawaiian Missionary Society at Honolulu. They furnish themselves with trade from whaleships in this way to enable them to get provisions from the natives. I sent Mrs. Kekela some calico for a dress, as I had given one to Mrs. Kaivi before. We have seen Hood's Island, Tahuata, or St. Christina, and Magdalena, or Fatu Hiva, today. About four o'clock the missionaries left us, and we said *aloha* to the island of Dominica. About sunset passed Hood's Island; it is a small island and uninhabited. There are two small islands in this group (I cannot now recollect the names) that are not inhabited by live men, but it is their belief that the spirits of their dead do there congregate.

FEBRUARY 18. This morning saw Dominica, Hood's Island, Ua Huka, or Washington Island, and Ua Pu. In the afternoon we were very near the latter island so that we could see the villages. As it was too late to send a boat in, Samuel decided to lay off tonight and send a boat in in the morning. With the exception of a few valleys that are green and thrifty-looking, the island appears barren and rocky.

FEBRUARY 19. Sent a boat in with a little trade to see if we could get a few hogs and some bananas, but nothing could be obtained. A canoe came off to us with natives, also a boat. The latter brought a hog to sell, which we bought for three fathoms of cloth. While the boat was ashore, one of our Kanakas, Johnny Boy, ran away. It is bad enough for a Kanaka that has been brought up among partially civilized people to run away in such a place as this, but that white people and Americans should choose a home among savages and cannibals is surprising. Captain Diman had three to desert him at Oomoa. After four days had passed, one repented and turned back. The others kept their hiding places.

FEBRUARY 20. Saw Ua Pu, Nuku Hiva, Hergest's Rocks, and Robert's Islands, which is the last we shall see of the Marquesas group. We obtained a considerable fresh [supply of provisions] here: [16] twenty-six hogs, forty fowl, two thousand coconuts for the hogs to feed on, plenty of bananas and plantains, breadfruit, papayas, a few pineapples, and a few sweet potatoes. The milk of a young coconut is delicious, and Minnie and myself have quite a feast with it. We also obtained a few sour oranges; there were no sweet ones to be found. I hoped to get some limes but was disappointed. Captain Diman sent me two bottles of lime juice, which was very acceptable, as I do not like to drink clear water now, it is so warm and poor.

FEBRUARY 24. Crossed the line today for the fourth time since leaving home.

FEBRUARY 25. Fifteen months of our voyage expires today, nearly half, perhaps.

FEBRUARY 26. Saw blackfish, lowered the boats for them, and they disappeared. Succeeded in bringing one little porpoise to the ship. Saved the tenderloin for sausage cakes and gave the remainder to the hogs. The last of Minnie's pigeons has flown. We missed him tonight; had been walking around by himself for several days. We were sorry to part with him.

FEBRUARY 27. Quite a strong breeze. Killed a hog in the afternoon.

MARCH 4. Have had strong trade winds for several days so that we have made rapid progress in our passage; are about three days sail from Maui, which is to be our stopping place.

MARCH 6. Saw a sail which appeared to be going to Hilo. Saw the island of Hawaii about noon. Saw another ship in the afternoon. Saw Maui in the evening.

MARCH 7. Lay to a few hours in the morning waiting for daylight to go through the passage. Arrived off the harbor about nine o'clock. Soon the customhouse officer came on board and shortly after we anchored, making the thirteenth whaler in port. After dinner Samuel went onshore to get letters if any were to be found. I remained on board, as I did not care about going ashore on the Sabbath. About four o'clock Samuel returned, bringing letters for Mr. Nickerson only. I was greatly disappointed, although I feared as much, as we were in several weeks earlier than we anticipated when leaving the Islands.

He told me that Mr. and Mrs. Bigelow with Lizzie were impatiently awaiting our arrival and I must prepare immediately for the shore, as the wind had commenced blowing and it would be so rough probably the next day that I could not land if I wished. So not caring to pass another day on shipboard when the pleasure of female society was proffered me and the meeting with friends whom I had learned to love and respect, I speedily finished my preparations; and we were soon on our way to Mrs.

Bigelow's, which will be our home for several weeks. Found them seemingly very happy to see us. Was sorry to learn that Mr. Gilman had left about a week previous for the States, where report says he is bound in search of a wife.

It appears very natural to stop at the old straw cottage again. Mr. and Mrs. Bigelow have broken up housekeeping in their old establishment and keep Mr. Gilman's house open for the accommodation of captains and their families during the shipping season. After that season is past, they, Mr. and Mrs. Bigelow, will also leave for the States, where they intend taking up their abode, provided the change of climate will not be too much for them.

MARCH 8. The most of my acquaintances called upon me today. There have been a few added to the circle of foreign residents since we were here before, which additions are highly prized: Mrs. Chandler, the lady of the American consul; Dr. White, lady, and daughter, of San Francisco, an assistant of Dr. Dow; and Miss Chamberlain, a schoolteacher. One of Mrs. Bishop's children, little Charlie, has winged his flight to an eternal world since we were here before, one short year ago.

MARCH 10. Passed the day with Mrs. Bishop. Had a very pleasant visit. She has a little motherless child with her, two years old— little Dora, daughter of Captain Fish of the *Corea*, of New London. Mrs. Fish died in Honolulu, where she left an infant three months old. Tears filled my eyes as I looked upon the little motherless Dora and thought what must have been that mother's feelings, to die and leave those little ones among strangers in a strange land. I almost longed to take her to my home and to my heart. In the evening stopped with them to a prayer meeting, where we met Mr. Baldwin, the missionary, and family. They were on a visit to the States when we were here before so that this is the first time we have met with them.

MARCH 11. Passed the day with Mrs. Brayton. Dr. White's little Mary was there to meet Minnie, and they had a royal time together playing to their hearts' content.[17] Our second officer, Mr. St. John, has been out of health for some time. Yesterday he went to consult a physician who told him that he had a disease of the heart and the sooner he could get home the better. So Samuel felt that he must give him his discharge, and he is now in the hospital. He has always treated me well, and I shall be very sorry to part with him. He has our best wishes for a safe return and speedy recovery.

MARCH 12. This morning a schooner arrived with the California mails, bringing us a number of those inky messengers of love and affection from friends far away: one from S. P. Bourne, Celia, and Celia Maria; one from Sarah and a note from Elisabeth Robinson and a note for Minnie from Willie; a letter from brother George from New Bedford; and one from Sandwich from Lizzie. Not a word from Father, Mother, Willie, or Cynthia. I know it is because we were in earlier than we intended, but I am extremely sorry. Lizzie wrote that my dear father's health was poor, but she had seen him much more feeble than he then was. I think much about him and hope and trust that he may yet be spared to his family these many years. Times have been very hard for the last winter at home. Everyone has been more or less affected, but fortunately we knew nothing of it until they were growing brighter. He who tempers the wind to the shorn lamb[18] has kindly given them a mild winter, so that there has not been so much suffering as if the winter had been so severe as for two winters past. I was pained to hear of the death of our neighbor, Mrs. Swift. Her death comes nearer than any that has transpired since leaving home, and it leaves a vacancy that can hardly be filled. She was a kind neighbor and loved and respected by all.

This afternoon I went on board the *Addison* with Minnie and Lizzie Bigelow. We saw the *Young Hero*, of Nantucket, Captain Long, getting under way, and as we were returning in the boat, she ran into the French whaler *Napoleon 3rd*, slightly damaging the latter and the former to the value of eight or ten thousand dollars, as was judged.

MARCH 14. Went to church once again this morning, for which privilege I hope I am truly thankful. When at home I always liked to attend church and was never in the habit of letting trifles absent me from the house of God. Still I think I never realized what a privilege it was until since I have become a wanderer upon the sea. Mr. Bishop has a small congregation, and sailors generally do not attend. I do not think he is exactly fitted to their wants.

Today I was made very happy by the arrival of the *Speedwell*, Captain and Mrs. Gibbs. She and I were schoolmates together, and with what pleasure shall we renew our acquaintance in this far-off island of the sea. Just before sunset, went down to Mrs. Brayton's to see them. Found them well. Mrs. Gibbs looked very natural but had grown to resemble her mother very much since I last saw her. They stopped at Fayal, where they saw our brother Thomas and wife. Brought us letters from them. They have been there several months while their ship has been out on a short cruise. Mercy has another little daughter born at that place. They had no name for it unless they decided to call it "Crianna," which they thought some of doing, as it possessed the accomplishment signified in that name to a great degree.

MARCH 15. Last night the whole town was alarmed by the sound of fire, which proved to be the *Young Hero,* set on fire, as was supposed, by some of the crew. They were helped by the crews of all the ships in the harbor, but it is still burning, and they will probably lose the ship. Mrs. Gibbs passed the day with us at Mrs. Bigelow's, and we passed the time very pleasantly in conversing of bygone days.

MARCH 16. Last night we were awakened by the sound of "The fire has burst through to the outside of the ship!" We got up and looked out of our window, which commanded the whole view of the harbor, and found it to be even so. It was a grand sight and still a very melancholy one. This morning it is burning with redoubled fury. As I sit by my window writing, looking up, I have seen the three masts fall one after the other, and now nothing remains but the hulk. Minnie has been in tears all the morning. It makes her feel so sad to see the destruction of a noble ship. What would I give to know the feelings of the man or men who could thus wantonly destroy her. Can it be possible that they are enjoying it? I think not. Captain and Mrs. Gibbs, Samuel, Minnie, and myself took tea with Mrs. Bishop this afternoon.

MARCH 17. Went on board the *Speedwell* this P.M. with Captain and Mrs. Gibbs, Mrs. Brayton, Lizzie Bigelow, [and] Minnie. I procured some books in exchange for some which I am to let her have. Had a very pleasant time, except that Mrs. Brayton was seasick. I had the pleasure of seeing Mr. Shiverick, their third officer, a Falmouth man, and of conversing upon home matters, which is very pleasant. A hand organ on board much delighted the children. Minnie could hardly be convinced that there was no one near to take the money.

Gifford has asked his discharge today, as he does not like whaling and cannot feel interested in it. I think Samuel will decide to give it to him, as he will not make a whaleman. I am sorry, for it is a very miserable place to leave a young man, and I think he is now a likely young man with good principles.

MARCH 18. The *Benjamin Tucker* arrived today, bringing as passengers Captain Andrews, lady, and a pair of twin boys, who were wrecked in the brig *Francis* on the coast of California, living in a tent on the sand for four weeks before they were taken off. They are going to occupy the next house, taking their meals with us. This P.M. Mrs. Gibbs, Samuel, Minnie, and myself went on board the *Addison* to see what I had for her. We intend leaving for Oahu tomorrow, and Miss Chamberlain, the teacher, will accompany us, as it is her vacation and much pleasanter on board a ship for passengers than those little native schooners.

MARCH 19. Was out this morning making my good-by calls when Mrs. Chandler told me that she had just seen my husband and that he informed her that we were not to leave today, as the sailors were superstitious in regard to sailing on Friday, as it was on the Friday before that the *Young Hero*'s trouble commenced; so he decided to humor them, as he was in no great haste. This morning the *Omega*, of Edgartown, of which Mr. Whittens is mate, arrived. He brought letters for Minnie and myself from Sarah and Willie, which were very acceptable even if we had received later intelligence from home. He said he would come up and see us if he had time before we left, which I hope he will do, as I should like much to see him and talk of his wife and Lizzie. I think much of them.

MARCH 20. Mrs. Andrews and children came up to the house today for the first time. She appears like a very interesting woman. She formerly belonged to Nantucket. We left our kind friends in the afternoon, after bidding an affectionate adieu to our worthy host and family, who leave for the States in about a month.

MARCH 21. This morning immediately after breakfast went a-shore. Found that Mr. Butler, with whom we stopped before, had failed and gone to Oregon. So were obliged to look up a new boarding place, which Captain Spencer very kindly undertook for us and was soon successful in finding a room for us at Mrs. Humphreys'; and we take our meals at Mrs. Carter's, a custom which prevails extensively at the Sandwich Islands. Captain Slocum insisted on our going immediately to his house to dine, which we accepted although it was Sunday, as I wanted to see his wife and learn of the welfare of my friends whom I had met here in the fall. Mrs. Slocum has failed since we last saw her, and I am fearful that she will be spared to her friends but a short time. Her disease, as she herself told me, had made and was still making rapid progress. We learned that Mrs. Coggeshall died in about a week after we left last fall, and in a few days after her husband left. Mrs. Slocum is at housekeeping and very pleasantly situated. Minnie was delighted to see Mr. Howland and Henry again. I did not get my trunks up to the house in time to change my clothes for church so that I was deprived of that privilege. Samuel attended church in the evening; I did not go, as I did not think it best to take Minnie out in the evening air. She has been quite unwell for several days and, I think, has had a slight touch of the "boohoo" fever, which attacks strangers almost invariably.

MARCH 22. Called to see some of my acquaintances today and have been engaged in shopping for myself and Mrs. Bigelow. We expected to leave tonight, but shall not get away until tomorrow, as we have had a chain to ship and our bone to get ashore.[19] The present prices of bone and oil are very low, and Samuel puts on a long face when he thinks of what he shipped last fall which is so soon to arrive. I met Gifford in the street today. He came from Maui Saturday and is thinking of going to

California. I was very glad to see him and gave him some good advice, which he took very kindly. Captain Ludlow passed the evening with us and a Mr. Smith who was with Samuel in the *Eliza Adams*. Captain Slocum very kindly sent up his horse and carriage for us to ride, which we were very happy to take; but as it commenced raining very soon after, our ride was necessarily cut short. Mr. Flintner called up to see us and presented Minnie with a very pretty fan.

MARCH 23. Went out in the morning to make some calls and stopped at Mr. Damon's until Samuel called for me to go on board. It was very rough, and I was glad to get on board the ship. Left about twelve o'clock. Just before we left Mrs. Carter sent Minnie a hen of a very peculiar kind, its feathers appearing to grow the wrong way, all in a heap. She calls it Frizzle. When we arrived on board, the cooper informed us that we had six little pigs, a circumstance that pleased Minnie, of course.[20]

FOURTH CRUISE

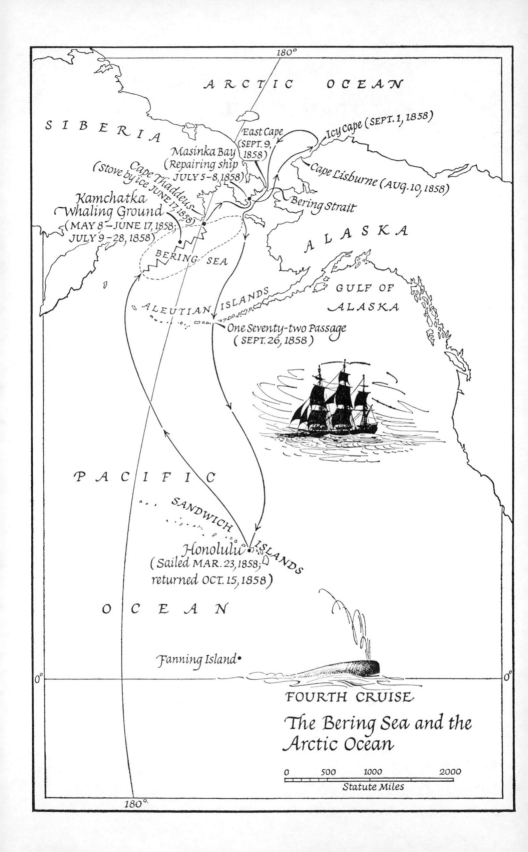

ARCTIC OCEAN

SIBERIA

Icy Cape (SEPT. 1, 1858)

East Cape
(SEPT. 9,
1858)

Masinka Bay
(Repairing ship
JULY 5–8, 1858)

Cape Lisburne (AUG. 10, 1858)

Cape Thaddeus
(Stove by ice JUNE 17, 1858)

Bering Strait

Kamchatka
Whaling Ground
(MAY 8–JUNE 17, 1858;
JULY 9–28, 1858)

ALASKA

BERING SEA

GULF OF
ALASKA

ALEUTIAN ISLANDS

One Seventy-two Passage
(SEPT. 26, 1858)

PACIFIC

SANDWICH ISLANDS

Honolulu
(Sailed MAR. 23, 1858;
returned OCT. 15, 1858)

OCEAN

Fanning Island

FOURTH CRUISE

The Bering Sea and the
Arctic Ocean

0   500   1000   2000
Statute Miles

The Bering Sea
and the Arctic Ocean

MARCH—OCTOBER 1858

————◆◆◆◆————

MARCH 28. Have had very rough weather with a strong breeze ever since we left Oahu until today, when it is smooth and pleasant. We are engaged in washing. Minnie met with about as severe an affliction as she ever experienced today. She lost her Frankie overboard, a doll that she dearly loved for its own sake and the more because it was Grandma's Annie's.[1] She cried for a long time and wrung her hands[2] in the greatest agony. She insisted so much upon having black clothes made to wear that I was obliged to get a piece of black ribbon to tie on her arm to pacify her.

MARCH 29. Had another addition to our family today of six more little pigs. The others are running about deck and are very cunning. Minnie thinks there never was anything prettier.

APRIL 6. We have had very pleasant weather for the last week until yesterday, when we were visited by a drenching rainstorm, and today it is not much better. The weather is growing cooler also. We are now where Samuel thinks there is a prospect of seeing right whales. We shall have a long cruise and sincerely hope it may be a successful one. We have some fruit left yet, although there was but very little to be procured at the Islands, as it was early. Of vegetables we have sweet and Irish potatoes, onions, and pumpkins; of fruit, bananas and oranges. We bought some delicious oranges at Oahu, and Captain Freeman sent me a basket at Maui. Captain Barber sent me a California cheese and a half bushel of figs. Mr. Bigelow presented Minnie with a tin of gingersnaps and gave me two dozen tins of preserved fruits, which—with crackers, preserved meats, codfish, fowls,

[85]

and hogs, beside our common fare—I think will make quite a bill of fare for the season. I also have a good supply of books and papers, and could I only have had one more package of letters from home, my wants would have been all supplied. Samuel thought it hardly safe to entrust them to the care of anyone coming after us, as it was uncertain about seeing them, but I can but hope that someone will bring them along. This morning we had an addition again to our family of five pigs, which is rather more than we care about at this time.

APRIL 11. Nothing of interest has transpired for the last week. Have had rough, windy, drizzling weather about every day. It is also quite cool, and a fire which we have now in our cabin is very comfortable as well as cheerful. Have also had an addition of five pigs which were very short-lived, as we already had more than we could accommodate.

APRIL 16. Have had damp, rough weather during the week, and today we have snow and hail squalls. At times the snow flies right merrily.

APRIL 18. Quite warm and pleasant weather. Went on deck in the afternoon and had quite a promenade. How much I have thought of loving friends far away today, and I doubt not but we have been thought of with much affection by them as they went up to the house of God, and wished that we might bear them company. I passed the most of the day in reading. Sometimes I write a little.

APRIL 21. Foggy this morning but soon cleared away, and we have had a fine day. Occasionally we hear the cry from the masthead of "There blows!" but it proves to be nothing more than a humpback or finback, while the kind that we are in pursuit of remains as yet unseen, and we still go on our way through the waters. A good season's work, that we may go home, seems almost too much to hope for.

APRIL 25. Foggy as usual. Have had no observations for five days, but we have plenty of sea room as yet. This is the Sabbath. Cold, dreary, and uncomfortable. Our friends at home

have twice wended their way to the house of God, and the blessings they have there sought for themselves, they have alike
sought for us, the absent, deprived of like privileges; and as
their eyes are now closed in sleep, perhaps they are dreaming
of loved ones on the sea. I love to think that the same Eye
watches over us and those dear faraway ones, and that the same
Arm is outstretched over them that protects us. We are alike
under His care whether on the land or on the sea.

APRIL 27. A bright day, clear and cold. Have been able to get
good observations today, which prove us to be about where
Samuel supposed. For the last two weeks we have had very
smooth weather, which we hardly expected here, although
very acceptable.

APRIL 29. Quite a severe gale came on last night, which has
blown with increasing force through the day, attended with
some rain.

APRIL 30. The wind blew very hard through the night and a part
of the day. Afternoon, wind abates and clears away, quite pleasant.

MAY 2. Cold with rain, snow, and hail. Considerable ice made
on deck last night, and this morning Minnie had a fine time
getting ice and making snowballs. Minnie's Frizzle has departed
this life. Probably the change of climate was too much for her.
Have seen a few finbacks today, which is thought to be a very
good sign.

MAY 3. This morning we heard the pleasing sound of "Sail O!"
which assured us that we were not alone upon the ocean. After
tea we spoke the ship, which proved to be the *Champion*,
of Edgartown. Captain Coffin came on board and passed the
evening with us. We have decided to keep together for the
present, as it is more pleasant to go in among the ice with company than alone and unattended.

MAY 4. A heavy gale, which continued for the day. The *Champion* quite near us, both laying to.

MAY 5. Pleasant weather. Captain Coffin came on board and passed the day with us. Had a nice time. He brought the daguerreotypes of his wife and boy for me to see. Saw two ships in the afternoon bound to the northeast. Did not speak them.

MAY 6. Saw several pieces of floating ice today, the first we have seen. It cautions us to be careful. It is well for us that there is so much daylight. The sun rises about three o'clock in the morning and sets at nine in the evening, so that there is only an hour or two of darkness. We are bound to the coast and from thence to follow the ice along to Cape Thaddeus.

MAY 7. Another gale, but quite a comfortable one, as the ship lay very steady. Minnie has been quite unwell for several days with a severe cold, headache, earache, and throatache. She and Samuel had a touch of the boohoo fever after leaving the Islands (to which most foreigners are subject). Otherwise she has enjoyed excellent health since leaving home.

MAY 8. The coldest day we have yet experienced; ice made on deck quite fast. About three o'clock P.M. raised two sails. Soon after raised two more, and presently one alone. They were all to the windward, and we spoke none of them. Our consort is quite near us. After tea he lowered his boat and made us a call. It seems very pleasant and homelike to have him call so often. We killed two hogs today.

MAY 9. The *Champion* the only ship in sight in the morning. About nine o'clock raised two more, but no whales yet seen or heard of.

MAY 10. In the afternoon Captain Coffin came on board. Went near enough Saturday to one of the ships so that he could read her name, which he found to be the *Majestic*, just from home.

MAY 12. Kept headed in through the night; in the morning found ourselves among the ice among ships. The *Addison* with her consort decided to run along a little farther and see what was to be seen, as there were three ships farther in the ice and one had her boats down. Soon afterward the *Champion* repented and turned back, and we kept on alone. After dinner we saw a mussel digger, which we suppose to be the same one that the boats were in pursuit of. Spoke the *Gay Head;* Captain Lowen came on board and made us a short call. I was very glad to see him, as I saw him on Kodiak last season. There are ten ships around us, of which are the *Marengo,* the *Omega,* of Edgartown, *America, John and Elisabeth,* and two French ships. I was very glad to hear of the *Marengo* being so near. I hope we may have an opportunity of seeing Mrs. Skinner, also of seeing our neighbor Mr. Whittens in the *Omega.* As it was thick and coming on to blow, we all started to leave the ice.

MAY 13. This morning found ourselves near the *Champion* again. The wind blew quite a gale last night, and it is thick and foggy today.

MAY 14. Another blow last night and thick today. No ships in sight. Quite a snowstorm in the afternoon.

MAY 15. Clear and cold. Are working our way towards the ice.
P.M.   Saw a ship and saw some floating ice. After tea spoke the ship *Milo;* Captain Sowle came on board. He is a sperm whaler, thirty months out; has 900 [barrels] sperm and 600 whale. Had not received a letter from his wife during his absence. Had been in no place that he could get papers or news from the States. Had seen no ships and was, as he said, ignorant of everything that was going on. I looked him up all the late papers that I had, which I presume were very acceptable. At nine o'clock three other ships were in sight.

MAY 16. We are again in the ice. There are quite large pieces floating about and long pieces of field ice that has not been broken up; but they say there is but very little depth to it for this season of the year, and everything so far indicates a mild season. We have heard of no one as yet getting a whale, although Captain Lowen reported that one of the French ships had seen two. I hear that the *Speedwell* is around us. Hope we may be so fortunate as to fall in with her occasionally. Six ships in sight this noon; the *Milo* close by us. About six o'clock a real bowhead was raised, and three of our boats beside several from other ships went in pursuit of him, but he went under the ice and disappeared. The sight of the creature pleased them wonderfully, even if he was not to be taken.

MAY 17. The good old *Addison* has taken a bowhead, the first that we have heard of being taken. The boats were down from several ships near us, and so we thought our boats might as well be down also, even if we could see nothing. Our boats had not been down more than ten minutes before the whale came up between our bow boat and a boat from another ship. They both started for him, but our boat, having the best chance, struck. He ran under the ice soon after they fastened, but our brave crew were not going to give him up so, so two boats went around on the other side of the ice to lance him and send him back, which they finally did after having quite an exciting time. Mr. Nickerson got out of his boat and went on the ice to try to shoot him, while another boat's crew from another ship landed and snowballed the whale, probably wounding him severely. An officer from the *Milo* wished an opportunity of greasing his lance, which they afforded him. The *Saratoga, Milo, John and Elisabeth, Gay Head, Majestic,* and two more are close by us. Most of them been chasing all day without success. Spoke the *Milo* this morning. We have had very delightful weather for three days past. We hope it may continue. This P.M. all hands have been busily engaged in cutting him in.

MAY 18. The *Gay Head* took a whale at 10 P.M. last evening. Samuel went on board the *Milo* in the morning to procure some cutting spades if possible. Captain Sowle sent Minnie a jar containing about two quarts of raspberry jam, which was very nice. Failing to procure what he wished, he went on board the *Saratoga.* Captain Slocum sent us some fresh dates, different from any that I ever saw. In the afternoon he went on board the *Majestic,* where he was successful. About 4 P.M. saw a bowhead. Boats from all the ships went in pursuit of him, but he made his escape by going under the ice. Five ships have been added to our company today; two of them have been reported as the *Caravan* and the *Marengo.* We have the most delightful weather I think that I ever experienced, still, clear, and comfortably warm.

MAY 19. A thick fog, so thick most of the time that we could not see a ship's length, which, considering our situation—so small a place to work in and so many ships—was rather unpleasant. The other three ships that we saw yesterday were the *Champion, Hudson,* and the bark *Fortune.* The boats from the most of the ships were off this morning, and it seemed very lively to hear the horns and the guns informing the boats of the whereabouts of their respective ships. Our boat spoke the *Marengo,* and we received the compliments of Captain and Mrs. Skinner. The *Majestic* got a whale last night, so that there are now three ships boiling. We are nearly through now. Our whale turned out to be rather a poor one, but small favors thankfully received. Several ships are now on their way in where we are. The whale made 67 barrels.

MAY 20. Quite clear and cold. The *James Maury,* Captain Curry, is quite near us; came in last night. Captain Slocum made us a short visit in the morning. We gave him a piece of fresh pork and three little pigs. About noon the ships began to work in the ice and, after going through several fields of rotten ice, found ourselves in clear water again. We are surrounded by ice but have a larger place to get about in. Are nearer the land than we were before. Saw a ship at a distance which appeared to be cutting in. Captain Slocum spoke the *Speedwell* about a week ago. He thinks she is one of the ships in sight.

MAY 21. Had quite a hard snowstorm which lasted all night; thick and cloudy this morning. Spoke the ship which we saw cutting in yesterday, which proves to be the bark *Fortune,* Captain Anderson, boiling. Another ship near us which we supposed to be the *Rambler.* We afterward found it to be the *Mary,* of Edgartown. A bowhead was seen in the forenoon, and boats from all the respective ships went in pursuit of him. The *Majestic's* boats were the fortunate captors, so that she now numbers two whales. Our boat spoke the *Omega* while out, and Mr. Whittens sent his respects to us. I hope he will be able to come and see us. Had quite a severe snowstorm for most of the day. In the afternoon a gale came up and lasted for several hours. There is not much sea here while we are surrounded by ice, so that we lay very still. The *Omega* reports one whale.

MAY 22. Boats were off once but without success. After tea Samuel went on board the *Omega,* and Mr. Whittens came here to see us, bringing the daguerreotypes of his wife and Lizzie. Had a very pleasant call from him. It seems very pleasant to see and converse with anyone who knows my friends, even if they are personally strangers to me.

MAY 23. Another whale belongs to the *Addison.* Took him alongside about two o'clock, and they are now engaged in cutting in. The *Gay Head* appears to be engaged in the same manner. Sixteen ships in sight. Cold and rather cloudy, but very smooth. Yesterday we took a seal. The size of it surprised me very much, but I am told they are to be seen here very much larger. This was the size of a large dog. They are very ugly-looking creatures. I have seen many small ones.

MAY 24. A strong breeze in the morning. Commenced boiling. In the afternoon moderated. Eleven ships in sight. *Gay Head* close by us. *Saratoga* came down to us, and Captain Slocum came on board for a short time. Soon after he went back to his ship, they raised whales, lowered their boats, and succeeded in taking one, to the satisfaction probably of all concerned. The *Caravan* took one yesterday also, and there is a bark boiling in sight. Delightful weather, smooth and clear.

MAY 25. A fine morning, still and clear. The boats have all gone in the ice to look for a whale. Ships around us in all directions, seven of them boiling. Boats returned about two o'clock having seen nothing. Afternoon, spoke the ship *America,* Captain Bryant; one whale [this] season.[3] After tea Samuel took Minnie and went on board the *Gay Head* to make a short call. Minnie had a fine time and came back very much delighted with her visit. Eighteen months of our voyage expires today.

MAY 27. Samuel and Minnie went on board the *Saratoga* this morning. Stowed down our oil today: 95 barrels.

MAY 28. The ships are all going out of the ice to get into the land at the eastward, as it is an open sea there, and beat our

way up towards Cape Thaddeus. Land plain in sight. Minnie
has dreamed of seeing Asia several times, and now she has a
view of the coast. Eleven ships in sight.

MAY 29. Captain Sanborn of the *Omega* came on board and
passed the most of the day. In the afternoon lowered the boats
and sent them in the ice to look for a bowhead. Saw plenty of
walrus on the ice and in the water. The waist boat killed one,
but he was so large they thought it would take too much time
to tow him to the ship, so they cut off his head and left his
body on the ice. They judged the weight to be about eight
hundred pounds. The head is a very frightful-looking thing
but has a splendid pair of tusks. Towards night Captain Slocum
came on board for a short time. Captain Sanborn says that a
schooner is to leave the Islands in June with potatoes and letters
for the Arctic fleet. I hope it may be even so and that ours may
be of the number.

MAY 30. A thick fog. The horns were going through the morning
quite merrily from the ships around us. Afternoon cleared up.
Samuel went on board the Bremen brig *Antilla* thinking we
might obtain some late papers from the Islands, but she left
about the time that we did. As they were all Dutch[4] on board,
he made rather a formal call. Fifteen ships in sight.

MAY 31. Quite a strong breeze and a thick fog. A number of
ships around us, but they cannot be seen unless they are close
by us. Spoke the *Mary*, Captain Jenks, in the morning.

JUNE 1. How I wish I could enjoy this month at home, by far
the most pleasant of the year to me. Our little village at this
time presents a delightful appearance to my imagination. The
earth that a little while ago was barren and desolate has laid
aside her mantle of snow and put on a robe of richest green.
The trees that spread out their naked arms have adorned themselves with new foliage, while the whole air is fragrant with
flowers and redolent with the songs of the birds. A thick fog
still. Samuel went on board the *Omega* and took tea with Captain Sanborn.

JUNE 2. Foggy still. Ships all around us, but nothing going on except gamming. That appears to be the order of the day.

JUNE 3. A thick fog. Spoke the *Milo* in the morning. Samuel went on board for a short time; found Captain Green of the *Rousseau*[5] there. *Milo* had taken one whale, *Rousseau* nothing. As Samuel went away, he told me to prepare myself for a gam; for when he came back, he was going to hunt up the *Marengo,* as she had been in sight in the morning. I needed not a second invitation but prepared Minnie and myself accordingly, though half doubting whether we should succeed in the attempt. He came back, and it cleared up so that we could see the *Marengo* a short distance from us. We went on board and passed a very pleasant day with Captain and Mrs. Skinner. This is her third voyage north. Quite an experienced sailor.[6] While we were there the *William C. Nye* spoke the *Addison,* and finding we were on board the *Marengo,* he went there too. Samuel found an old shipmate in Captain Soule, and they were very happy to meet. In the afternoon Captain Sanborn of the *Omega* came on board, and we had quite a merry time. The captains decided that it was worth one whale to see two ladies together. The *Marengo* has taken nothing as yet and the *William C. Nye* one whale, the *Omega* a finback which yielded about 30 barrels. Just before we left the *Marengo,* the wind began to breeze and blew quite fresh for the night.

JUNE 4. A strong breeze and thick fog. Four ships near us. I forgot to mention that Mrs. Skinner and myself made an exchange of articles that we most wanted. I wanted a skein of red sewing silk very much (I had a plenty that was too light), which she could supply me with, while she wanted a skein of blue yarn, which I had for her. She presented us with another lot of those Magdalena Bay figs. I venture to say that we fare much better for figs than though we were at home.

JUNE 5. Rather thick today, but the wind has moderated. Land has been in sight for the most of the day, the shore along Cape Thaddeus. We were about twenty miles from the land at one time, but it was so very high it appeared as if it were not more than three or four miles off. We want now to get the other side between Capes Navarin and Thaddeus, where the whales are supposed to be, as soon as the weather clears. After tea spoke the *Christopher Mitchell*. Captain Manchester came on board and stopped until sunset, which was about ten o'clock. We had a letter on board for his cabin boy; eighteen months old, but he said it would be news to him as he had not received a letter this voyage. He has been in the Indian Ocean. Heard of Captain Frank Smith wanting two whales to fill, so I presume he is with his family by this time.[7]

JUNE 6. Foggy as usual and a strong breeze. We were all surprised and pained this morning to learn that Minnie's little kid Billy was found dead in his house. We think he must have had a fit, as he was well to all appearance last night. It was a sad thing to Minnie, for she dearly loved him, and indeed he was a great pet with us all.

P.M. The weather appears to be clearing and more settled. Hope we may have it pleasant tomorrow, as I have been waiting some time for a good washing day.

JUNE 7. Clear and bright. Have done a large washing and feel well satisfied with my morning's work. We are between Capes Navarin and Thaddeus, off the bay of Archangel Gabriel, the name laid down on the chart, a very singular name for a bay, to say the least. Five ships in sight, but we are disappointed in not seeing the whales. About eight o'clock P.M. saw one whale and lowered the boats without success.

JUNE 8. Lowered the boats three times for one whale, but they could not get near him. Two ships in sight. Samuel is quite undetermined where to go now. He had calculated upon seeing ice and whales off Thaddeus. We are now looking around for ice, thinking if we find it we might find whales at the same time. About eight o'clock spoke the *William and Henry*. Captain Grinnell came on board and stopped until ten. Just as he left in his boat, a thick fog set in which shut his ship from our sight.

JUNE 9. A pleasant day, but no whales. Two ships in sight. Wind ahead, and we are beating our way again towards Thaddeus, as the ice is so thick in the sea that it is impossible to get through it.

JUNE 10. Spoke the *Christopher Mitchell* about four o'clock this morning. Did not gam, as there was a strong breeze. Had quite an unpleasant day, foggy and windy.

JUNE 11 and 12. Same as tenth, with some rain.

JUNE 13. The fog has left us, but it is cloudy. We are near the ice to the eastward of Thaddeus. Eight ships in sight. Passed a clipper bark this morning. Yesterday I had a severe attack of sick headache, which lasted me through the day. I was never troubled with that complaint until quite recently, and I find it anything but pleasant. I lay it to drinking chocolate in the morning and am resolved to give it up for the present to see what effect it will have.

Afternoon. We have had some rain since morning and quite a strong breeze. Spoke the *Omega*, of Fairhaven. Captain Whalon came on board, but as we were going in opposite directions, his call was short. He has left his wife at Hilo this season in company with eight captains' ladies. I suppose they intend having a nice time, but I accompanied Samuel that my little family might be an unbroken one, and nothing but sickness will cause me to change my views.

JUNE 14. Calm, warm, and some part of the day foggy. Came up to very heavy solid ice in the afternoon. When we first came up here, everyone said they never saw such thin open ice so early in the season, and it was when we first saw it, but all that we see now is uncommonly thick for the season. It must have been a severe winter. According to appearances it will be some time before anyone gets through into the [Bering] Strait. No ship in sight today, the first day for a long time that we have been alone.

JUNE 15. Clear and a strong breeze. We are near the land. Several ships in sight. Some parts of the day foggy. After tea P.M. spoke the *Christopher Mitchell*. Captain Manchester came on board and spent several hours with us. He has taken nothing as yet and is getting rather downhearted. He brought me some tamarinds which he put up from Lombok, New Holland, which were very nice. Heard of the *Speedwell* having two whales. He told us also of the ship *Eliza F. Mason* that he spoke several days ago, where the captain had his wife on board and a little infant. That was very delightful news for Minnie to hear, and I presume she will keep a sharp lookout for the *Eliza F. Mason*.

JUNE 16. Foggy in the morning. P.M. cleared up. Eight ships in sight.

JUNE 17. A sad accident happened to us this morning. In a thick snowstorm we hit a lone cake of ice. No one saw it, neither had any been seen during the morning. We were not aware that there was any within six miles, at least. The first thing I did was to get Minnie up and dress her. We were at breakfast, and I generally let Minnie sleep in the morning, as we breakfast early. I was very calm and composed while dressing her and was ready to collect my things preparatory to leaving the ship, as I expected we should be obliged to do. The ship was stoven some on her larboard bow, causing her to leak a little; but Samuel thinks when he can get up to the land into a bay where we can anchor to repair her a little, it will be perfectly safe to continue on whale ground for the season. Captains Freeman of the *Tybee* and Smith of the *Fabius* were on board during the day, and they considered that it was perfectly safe to do so.[8] I believe I am truly thankful that it is no worse, and I retire to rest with a feeling of gratitude that the *Addison* is still my home. There are plenty of ships in sight, and I know that I should suffer for nothing; but for Samuel's sake especially am I thankful.

JUNE 18. The noise of the pumps kept me awake through the night. She does not leak much, but we are anxious to get into the bay, when the ice will let us; but we have found no opening as yet. I can see that it worries Samuel very much. I am extremely sorry that any such thing should have happened, as he has been so careful all the season; but it was no fault of his, and I try to comfort him all I can.

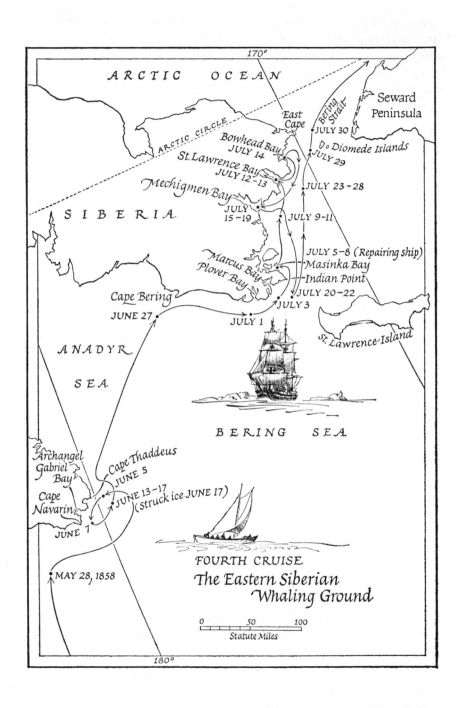

ARCTIC OCEAN

170°

ARCTIC CIRCLE

East Cape

Bering Strait

JULY 30

Seward Peninsula

Bowhead Bay
JULY 14

Diomede Islands
JULY 29

St. Lawrence Bay
JULY 12–13

JULY 23–28

Mechigmen Bay

SIBERIA

JULY 15–19

JULY 9–11

JULY 5–8 (Repairing ship)
Masinka Bay
Indian Point

Marcus Bay
Plover Bay

JULY 20–22

Cape Bering
JUNE 27

JULY 3

JULY 1

ANADYR

SEA

St. Lawrence Island

BERING SEA

Archangel
Gabriel
Bay

Cape Thaddeus
JUNE 5

Cape
Navarin

JUNE 13–17
(Struck ice JUNE 17)

JUNE 7

MAY 28, 1858

FOURTH CRUISE
The Eastern Siberian
Whaling Ground

0   50   100
Statute Miles

180°

1858

JUNE 19. In the morning Samuel went on board the *Omega* to get some spikes and boat boards. When he returned, Captain Whalon and Captain Manchester of the *Christopher Mitchell* accompanied him. In the afternoon spoke the *Rousseau*. Captain Green came on board, and afterward spoke the *Speedwell*. Captain Gibbs came on board but did not bring his wife, as they had company and he thought we had enough, but wished us to go there. Samuel did not care about leaving his ship, and I did not want him to, as Mr. Nickerson was away. I felt very much disappointed and tried to persuade Captain Gibbs to go back after her, but it was useless. We could hardly understand it, but perhaps she can satisfactorily explain it when I see her; at any rate, I have been anticipating seeing her all the season, and she has done the same.

JUNE 20. A very heavy sea today. We have found another small leak which they have been trying to stop and have been quite successful. This P.M. she does not leak as much as she has done. They have also been putting canvas on the outside. I think Samuel feels easier today than he has done. Signalized the *Saratoga* this forenoon and spoke the *Tybee* in the afternoon. Captain Freeman has one whale this season, Captain Smith nothing, Captain Manchester nothing, Captain Green ditto, Captain Whalon one whale, Captain Gibbs has taken three.

JUNE 21. A very heavy sea and quite a gale. I felt anxious, not knowing how our ship would stand such a heavy sea, but she withstood it bravely; leaks no more than in a calm. Spoke the *Tybee* again today. No gamming, as it was too rough.

JUNE 22. The wind and sea has abated, and we now have a thick fog. Three ships in sight. About teatime spoke the *Ocmulgee*, of Edgartown. Captain Greene came on board and passed the evening. He is a New London man and is well acquainted with Thomas, Mercy, and her mother's family. I like to see anyone that knows persons with whom I am acquainted. He has been on Kodiak this season and just arrived here; has taken nothing.

JUNE 23. The *Ocmulgee,* a Frenchman, and one other ship have gone in the ice, and it being for the most part of the time a thick fog, Samuel deemed it not advisable to follow them. So we are now wending our way back toward Thaddeus again where we suppose most of the fleet are.

JUNE 24. All day we have been, as it were, alone upon the waters. Not a ship to be seen. It seems very lonely now to be alone after seeing so many ships. We do not leak but little now. When we can get in the bay to patch up on the outside a little, we think we shall get along nicely.

JUNE 25. Saw a ship and a bark. After tea they came down and spoke us. Captain Brownson of the bark *Baltic* and Captain Barber of the *Benjamin Tucker* came on board and passed the evening.

JUNE 26.[9] Captains Barber and Brownson came on board and passed the day with us. Captain Barber brought me a box of figs and a bag of raisins, and Captain Brownson brought me two jars of preserves. We also procured two late papers from them, a New Bedford paper of February 5 and a New York paper of March 6. We have more favorable news in regard to times than when we left the Islands. The bone which we sent home by the *John Land* had arrived safely, but no sales for bone. Oil had advanced in prices. Ours had not then arrived per *Harriet and Jessie.* I trembled when I took up the New Bedford paper to read the record of deaths, but I found no dear name to me therein recorded. A thick fog still prevails and appears likely to continue for several days yet to come. Neither of the ships have taken anything this season.

JUNE 27. Foggy still. Three ships in sight.

JUNE 28. Cloudy but not thick. Cape Bering in sight, also six ships. In the morning there was one quite near us, which Samuel thought to be the *Eliza F. Mason;* and as Captain Smith had his wife and child on board, I anticipated a gam. We drew quite near together by noon, and as it was nearly calm, we concluded to get in the boat and go to them immediately after dinner. When Minnie and myself were fully equipped and our bonnets and cloaks on, all ready for a start, we made the discovery that it was the French ship *Caulaincourt*. Samuel concluded to go on board, and to make up for Minnie's disappointment, he let her go with him. They returned about teatime, and Minnie was highly delighted with her visit. They dined on board at four o'clock and came back immediately after dinner, which occupied an hour and a half. Minnie brought home a dozen New Zealand apples, some fancy pictures, and a live kitty, which she has named Coda after her kitten she left at home. Captain Labaste is just from New Zealand; has taken no oil this season.

JUNE 29. Had a nice washing day, for which I have been waiting for over a week. Five ships in sight, also land.

JULY 1. Off the coast near Plover Bay, where we hope to anchor and repair the ship, provided there is no ice in the bay.

P.M. A dead calm with a strong current drifting us away from the land. Samuel decided to anchor after tea, which we did in seventeen fathoms of water.

JULY 2. Sent Mr. Chappell with his boat's crew off at two o'clock in the morning on an exploring expedition in Plover Bay. The natives were off in the morning killing walrus. Afterward they came on board the *Addison*. They are rather a short, thickset race with prominent cheekbones, black hair closely shaved on their heads, except their foreheads, and a yellow complexion. Minnie and myself attracted much attention from them. They were dressed in furs and skins.

In the morning we were surprised to see a long strip of ice drifting with the current from the Anadyr Sea directly toward us. Samuel had a spar put out to protect our weak bow, but about noon a slight breeze sprang up, so that we weighed anchor and went out of the way of the ice.

P.M. Mr. Chappell returned and reported ice still in the bay. Another load of Eskimos came on board, which consisted of seven men, one of which we took to be a man of rank by the attention which was paid him by the others, and one woman. She was dressed nearly like the others. Some had on coats or robes made of the skins of birds with the feathers attached. They brought off some trade, but it appeared to be impossible to make a bargain with them.

Another ship anchored near us last night, which we spoke today and found to be the *Benjamin Tucker*. He has seen whales every day for several days. Mr. Chappell saw one today while going in the bay. Both ships are to anchor again tonight; then we are going to see how the next bay looks. Another load of Eskimo men and women came off about teatime. They can understand but very little English, and their language is perfectly unintelligible. Another ship in sight.

In the evening Captain Barber came on board. He informed us of the loss of the French ship *Napoleon 3rd* in the ice on the twentieth of May off the island of St. Paul. All hands saved and 500 barrels of oil taken out by the *Braganza* and the *Hercules*. Had 1,200 on board. A boatload of natives came off towards night, consisting of men, women, and children. They left about nine o'clock but could not find the shore on account of a thick fog which set in about the time they left. In the course of the night two other boats came off. Their boats are made of a wooden frame and covered with skin.

JULY 3. A thick fog and a heavy swell alongshore. We dragged our anchor a little in the morning but helped that very soon by giving her more chain and fixing the yards. Two ships in sight. One proved to be the *Erie*. Captain Jernegan came on board for a short time to get information. He thinks there must be plenty of whales here by and by; says he has seen hundreds at the south working north since we last saw him two weeks ago. We are laying off Marcus Bay. When the fog lights up a little, it looks as if there were ice in the bay. There is one other bay around the point which Samuel will try next, and should there be ice there, I suppose we must wait patiently until it leaves one of them. A strong breeze sprung up in the forenoon.

Four o'clock P.M. Saw a large body of ice coming down toward us so were obliged to weigh anchor and go to sea. Shall lay off and on through the night.

JULY 4. Lay off and on through the night. A thick fog and strong breeze, land on one side and ice on the other. Samuel was up for the most of the night. The same weather the most of the day. It will be a great relief to us all when we can get in and repair the ship. She does not leak any more, but we feel anxious in a gale of wind and a heavy sea, not knowing how much she will bear. This trouble with the absence of whales wears upon Samuel. He grows thin and has lost his appetite, but it may be that all will turn out right in the end. We have heard of but three that have taken three whales and but a few that have two. It has been thus far a very icy season, and the whales, it is supposed, have been in the ice where ships could not go. It is about time for the ice to break up now, if it is to break up this season.

The Fourth of July today and the Sabbath. How different our situation from our friends at home! A gale of wind with ice and land to avoid. The ice probably would be a refreshing sight to them. Probably the celebration, if there is any to come off, will take place tomorrow. We had a turkey stuffed and roasted with wild ducks, which are very plenty here. Perhaps tomorrow we may get a whale. Spoke the *Benjamin Tucker* in the afternoon. Samuel went on board to tea. As it cleared away a little, they decided to start for another bay.

JULY 5. Thick and foggy through the night. Lay off and on under short sail. Lost sight of our consort until about noon, when it cleared up a little, and we found him anchored about two miles from us. Twelve ships in sight, some of them anchored at various places along the coast. The *Rousseau* passed very near us. As it cleared up, the *Benjamin Tucker* weighed anchor, and we proceeded together around the point to look for Masinka Bay, as it is called, which is the Eskimo name for "good." [10] We were obliged to pass through a little ice, which was very thin, but we have now arrived safely at the desired harbor and are snugly anchored and tomorrow morning shall commence operations. Hope we may find it no worse than we fear. Another ship entering the bay tonight. A canoe of natives have just arrived, and I will leave off to go up and see them.

JULY 6. Commenced breaking out and arranging matters preparatory to repairing the ship. Procured a carpenter from the *Benjamin Tucker* and carpenter and blacksmith from the *James Maury*, who is anchored near us.

P.M. They have got her out of water as much as possible on the larboard bow, so that our position on board is not very comfortable. I have had invitations to go on board the other ships, but I think I can stay here very well. Captains Barber and Curry were on board all day. We have had fine pleasant weather through the day, but all outside the bay there is a thick fog bank. I would hardly believe there could be such a difference. The *James Maury* has taken two whales this season.

JULY 7. About one o'clock in the morning they awoke Samuel by telling him there was plenty of ice drifting toward us. He immediately got up and went on deck and found that the ice was too heavy to drift through and we must get under way, which we did, also the *Benjamin Tucker*. The *James Maury* lay still, as he could clear the heavy ice. After the ice had passed and we saw no more coming, we concluded that was the last installment and decided to go back and anchor again, as we were in no condition to go to sea, as we were heeled over to one side very much and down at the stern. When we were in the ice, we slipped our anchor,[11] and when we went back after getting through the ice, we recovered it again.

We had a fine day, this day. Captain Barber came on board and invited Minnie to go on board and dine with him on roast turkey, which she was delighted to do. About noon the *Caravan*, Captain Bragg, came in and anchored. Minnie returned about four o'clock with a bouquet of beautiful flowers which she plucked from the shore, having been there with Captains Barber, Curry, and Bragg. She visited the Eskimos in their huts, which were poles set up and covered with skins. Their winter residences are underground. They were cooking a piece of walrus meat in oil while she was there. They offered her a piece, which she declined. They think much of her. The little children that come on board run about with her.

The children, even infants, are dressed the same as their parents. The females wear loose pants "à la Bloomer," and the males wear tights, which is the only difference perceivable in the dress of the two sexes. The men have their hair shaved on their heads, except around their foreheads, and the women have theirs cut short around their forehead and two long braids behind. They wear no covering on their heads, but the other parts of their bodies are well covered, wearing two or three sets of skins. Their wants consist mostly of tobacco and rum. They caught Minnie's name and would call to her every time she came near them, "Minnie, silopa!" which means tobacco; "Minnie, rum! Minnie, teteta!" which being interpreted signifies needles. She would not allow them to kiss her if she could possibly avoid it, which they all wanted to do, and many were the struggles which she had to get away from them, and sometimes in vain. As for myself, I was obliged to come forward when they were on deck, or I should have had the cabin filled with them. They would come to the gangway and cry out, "Woman! Woman! Woman!"

I would like to have gone ashore with Minnie and the captains. Captain Barber said he would have called for me had he known how it was ashore, but he thought it might be wet. He has invited me to go with him tomorrow, which invitation I shall be happy to accept.

JULY 8. About nine o'clock last evening we saw ice again coming towards us. We took up our anchors and tried to get under way; but as it was a dead calm, we found it best to let go again, for if we drifted with the ice, there was danger of going ashore. The first flow of ice that came to us was not bad, quite thick but considerably broken up. After that it came on pretty bad. We were obliged to have men out on the ice cutting our way along, until we came to a field that it was impossible to get through. Just then there came on a slight breeze, so that we slipped our anchor, and turning around a little, we cleared all of that except the point. Then we put down our large anchor and drifted through the remainder, some of which was very heavy, solid field ice two miles in length. After cutting, spading, sawing, and pulling with ropes, we finally worked through the last of it about four o'clock in the morning. It was a night of hard work and anxiety. We were afraid mostly of staving our ship again. There was also danger of dragging our anchor and going ashore. The *James Maury* got into the worst ice. She and the *Caravan* came very near running together and also going ashore. The *James Maury* lost one anchor and spoiled another, and the *Caravan* broke his large one.

After we cleared the ice, we went back and recovered our anchor for the second time. We had but one anchor out, which held us very well. The others had two out and dragged rather more than we did. It was a serious time. I was up and down, on deck and below, all night to see how matters were progressing. Samuel thought I ought to go to bed and sleep, but I knew that I could not sleep should I go to bed.[12] When I say I was on deck and below all night, I must explain that the nights are very different from our nights at home. There was just about one hour between sunrise and sunset, and the remainder of the time was a clear, bright sunshine. We had about finished the outside of the ship, so that we could right her up and make our departure, which we were very glad to do, not deeming it a safe place to lay, although it seems as if there could be no more ice to come from the little bays around where we suppose that to have come from. After we got out of the bay and got things upright a little, all hands had a watch below (except enough to work the ship), which they very much needed.

JULY 9. The *Caravan* is out of sight. Captain Barber gammed with us, and we spoke the *James Maury*. Off Mechigmen Bay two canoes of natives came on board with bone and walrus teeth but would not trade unless we would give them plenty of rum. It is extremely hard to make a bargain with them. They are great beggars and great thieves. One of them offered me a piece of walrus meat cooked in oil for a little cuff pin which I wore around my neck in a velvet. He appeared to be surprised to think I refused it. Probably he thought it would be a grand bargain for me. We saw the little children gnawing on a piece of raw blubber with as much satisfaction as a child at home in having any dainty morsel. In the afternoon had a strong breeze. About teatime it moderated and commenced raining.

JULY 10. Samuel went on board the *Benjamin Tucker* in the morning and stopped until after dinner. Mr. Paine, the mate, came on board. About five o'clock it came in thick and rainy, and we anchored in seven fathoms of water. A French ship lays quite near us. After tea Captain Barber came on board, and soon after we had a visit from Captain Hache of the French ship *Jason*, seven months out, clean. He has been in the ice, lost his cutwater, part of his stern, sheathing and copper, etc., but does not leak. The *Caravan* has lost her cutwater. The *Mary*, of Edgartown, has got stove in the ice so that she leaks quite badly. Our leak is nearly stopped now—unless it breaks out in some new place. She leaks perhaps eight or ten strokes [of the pump] per hour. Heard from the *South America, Nassau, William Thompson,* and *William Tell.* Nothing [this] season.

JULY 11. A hard rainstorm through the night. This morning it cleared up with a north wind, the first time for a long while that we have had the wind from that quarter. We took up our anchor after breakfast and are now cruising round on the lookout for bowheads, as it is about time for them to begin to be along here. Saw a plenty of mussel diggers, or California grays, this morning.

Afternoon. Samuel went on board the *Benjamin Tucker* to see who was gamming with him and to learn the news. Stopped to tea, and Mr. Paine, the mate, came here. Seventeen ships and brigs in sight, most of them coming down the Strait. Samuel learned from Captain Sarvent that a number of ships had been up in the Arctic and down through the Strait again, as there were no whales there. We are pretty well satisfied that there have been but a very few to go through and a large body of whales is yet to come and they must pass this way to get there. In the evening Captain Barber gammed with several ships on board the *America.* She has taken nothing since May; has three whales, the *Japan* nothing, *Hudson* one whale, *Helen Mar* nothing, and *Arnolda* nothing.

JULY 12. Most of the fleet we saw yesterday have gone south, but the *Benjamin Tucker* and *Addison* have decided to stop around here for a few days and go around in the bays. Captain Barber came on board in the morning, but it came on so rugged that he soon left us. During the forenoon we had a strong breeze and a heavy sea. Spoke the *Emerald,* Captain Hallock, from the Arctic going south; nothing [this] season. In the afternoon worked up in St. Lawrence Bay and found the weather very delightful. About 5 P.M. anchored in twenty-three fathoms of water in company with the *Benjamin Tucker* and the *Goethe,* Captain Austin. He is just from Kodiak with three whales; reports whales quite plenty there but difficult to take. We are to send boats farther up the bay, prospecting, and oh, that they might find one bowhead to cheer our hearts!

JULY 13. The anniversary of our wedding day, being eleven years since we were united in the holy bonds of matrimony, and eleven happy years have they been to us. Two boats left the ship in the morning. Were gone through the day. About seven o'clock Mr. Nickerson returned in Mr. Brown's boat, leaving his boatsteerer laying by a whale called a mussel digger, ripsack, devilfish, or California gray. We had previously anchored, as it was a calm and we could make nothing, but we got under way to try to beat down to where they were. As it was impossible to do so, we anchored again that we might be able to hold our own. We had Eskimos in great numbers on board through the day, men, women, and children. Minnie had a grand time running races with the children. They appeared to be quite playful. Samuel purchased about eighty pounds of walrus teeth and two splendid bearskins of them. We saw two bears on a hill from the ship last night which looked to be enormous. About 9 P.M., as it was coming in foggy, sent Mr. Chappell out to Antone's assistance with orders to leave the whale if necessary.

JULY 14. Weather thick and foggy during the night. Heard nor saw nothing of the boats. After breakfast got out our big gun and fired so as to guide them to the ship. We suppose they stopped on board some ship, as there were several near the whale. About nine o'clock the boats returned, leaving the whale anchored and a waif in him so that no one might claim him. Soon after, a slight breeze sprang up, and we got under way. Captain Barber made us a short call. At 12 M. found the whale, got him alongside, and commenced cutting in. They do not make much oil, but every little helps in these hard times. There appears to be a great many of them around, but they are generally hard to take and more dangerous than other whales, often chasing and attacking boats.

Afternoon. Fog cleared away and very pleasant. The *Benjamin Tucker* lowered for mussel diggers; fastened to a cow and calf. The latter sank. Samuel went on board at 8 P.M. and stopped until 10. The *Benjamin Tucker* got his whale alongside about that time. We are now in what they call Bowhead Bay, nearly off East Cape and in sight of the Diomede Islands, which are situated nearly in the center of the Strait. Shall not anchor unless it comes in thick.

JULY 15. Captain Barber came on board in the morning. Is not as well pleased with his whale as he expected to be. It has turned out to be a dry-skin, and he will be under the necessity of throwing it all away. We have had natives off in great numbers today, and if they could procure a piece of our blubber to eat by fair means or foul, they devoured it with a great relish. If Samuel had allowed them to take it as they wished, we should have had none left. It is sickening to see them. They brought some specimens of their workmanship off today in the shape of ivory images, which were really quite skillful.

P.M. We are working down off Mechigmen Bay again. Five ships in sight. About teatime had a call from Captain Sanborn of the *Omega* and Captain May of the *Dromo*, of New London; has taken no oil this season. The *Omega* has one whale. They give the same report in regard to whales that we have heard for some time: none to be seen. At eight o'clock P.M. we anchored in Mechigmen Bay where we expect to water tomorrow. The *Nassau* is anchored near us. Captain Murdock came on board after we anchored. He is getting water also. We have both sent rafts inshore tonight. Captain Murdock took the captain of the French ship *Napoleon 3rd*, which was lost in the ice, off from St. Paul Island, where he went with his boat's crew, and put him on board the *Nil*, a French whaler.

JULY 16. Sent rafts inshore for water, but owing to the low state of the tide it could not be got off until this afternoon, one boat staying by the casks until another went to relieve them. Just after dinner our eyes were gladdened by the sight of a bowhead. Sent three boats off, but without success, as they were going too rapidly to stand any chance of getting near them. In the afternoon Captain Murdock came on board for a short time. His water they found to be too brackish to use, so that he will be obliged to send in again. Ours we found to be a little brackish, but as we only needed a little, we can get along without being obliged to drink it. The men that were ashore brought me three bouquets, which are very pretty indeed. Since we have been around the land, I have had over thirty different varieties brought me. It looks strangely to see them growing by the side of a snowbank. They must come forward very rapidly, as their seasons are so short. After tea lowered again for bowheads with like success. Finished boiling today. The whale made 25 barrels.

JULY 17. Got up this morning and was told to look out of the cabin window. Saw a strange ship had come in and anchored during the night. I inquired who it was and was told that it was the *Marengo*. "Well," said I to myself, "I guess I shall have company today." So I went to work after breakfast to clean up my cabin and make things look as pleasant as possible. As their boats were all out watering and whaling and we had one boat on the cranes, I invited Samuel to go on board and bring them to pass the day with us. He soon returned bringing Mrs. Skinner with him, but the captain was so much interested in looking out for whales that he could not accompany her just then.

About noon the *Omega* and three black clippers, the *Eliza F. Mason,* the *Gay Head,* and the *Speedwell,* came in and anchored for water, so that there were four ladies in the bay. I was in hopes that Mrs. Gibbs would have come here, but she may have been on board the *Eliza F. Mason.* I should have looked her up if I had not had company, and I thought they might lay there all night; but while we were at tea, they got under way and came down across our stern and spoke us. He has given up all hopes of getting anything in the Arctic and is now bound south, either to Bristol Bay or the Okhotsk. I hope he may be successful, but I should be sorry for Samuel to leave this region now, as there have been a great many whales seen and they must be going north sometime or other. There have been a great many seen around us today, but they have been going with such rapidity that it was of but little use to have boats down, although we have had two and three down all day. Just before Captain and Mrs. Skinner left, Captain Sanborn came on board and reported that he had been fast to a whale but lost him. He also reports that there have been five whales taken in the Arctic.

JULY 18. Minnie's birthday—seven years old today. How time flies! She feels quite old and has been telling me how it amuses her to think how foolish she was in her "younger days," when she first came to sea, for instance. There have been nine ships in the bay today. Most of them came to an anchor, as it is a gale of wind and outside a heavy sea. The *Nassau, Omega, Marengo, South America, Benjamin Tucker, Gay Head, Dromo,* the French ship *Manche,* and the *Addison* brings up the list. After we had retired for the night, which was quite early, the captain of the *Manche* came on board to get information in regard to whales. He has not seen one for two months. Samuel got up to receive him, but he did not stop but a few minutes, as Samuel told him that the *Nassau* had taken off the captain and boat's crew of the *Napoleon* from St. Paul; and learning that he had French sailors on board which he would like to dispose of, he left us and went to him, as he was in want of men.

JULY 19. All the anchored ships got under way in the morning except the *Omega,* Captain Sanborn. In the forenoon the *Marengo's* boats went down after a bowhead, which they fortunately captured, and got him alongside about 2 P.M., the first whale they have taken this season. Saw the *Nassau's* boats chasing a mussel digger. About teatime spoke the *Omega,* of Fairhaven. Captain Whalon came on board for a short time. He has been in the Arctic and out again like a great many others without seeing anything. Left nine ships anchored off East Cape yesterday morning. A strong breeze through the afternoon, still increasing.

JULY 20. Lay off and on the bay during the night, but as there was a strong breeze and a heavy sea, Samuel decided to run off before the wind and go down to Plover and Marcus Bays to see what was there. He is almost discouraged today in regard to getting any oil. Sometimes thinks he will start immediately for Bristol Bay, right whaling. I must confess that prospects look very dark just now, but may it not be in this case as in many others that the darkest time is just before day? Anchored about 8 P.M. off Marcus Bay in company with the *Harmony,* Captain Austin. Having a terrific gale from the north. Saw seven bowheads a short time before we anchored, which looked quite encouraging.

JULY 21. Began to drag last night soon after anchoring, so put down the second anchor. The wind came in squalls with great violence, but we lay very still. It blows strong this morning but with less force than through the night. Find the *Harmony* close by us this morning. She dragged considerably through the night.

P.M. The gale abated, and after tea we took up our anchors and started to go around Indian Point, which is a long low point of land reaching out fifteen or twenty miles into the sea with huts on the point. The *Harmony* left several hours before us.

JULY 22. Saw a ship this morning quite near. We soon proved it to be the *Champion,* Captain Coffin, our former partner. Captain Coffin came on board, and we were very happy to see him, as it had been some time since we had either seen or heard from him. He has taken nothing this season; is feeling rather low about these days but hopes better times are coming.

JULY 23. Foggy for the most part of the night and a greater part of this day. No land could be seen, and the only way we could tell where we were was by using the lead and line. About 4 P.M. it cleared away so that we had a view of the land and found ourselves just where Samuel had predicted, off St. Lawrence heads. Have been any quantity of mussel diggers around today, and we have had four boats in pursuit of them without success as yet. Captain Coffin informed us that Captain Gibbs of the *Speedwell* has given up his intention of going south and has returned to the bays again to look for bowheads. May success attend him. In the evening Samuel went on board the *Champion* for a short time.

JULY 24. Pleasant weather with a light breeze. Several ships in sight; *Champion* close by.

P.M. Saw the *Marengo* [and] a clipper at a distance which we could not make out. About 8 P.M. a boat lowered from the clipper and came towards us. When it came near, we found it to be Captain Gibbs and wife of the *Speedwell.* I was extremely happy to see them. They stopped until half-past eleven, and I enjoyed their visit very much. Captain Gibbs has decided to stick to the Arctic this season, oil or no oil.

JULY 25. Calm as a clock. The *Marengo, Speedwell, Champion,* and the French *Caulaincourt* close by. About 10 A.M. Captain Gibbs set his signal for us to come on board, so we, nothing loth, prepared ourselves and started. Soon after our arrival Captain Skinner and wife came and in the afternoon Captain Coffin of the *Champion* and Captain Labaste of the *Caulaincourt*. He has taken two whales since we last saw [him]. There has been a small cut in the Anadyr Sea, but we were not there to take a share in it. The *William Thompson* took three whales which made him 500 barrels. He stands number one on the list now. The *Christopher Mitchell* took two whales, the *Baltic* one, *Saratoga* one, *Hercules* two. The *Addison* as yet can boast of only two and a mussel digger. We had a grand visit on board the *Speedwell*.[13] It is not often that three ladies can get together. Mrs. Gibbs has a pleasant cabin and fine accommodations. Soon after we arrived on board, a ship which was near us set her signal and hauled up her mainsail for us, so we went down and spoke her. She proved to be the *William Rotch*. Captain Ellison came on board for a few minutes. He is just from New Zealand, two years out, with about 300 barrels of oil. He said he saw a little girl on the house, so filled his pockets with oranges for her.

I saw a piece in the *Friend* today on board the *Speedwell*, which purports to be my testimony in regard to the influence of missionaries. I recollect of telling Mr. Damon that I was very much disappointed in regard to the natives when I first arrived at the Islands; they were not nearly so far advanced as I expected to see them. I did not for an instant think that the statements that were made were untrue, but that I had set my standard of excellence too high, had formed too exalted an idea of them. "But," said I, "since I have been at the Marquesas Islands and see how low and degraded they are there, I can form a better idea of what has been done here." Well, it seems that Mr. Damon thought that he could make that tell in print, so has written a long piece in which anyone would infer that I was always rather an enemy to the missionary cause than otherwise; but since I had been to the Marquesas Islands and seen the natives uncontaminated by missionary influence, I was compelled to acknowledge that, after all, the missionaries had done some good. It made me feel very sad and caused me to shed some tears, because I think it places me in a false position. I have always been friendly to the missionary cause, have belonged to missionary societies, and have always given all that I felt able to assist both home and foreign missions. I have read too many books to doubt for a single moment that they have been instrumental in doing much good. Mr. Damon must have drawn a wrong inference altogether from the remark which I made.[14]

JULY 26. A strong breeze, afternoon increasing. Three ships in sight.

JULY 27. As we drew near the land, the gale moderated. Quite calm inshore. Spoke the *Nil,* a French ship. Samuel went on board for a short time. Captain Morel, late of the *Napoleon 3rd,* returned with him and stopped a short time. I wanted to do something for him, but he said that he saved his clothes. Samuel gave him some tobacco. We heard by him that the *Jason* had a boat stoven by a mussel digger, one man killed and four hurt. The *America* heard from with four whales. Heigh-ho, when will the *Addison* have four?

P.M. The *Marengo* close by us. Mrs. Skinner and I waved handkerchiefs. Samuel went on board for a few minutes and took Minnie with him. I sent Mrs. Skinner some cookies, and she sent me some figs.

JULY 28. Laying off and on shore. Pleasant inshore and a gale of wind off. Ten ships in sight.

JULY 29. Beating up the Strait in company with six other ships. Land in sight on both sides and the center of the Strait. America on one side, Asia on the other, and the Diomede Islands between.

P.M. Spoke the *Marengo,* and we ladies had another flourish of pocket handkerchiefs. Saw the *Speedwell* inshore cutting in a whale. Lucky man, may we go and do likewise. We had our boats out to try even to get a mussel digger, but 'twas of no use. Shall we get anything more this season?

JULY 30. Last night saw a bowhead and chased him. Saw another this morning. They are queer fish; you do not know how to make allowance for them. The boats went off some distance this morning, and the whale came up after a long time close by the ship. Sometimes they will go two miles under water. So we got nothing. A beautiful morning. I was on deck most of the forenoon. We passed East Cape where Augustus buried Mr. Eldredge, his mate in the *Awashonks* who was killed by a whale.[15] If we had known just the spot, I should like to have visited it for the sake of his poor wife, but it would have been a fruitless search probably to have attempted. We got through in the Arctic Ocean about noon. Eight ships in all, *Marengo, Speedwell, Addison, Nil, Caulaincourt, Baltic, Braganza,* and an unknown bark.

P.M. Spoke the *Braganza.* Captain Jackson came on board and passed the afternoon. Had the pleasure of seeing a bark cutting and boiling. That looks encouraging but is not a very pleasing sight to selfish mortals who want everybody to do as well as they and no better. I burnt my face very badly today in the sun, being on deck so much. Getting sunburnt in the Arctic Ocean sounds rather strangely, but true nevertheless.

JULY 31. The last day of July. Time flies, and in August now is our sole dependence. Oh, that we might get some oil! A thick fog and calm throughout the day.

AUGUST 1. The same weather continues, and what long faces greet my eyes. Everybody is discouraged. Samuel has held out wonderfully, until now he too has given up to the general feeling. How I wish that I could do something to enliven them. Whales will do it, and I don't know of anything else. "A whale, a whale, a kingdom for a whale!" [16] How I long to see pleasant looks and smiling countenances again. We have looked and searched in vain, and the rest of the fleet have done likewise. If we cannot find the whales, we cannot get the oil. The days of miracles have passed, or it might be supposed to be in the power of man to make them.

Spoke the *Japan* and *Tybee. Japan* has taken 100 barrels of walrus oil and the *Tybee* two bowheads. Afterward saw a bark boiling; went to her and found her to be the *Baltic.* Captain Brownson had just taken his whale in the fog, the only one that he saw. This makes him three. The bark that we saw the other day cutting and boiling was the bark *Emerald,* Captain Pierce. He has taken 300 barrels of California-gray oil.

AUGUST 2. Cloudy and rainy for the most part of the day. Captain Bryant of the *America* came on board in the morning. He left his wife in Maui this season and has had an infant born there since he left. He has received one letter from her since he left containing the sad intelligence that little Mary White (Dr. White's daughter) was very low with the dysentery and that they had given up all hopes of her life. She was Minnie's little playmate at Maui and a remarkably interesting child of five years. I sincerely hope that she has been spared to them. They have lost two children, and she is their all now. Captain Bryant has taken four whales this season, making him 350 barrels. Have seen nothing that looked like whales today.

AUGUST 3. The sun rose clear this morning, and we hoped to have a pleasant day, but the sky was some overclouded; and now it is a thick fog and the same for the remainder of the day.

AUGUST 4. Foggy in the morning as usual. About noon the fog cleared away some. Calm the greater part of the day.

P.M.   Cloudy. Spoke two ships, the *Dromo* and the *Majestic*. Samuel went on board the *Dromo* to learn what he could respecting the whales. Found that he had been to Cape Lisburne and as far north as the barrier of ice and had not seen a spout. Had spoken several ships also who had seen nothing. Captain May has taken nothing this season. A gloomy prospect, truly. Captain May informed Samuel that Captain Macomber of the *Majestic* was very sick; and after he returned from the *Dromo,* he went on board the *Majestic* to offer them any assistance and to express his sympathy. He found Captain Macomber to be a very sick man—took no notice of anything and was delirious for the most of the time. They think there is no chance for his life. Cause: He had become discouraged and taken to drinking until he knew not when to stop. Another warning to shun the intoxicating cup. He has a son with him about ten years of age. Oh, that his life may be spared.

Minnie has been rather unwell for a day or two with a cold. Her throat is rather painful. Her tonsils enlarge whenever she takes cold and are some inflamed. I trust it is nothing serious however. Heard of the *Metacom,* one whale, and the *Rousseau* with nothing.

1858

AUGUST 5. Cloudy with quite a strong breeze. About 10 A.M. spoke the *America;* Captain Bryant came on board and stopped until after dinner. He has been as far as the ice barrier since we saw him and has seen ne'er a whale. If we cannot get ourselves, it is a great satisfaction to know that others are not taking it in great quantities, in this ocean at least. Is it possible that our season's work can be reckoned at 200 barrels? Samuel is more fortunate than many others, for he has no home expenses to pay. Oh, where shall whales be found? Minnie's throat is better today.

P.M. Clear and bright with a strong breeze. Bound to the eastward to see what may be there for us.

AUGUST 6. Lay to in a gale through the day. The weather has been clear and bright. We have been east far enough and have seen nothing and are now going on what they call compass ground. No ship in sight.

AUGUST 7. A strong breeze in the morning; moderated towards night somewhat. Saw a clipper brig. Did not speak her. Are about on compass ground now but have as yet seen nothing.

AUGUST 8. Light wind and cloudy. About noon saw a bark. Soon after spoke her. She proved to be the *Harmony,* of Honolulu. Captain Austin came on board and passed the afternoon. He has taken four whales this season, three in the ice at the south in May. He was blocked in the ice for over six weeks and injured his ship considerably. Has lost one man overboard, a Kanaka. So ends this day without seeing whales, spouts, or anything indicating life.

AUGUST 10. This is the day that Samuel set to leave the Arctic, provided he saw no better chance than he has seen. We have been proceeding north for a day or two, or northeast, toward Cape Lisburne. Saw the land this morning, and about 10 A.M. commenced raising ships, two of them boiling. Soon after saw a carcass and soon after that raised two bowheads. Soon after we lowered, a bark's boats struck a whale; and that set the others in such commotion that it was impossible to get near them. Presently more whales came in sight, and we had a fair prospect of getting onto one, when another ship struck, and they all went to the windward with great speed. So ends our chasing for this day. Ill luck seems to attend us. Oh, Dame Fortune, just for *one* of thy smiles!

AUGUST 11. Lowered about five o'clock this morning. The bow boat went onto one, and the boatsteerer missed him. Oh, dear! They are boiling, chasing, and cutting all around us, and we can do nothing but chase. Lowered several times during the day without success. Samuel went on board the *Paulina*. They were boiling their first whale.

AUGUST 12. Eureka! Eureka! We have got a bowhead at last. The boats were out a number of times during the day, and in the afternoon we thought we should surely get one, as the whales acted very well, when presently a ship struck near us. So farther attempts with those whales were of course useless, and the boats came on board. All hands were completely discouraged and were ready to exclaim, "Can any good thing be for the *Addison*?" I was so disappointed that my sorrow found vent in tears. Soon after we raised a lone whale; gave all hands an early supper and sent them off. When in a short time the bow boat had the extreme good luck to get fast, what a joyful sound was that "A boat fast!" It was sweet music to our ears. It was a bad whale to kill—stove the larboard boat so that another boat was obliged to leave to bring the crew to the ship, which is rather an unusual thing for a bowhead to do. No one was injured. Got the whale alongside about half-past 10 P.M. May it be a precursor of many more. Eight ships in sight boiling.

AUGUST 13. A change has come over the countenances of our ship's company. Notwithstanding that they were up all night cutting in, faces long unused to smiles are radiant with pleasure, a sight that delights me very much. Minnie was so interested that she awoke very often through the night to enquire what progress they were making and if I was sure that they would save him all. The *Japan* and the *James Maury* are in sight this morning, both boiling. Lowered once today without success.

AUGUST 14. A strong breeze through the night from the south

with quite a sea. Moderated some in the forenoon. Saw whales once; lowered a couple of boats without success. Signalized the *William Thompson*. After that Captain Childs came on board. He is a Falmouth man. I had previously seen him at home and was very happy to renew my acquaintance with him in the Arctic Ocean. He brought his wife out with him and two children; but she was taken sick with a fever before his arrival at the Islands, so that he was obliged to leave her there with one child, and he has the other on board with him, a little boy four years of age. Minnie was very much delighted to have a visit from him, the first child she has yet seen at sea. We fitted him off with playthings, eatables, stockings, and mittens, which I thought he might need with no mother to look out for him. Captain Childs has taken five whales; is boiling two now which he took a few days ago at one lowering. We heard of Lewis by him as being seen on New Zealand in February cutting in a large whale, also that a little daughter had been added to their family.[17] Captain Childs brought me a nice piece of fresh pork, which was very acceptable.[18]

AUGUST 15. This morning early all hands were called to go out in pursuit of bowheads, and before I got up we had one alongside. What good luck! Saw the *William Thompson* take one in the forenoon, also a bark supposed to be the *Helen Mar*. All hands busily engaged in cutting him in.

P.M. Two boats went out after whales but returned without success.

AUGUST 16. Another whale alongside before breakfast, and when that was cut in we had another all ready to take in. Two boats went out in the forenoon and captured him. All hands were so busy that I took the steward's place down in the cabin in getting dinner and clearing away. The *William Thompson* has taken another whale today. Well, we are beginning to look up a little. Three whales in two days is doing well. May our success continue.

AUGUST 17. Thick, foggy, and drizzly for most of the day. Lowered one boat in the forenoon without success.

P.M. Captain Curry of the *James Maury* came on board for

a few minutes. He has taken five whales in all, three up here. Stowed down some of the oil that we had on deck, about 60 barrels. A little land bird flew on board this P.M., which I put in my bird cage and carried on deck, thinking it might be too warm for him in the cabin. He appeared very well, but in a few hours he died. He is the second one that I have tried this season, and now I shall give it up for this voyage.

AUGUST 18. Rather cloudy but not foggy. Spoke the *Omega*, Captain Sanborn; three whales this season. Saw whales this forenoon. Three boats lowered; one got near the whale, but the boatsteerer missed in darting. Stowed down 42 barrels in the afternoon. Cloudy and drizzly for the most of the day. Saw the *James Maury* take a whale today.

AUGUST 19. A calm through the morning and no whales in sight.
P.M. Spoke the *Baltic*. Captain Brownson came on board and passed the afternoon. He has taken three whales since we saw him, which makes him six the season. Towards night quite a strong breeze sprang up. Saw no whales for the day.

AUGUST 20. A dead calm for the most of the day and cloudy. About noon it cleared up so that we saw the land. We have got out of the way of the whales and are in a different position in regard to the land from what we expected. Stowed down 100 barrels of oil. About 6 P.M. a slight breeze sprang up.

AUGUST 21. Experienced quite a severe gale for a few hours this morning from the south. Stowed down our oil as fast as possible for fear that we might lose it; 117 barrels stowed down today. No ships in sight until about sunset, when we raised three boiling. So we hope we have got among the whales again. We begin to have an hour or two of night now. It is not very dark as yet, however.

AUGUST 22. Raised whales in the morning. Chased without success. Saw a bark cutting and a ship take a whale alongside. Eight ships in sight.
8 P.M. Have been chasing whales all day and have taken nothing. Have seen them cutting in all around us. Sixteen ships

in sight. We are further north today than we have yet been, nearly to Icy Cape. Our boats spoke the *Sarah Sheafe* today, Captain Loper; seven whales this season, one in advance of us.

AUGUST 23. Saw whales this morning, but they proved to be mussel diggers. Eight ships in sight, and a dead calm for most of the day.

P.M. Samuel went on board the bark *Mary and Susan*, Captain Stewart. He has taken nine whales, which made him 900 barrels. He says the ships that were cutting in all around us yesterday took their whales the day before, just after the blow. There were a great many around during the gale, and that was the cause of their being so stirred up the next day. Captain Stewart left his wife at Talcahuano.

AUGUST 24. A gale of wind from the northwest, which lasted about six hours, not quite as severe as the one we encountered a few days ago. No whales or ships in sight during the day. Thick and cloudy, also rainy, some parts of the day.

AUGUST 25. Cloudy and some rainy in the morning. The *Mary and Susan* close by us. How we want another whale! What can we do to obtain one?

P.M. Foggy and nearly calm. Seven ships in sight, two boiling. Stowed down the remainder of our oil today. It makes us 598 barrels this season.

AUGUST 26. Raised whales early this morning. The boats went out in pursuit of them. The waist boat struck one, but the iron drawed; consequently he was not for us. A strong breeze, nine ships in sight, the *James Maury* one with a whale alongside.

P.M. Eight o'clock. Plenty of whales in sight during the day, but none for the *Addison*. Our boats were back and forth from the ship all day. Saw the bark *Emerald* take a whale alongside and a ship, name unknown. The *Goethe* fastened but lost her whale, the same as we did in the morning. Long faces are again the order of the day. Samuel feels badly, for he thinks we ought to have had one for the chance we had. Well, we may have better luck tomorow.

AUGUST 27. Boats lowered early in the morning, but the whales disappeared. Saw none for the remainder of the day except mussel diggers. Some rainy.

AUGUST 28. Saw nothing that looked like bowheads through the morning, but an abundance of mussel diggers visible. A number of ships in sight, the greater part of them boiling. In the afternoon raised a bowhead and sent the boats out in pursuit of him. While they were out, five or six made their appearance, and we had the wonderful good fortune to capture one. We got him alongside about 7 P.M., so that we had more night work in cutting in. As Samuel was to be up through the night, I took Minnie in bed with me; but as she could not come without Billy Button, I had two bedfellows. After we had taken the whale alongside, Captain Soule of the *William C. Nye* came on board and stopped about an hour; and after he left, Captain Stewart of the *Mary and Susan* made us a call. They have each taken nine whales this season, while this one makes us seven. I wish that we had several more, but I believe I feel truly thankful for what we have done. It is so much better than we feared at one time. I think it will turn out to be quite a good season for whales to those who remained here, after all. Spoke the *Milo's* boats also today. She has taken nine whales.

AUGUST 29. A strong breeze and quite thick. Four ships in sight in the afternoon. No whales to be seen.

AUGUST 30. Damp, dark, and some rainy with a strong breeze. Three ships in sight and no whales.

AUGUST 31. Pleasant the first part of the day; latter part cloudy and some rainy. Nothing in sight, either ships or whales, the first time we have been alone for many days. Saw land this forenoon, about thirty-five miles north of Cape Lisburne. We have another shore bird now—one of the boatsteerers caught one a few days ago—which resembles very much in appearance a snipe. So of course it is not a remarkably handsome bird, but as it would eat and drink, I thought I would put it in my cage to please Minnie. I do not anticipate any sweet notes from him.

SEPTEMBER 1. Damp, disagreeable weather with a strong breeze. No ships or whales in sight. We have finished boiling, and it looks verily like the last of the season to me. We have been eating bowhead meat for several days, made with pork into sausage cakes, also fried, and it is really good eating, far before salt pork in my estimation.

P.M. Saw a ship which ran down and spoke us. It proved to be the *Milo*, Captain Sowle. Samuel went on board for a short time. He has not seen a whale since we took our last; thinks there is a general scattering of ships. They decided to steer off to the westward through the night and try a new place. I do not care much about going farther west, as there is a strong current and ships are often close into the land before they dream of such a thing. Several ships have been lost in that way.

SEPTEMBER 2. About the same weather that we had yesterday, with a thick fog for the most part of the day. We were engaged in stowing down the oil from our last whale, which amounted to 110 barrels, so that we have 700 barrels, the product of our season's work, which is a good average among the Arctic Ocean fleet so far as we have heard from. After tea spoke the ship *Emerald*. Captain Hallock came on board. He has taken two whales this season. He gave us the sad intelligence of the death of Captain Macomber of the *Majestic,* which took place on the next day after we saw him. His body was committed to the deep in a few hours after his death, as they were not able to keep him long enough to reach the land. I feel for his wife and family when they shall hear the sad tidings. May they find relief and comfort in Him who has promised to be the widow's God and the Father of the fatherless. He also reported the *Benjamin Tucker* to us with one whale. He has not left the Arctic as has been reported. In taking that whale he had a boat stoven and a man killed. Truly, "in the midst of life are we in death." [19] Reported Captain Childs of the *William Thompson* as having picked up a boat's crew belonging to the French ship *De Haut-poul,* which was fast to a whale and lost the ship during a fog. Have been with him a week and have not yet seen the ship. Captain Childs has taken eight whales.

SEPTEMBER 3. A thick fog until noon, when it cleared away quite pleasant. Saw the *Emerald* once during the day at a distance. Saw no whales. We have been very near the barrier, although we did not see it, as it was thick; but Captain Hallock says he was close by it the day that we gammed.

SEPTEMBER 4. Spoke the bark *Baltic* in the morning. Samuel went on board. She is boiling her eighth whale. She has been among whales this week, which school we missed. The *William Thompson* took two, which made him ten. Well, old *Addison*, this will never do for you to be so far behindhand. You must do your best to get two more. Heard from the *Hercules*, nine whales, *Nassau*, four, *Japan*, eight. Samuel feels so poor now that he wishes he had not gone on board, but we are not the worst off by any means. Many a ship's company would feel themselves to be well off if they had taken even what we have. Saw one whale in the morning, which made its appearance like a ghost and then vanished away. In the afternoon saw another, which we chased without success. As it was quite pleasant in the morning, I thought I would have a washing day, nearly a month having elapsed since my last; but soon after I got my clothes hung out, it commenced raining again. Towards night the wind breezed up quite strong with a heavy swell from the eastward.

SEPTEMBER 5. Quite a strong breeze through the night with rain and a heavy sea, which caused the old *Addison* to reel to and fro like a drunken man; but this morning it has moderated somewhat, but rain and fog abounds. Saw a few mussel diggers during the day and three ships, but *ourie* bowheads, as the Kanakas say.

SEPTEMBER 6. Rainy, foggy, and cloudy as usual, but the wind has gone down. It is very seldom in these days that we are able to get an observation. After tea it cleared up a little so that we saw three ships.

SEPTEMBER 7. A strong breeze with quite a sea during the night. This morning thick and foggy. About 11 A.M. saw the *Black Warrior*, of Honolulu, Captain Brown. He ran down to us and came on board. He has taken two whales this season. When he found that we were to leave in a few days, he went on board to finish some letters that he had commenced, that he might send them by us to the Islands, as he would go to Margarita Bay before going in. At 2 P.M. he returned with the letters and then went to the northwest. Soon after raised a bark which proved to be the *Paulina,* Captain Steen. After speaking, Captain Steen came on board. They report a number of vessels as having gone through the Strait, and we shall probably follow them the first fair day. The *Paulina* has taken five whales.

SEPTEMBER 8. Started today on our way out of the Arctic after it lightened up a little. Could get no good observations, so Samuel was obliged to act according to the best of his judgment. I shall be glad when we get safely through the Strait, although I should like much to have had a couple more whales before leaving. We may get one in Bristol Bay yet, as we go through on our way to the Islands and shall probably stop there a week or ten days.

SEPTEMBER 9. We kept on last night as long as Samuel deemed it safe, he sitting up until eleven o'clock; then wore ship for an hour or two. About 6 A.M. raised East Cape right ahead, which we were all very happy to see, as it showed us our position which we had not positively known for a number of days. Came through the Strait flying with all sail set and a strong northerly wind. We are now off St. Lawrence Bay, 7 P.M., with one sail in sight. The land along the coast looks barren, cheerless, and dreary, more so than when we came in, as it was warmer and pleasanter then. We miss those long days that we then enjoyed. Now we experience quite long dark nights.

SEPTEMBER 10. A dead calm. For the most of the day we have been moving quite lazily along, quite a contrast to the way our gallant *Addison* tripped over the waters yesterday. Two ships in sight, one the *Japan,* the other name unknown. We heard a report a few days since that Captain Grandsaigne of the French ship *Nil* was dead and that Captain Morel, formerly of the *Napoleon 3rd,* had taken command of her. He was quite unwell when we saw him, and the report may be true.

SEPTEMBER 11. Clear and pleasant but cold, a white frost in the morning. Eight A.M. we were off Indian Point. Saw the huts on it. It makes off a long way into the sea and looks strangely, as the land is so low. Considerable snow has fallen since we went through here on our way north, some of the mountains being thickly covered. We experienced a slight snow squall during the day. Saw St. Lawrence Island in the afternoon. Both ships out of sight, and we are again alone.

SEPTEMBER 12. A strong breeze with squalls in the morning. We are wending our way rapidly along. If the wind holds, we shall see [St.] Matthew, or Gore's, Island tomorrow morning, where we some hope to see right whales. Saw the island this afternoon but saw nothing living around it.

SEPTEMBER 13. Kept near the land through the night and are now quite near it on the other side. Three ships were raised from aloft, but they all proved to be rocks on Pinnacle Island, a small island close by the other.

P.M.   Saw finbacks and two right whales going to windward. We are now bound in the direction of St. Paul Island with a strong breeze and fine weather.

SEPTEMBER 14. Clear, bright, and pleasant. Have been expecting through the afternoon to see the island of St. Paul, but as it has not been quite clear in that direction, we have not as yet seen it.

6 P.M.   Heard the sound of "There blows!" from aloft, but they proved to be finbacks.

SEPTEMBER 15. Foggy through the day, regular Arctic Ocean and Bristol Bay weather. Luffed to at noon to catch codfish but did not get a bite. Hope that we may be successful in taking a supply while here.

SEPTEMBER 16. Foggy in the morning, but the sun came out occasionally through the day so that we were able to get observations. Have seen neither ships nor whales since we have been in Bristol Bay. The whales cannot be where they were last year, or we should occasionally see one.

SEPTEMBER 17. Saw the comet again last night.[20] We saw it for the first time in the Strait; have seen it whenever it has been clear. I wonder if our friends at home are looking at the same phenomenon? This morning it is clear again and pleasant. Nothing in sight except one solitary finback. Foggy in the afternoon.

SEPTEMBER 18. Foggy as usual again this morning. We are looking daily for the line gale, which I very much dread—especially on account of our ship, although she is in quite good condition. I hope we may be favored by moderate breezes until we arrive in port.

SEPTEMBER 19. Quite clear and calm in the morning but cloudy and some rainy for the remainder of the day. Could get no observations.

SEPTEMBER 20. Calm again and some foggy. Sun came out at times through the day. Lowered a boat in the afternoon to catch codfish; could get none, but afterward caught four from the ship.

SEPTEMBER 21. Calm in the morning and quite pleasant in the afternoon. Quite a strong breeze sprung up from the southeast, which was in a contrary direction from what we wish to get out.

SEPTEMBER 22. The breeze lasted through the night with some rain. A calm for the most of the day with a considerable swell, and we have been "rocking in the cradle of the deep"[21] rather more than we cared to or than was pleasant. I shall be heartily glad when we have a good day and a fair wind to get out, for we have seen neither ships nor whales since we have been here, besides being in fogs and calms for most of the time. The comet made its appearance again last evening; not bright, however, as it was rather cloudy.

SEPTEMBER 23. Calm and pleasant, not a bit of wind. When shall we ever have a fair wind to leave this ground? As there is no whaling to be done, we all feel in haste to be making our passage to the Islands. For the last few weeks I have been engaged at times in making a black silk basque for myself. After much tribulation and some tears on my part and a few scoldings on Samuel's that I did not have it done in port, I have at last completed it to the satisfaction of all concerned.

SEPTEMBER 24. A strong breeze from the eastward, and we are making the most of it in getting along toward the [One] Seventy-two Passage, where we expect to go out. The good *Addison* ploughs her way along right merrily through the waters. Saw the island of St. George this afternoon.

SEPTEMBER 25. The breeze still continues, but the wind is more to the southward; consequently not very fair. We are now about seventy miles from the passage. Twenty-two months today the *Addison* has been our home, and a pleasant home it has been to us for the most part of the time. May it so continue through the voyage.

SEPTEMBER 26. Raised three ships in the morning. We laid aback for the one astern to get up to us and were very glad to find our old friend and consort the *Benjamin Tucker,* Captain Barber. Captain Barber came on board and stopped until after dinner, when, as it was quite rugged, he thought it best to go back. Raised the land about 11 A.M. and came through the passage in the afternoon, so that we are now in the open sea again and can be said to have fairly commenced our passage to the Islands. Captain Barber has taken 400 barrels of oil this season—one bowhead and several mussel diggers. I am sorry for him. He deserves better success and has lost one man, a young fellow that he brought from home with him. The other ships that we raised this morning were the French ship *Caulaincourt* and the Oahu brig *Victoria.* Afternoon, a strong breeze and a heavy sea, which causes the *Addison* to rear and plunge as if she thought not of her precious cargo of human souls.

SEPTEMBER 27. Lost sight of the *Benjamin Tucker* during the night, and we are again alone. A strong breeze and a heavy sea.

SEPTEMBER 29. Weather still the same. We are getting along grandly in making our passage, but it is very uncomfortable. I tremble sometimes for the ship for fear she will give out, but Samuel thinks there is no danger. It will be a relief to me on that account to get in port. About sunset the wind increased to a gale.

SEPTEMBER 30. The gale continued through the night and has lasted through the day. We have been obliged to lay to, and there is no prospect of a change as yet. This probably is the line gale, as it is more severe than any that we have experienced.

OCTOBER 1. Moderated some during the night, and this morning we have a thick fog with some rain, a strong breeze still. There is one consolation: if the breezes continue, we shall soon be out of heavy weather and down in the delightful climate of the tropics.

P.M. Moderated, but foggy and rainy. The weather is considerably warmer than it has been.

OCTOBER 2. Last night we had quite a shower of rain with thunder and lightning. I heard the thunder and saw the lightning from the cabin, as I was in bed, for the first time in the voyage. This morning it is clear, bright, and pleasant with a mild breeze—so warm that we have no fire in the cabin and have open windows. Quite a contrast to the weather we have experienced for the last several months. It seems very delightful to us all.

OCTOBER 3. A fine breeze this morning, and we are getting all we can of it by putting out studding sails. We have not made much for the last two or three days. Saw a vessel this morning to the windward, which we hoped might be the *Benjamin Tucker;* but it proved to be the brig *Victoria,* Captain Fish, of Oahu.

OCTOBER 4.[22] Yesterday the brig rather beat us, but last night the wind hauled a little so that we beat her considerably. Fine weather and a good breeze, which sends the good ship on her way. I have been having a regular washing day, washing thick clothes to put up and thin ones to take out—hoods, sacks, thick dresses, etc.—getting out and doing up sunbonnets.

OCTOBER 5. In the morning the brig was out of sight, but in the afternoon she appeared again, having gained on us. This has been rather a squally day. Considerable rain has fallen, and everybody on deck is using an abundant supply of rainwater for washing purposes. Having stopped up the scuppers, they use the whole deck for one grand washtub. They all, especially the Kanakas, appear delighted to get in warm weather again. A fine breeze, and the *Addison* has been going at the rate of seven or eight knots.

OCTOBER 6. This morning we find that the clipper brig has beat us again. Another ship in sight. The ship came down after dinner and spoke us. She proved to be the *Abraham Barker,* Captain Slocum, from the Okhotsk Sea; three whales this season. He does not bring very flattering accounts from that region. A few ships have done quite well, but the most of the fleet are poorly off. Such news tends to make us feel quite well off, and I do feel that we have very much to be thankful for. It is so much better to go in port in our own ship with 700 barrels of oil and 10,000 pounds bone than it would to have gone in passengers, leaving the old *Addison's* bones in the Arctic, a fate which she very narrowly escaped. Captain Slocum sent us some coffee from his ship, which was very acceptable, as we have been without for several weeks.

OCTOBER 7. We have again beat the *Victoria*. The *Abraham Barker* and the *Addison* have kept very near together for the last twenty-four hours. A fine breeze, and the Sandwich Islands begin to look very near on the chart.

OCTOBER 10. This is the Sabbath, a day of rest for which I am truly glad. The past has been a busy week: washing and ironing all the thick clothing that we have been wearing for the season; then washing, starching, and ironing all the port clothes which are put by roughdry, which is no inconsiderable job; besides having the stove taken down and cleaning in every nook and corner. It all seems to come at once, for they all need warm weather; and when that arrives, we are not far from our journey's end. The *Abraham Barker* still near us. Parted company with the *Victoria* several days since astern. On another Sabbath, if nothing prevents, we can probably attend church. What a privilege we shall esteem it.

OCTOBER 12. Yesterday a sad event occurred which cast a gloom over our whole company—the death and burial of William Kalama, a Kanaka. He has been off duty some time; did not complain but appeared to be running down. Samuel gave him medicine and tonics. We had no idea that he was so low until they told us he was dead. He was on deck the day before. I went on deck at sunset to hear the funeral service read before he was consigned to the deep.[23] It seemed rather aggravating after being so long from home to die as it were within sight of it.

This P.M. Captain Slocum made us another visit. The wind has not been fair for several days. We shall not be able to fetch Maui, where Samuel intended to go first, and we shall have hard work to fetch Oahu unless the wind hauls. Have had no trades[24] as yet.

OCTOBER 13. Saw Oahu this morning. We have been going back and forth all day, beating, and are just about as near now at dark as we were then. I thought this morning that by this time I should have been made happy or sad by the reception of letters. Another ship has come up here today in the same predicament. Should we stop here several days with the wind as it now is, I expect there would be quite a fleet here.

OCTOBER 14. A.M.   Wind changeable so that we could get along but very little.

P.M.   Wind fair. Got off Diamond Head about dark. Lay off and on through the night. The *Marengo* close by us coming from Maui. Passed the clipper ship *John Marshall. Victoria, Abraham Barker,* and *Majestic* close by us.

OCTOBER 15. We were off Diamond Head early this morning. Captain Howland, the pilot, came on board. The steam tug is repairing some of her machinery, so that we are now awaiting her arrival.[25] Captain Slocum made us a call this morning as he went ashore. His ship lays off and on. Samuel has gone ashore to procure a boarding place for us and to get letters if there may be any for us; and I await their reception, oh, how tremblingly. The *Speedwell* has just passed us, so we shall probably find Captain and Mrs. Gibbs in port.[26]

FIFTH CRUISE

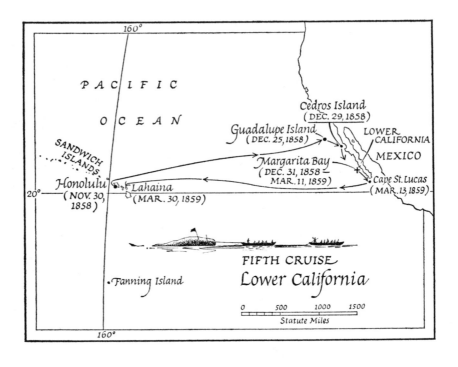

160°

P A C I F I C

O C E A N

Cedros Island
(DEC. 29, 1858)

Guadalupe Island
(DEC. 25, 1858)

LOWER
CALIFORNIA

MEXICO

SANDWICH
ISLANDS

Margarita Bay
(DEC. 31, 1858 –
MAR. 11, 1859)

Cape St. Lucas
(MAR. 13, 1859)

20°   Honolulu
(NOV. 30,
1858)

Lahaina
(MAR. 30, 1859)

FIFTH CRUISE
Lower California

Fanning Island

0   500   1000   1500
Statute Miles

160°

Lower California

NOVEMBER 1858–APRIL 1859

NOVEMBER 30. After a long period of silence I again resume my writing. Left Honolulu today after being a resident of that goodly city for a period of seven weeks. Our stay was prolonged so much beyond our usual time on account of repairing our ship, which has been thoroughly done, and now we think she is in a sound condition and will prove seaworthy.[1] May she for the future keep clear of all ice, shoals, rocks, and quicksands and bear us safely on until we shall reach the port of home.

Time passed very pleasantly to us while in port. Minnie's delight was unbounded at meeting with children again of her own age, which she found at Mr. Whitney's, where we boarded, also at Mr. Damon's,[2] where we occupied a room. We formed many pleasant acquaintances, especially among captains and their ladies, at one time there being twenty-one ladies in port. Three of the ladies came in with infants that were born at sea in the northern regions during the season: Mrs. Smith of the *Eliza F. Mason* has a son, Mrs. Green of the *Sheffield* a daughter, and Mrs. Taber of the *Adeline* a son. They are called young "bowheads" by the captains.

We received an abundant supply of letters while in port, more than we could reasonably have expected, and they were mostly filled with good tidings with the exception of our dear niece Celia Maria, whom we left in the full bloom of health and vigor and who is now in all human probability fast passing away. God help those parents if called so soon to part with their only child. I can hardly endure the thought that we can never look on her bright face again, but there is consolation in the thought that our loss will be her exceeding gain; in her young days she gave herself up to her Heavenly Father and, we trust, has ever since been an humble follower of the meek and lowly Jesus. I sent letters home to all the family on both sides, having an opportunity of sending by three different mails, and I can imagine how thankfully they will be received. I was so happy that we could give them good tidings in regard to health and comfort. Truly we are blessed when we can give and receive such good tidings of friends and kindred.

We had several very pleasant gatherings while in port: a meeting of the Strangers' Friend Society, a party of a few friends at Mrs. Edwards', a very pleasant gathering of the wives and children of the captains in port at Mr. Damon's, and the most pleasant of all was a visit to the Parry, as it is called, across the valley at the other side of the island. The party consisted of about twenty couple, all on horseback except Captain and Mrs. Weeks of the *Scotland* and Samuel and myself. As we ladies were novices in riding, we went in carriages. It was prophesied that we could not go within four miles of the Parry in carriages, but we were determined to make the attempt even if we had to walk the four miles. We left our carriage within a half of a mile of the place, and if we had walked the four miles, we should have been amply repaid for our labor in viewing the fine prospect before us. On our return stopped at the halfway house where refreshments had been prepared for us by Captain Spencer. The time passed so pleasantly with us that it was nearly dark before we separated. It was a pleasant little excursion that I shall always remember.

Mr. Nickerson left us to go home while we were in port, and as our second and third officers were seasoners, we have an entire new set in the cabin, Mr. Forsyth, Mr. Huntley, Mr. Parker, and Mr. Crocker. Samuel also discharged his steward, which delighted me very much. We have one now who appears something as a steward should, and we certainly find a great difference in the quality of the food which is placed before us. May it long continue to be so. George, our cabin boy, has gone forward. He is a smart fellow, and it was hard for him to be washing dishes or trimming lamps in the cabin when he might have been on deck pulling ropes or at the masthead looking out for whales; so when we were in port, Samuel thought he would promote him, which he did to his great joy.[3]

While in port, Mr. Damon proposed to me that the wives of captains in port should contribute towards purchasing a new carpet for the Bethel Church, which was very much needed. He wished me to mention it to the ladies, which I did with the assistance of Mrs. Captain Swain and succeeded in collecting about $70, which will probably be sufficient for recarpeting the church.

A few days before leaving port the sound of sorrow was again borne to us from the sea. The bark *Rajah* was wrecked in the Okhotsk Sea; the captain, one or two officers, and ten men were lost.[4] As Mr. Damon on the next Sabbath prayed so earnestly for the wives and families of the lost ones, the thought came over me how little those faraway ones realized the prayers that had ascended for them on account of their loneliness and bereavement. God be with them to comfort and protect them when the sad tidings shall reach them.

DECEMBER 25. When I left port I congratulated myself that I had been in Honolulu for seven weeks and escaped the "boohoo," or "Maui," fever, to which all foreigners are subject. But my congratulations came too soon, for after being at sea several days, the boohoo seized me, and I was sick enough; was obliged to keep my bed for a week. It is said to be a mild form of the Panama fever. There is nothing dangerous about it, but it is the most uncomfortable fever one can have, such weariness and awful aches in the bones that it is impossible to describe. Minnie had a very bad cold, and I feared that she would have an attack of it, but she escaped. We have all been afflicted with colds almost constantly ever since we arrived in port, and they seem still to continue. For the whole season north we were not troubled at all, and it seems strange to have so many in comfortable weather.

Minnie hung up her stocking as usual last night and was fortunate in finding it quite well filled with the usual supply of candies, nuts, and oranges, also a book and transparent slate from me, and a $2.50 gold piece from her papa. A few days ago Mr. Forsyth, our mate, gave her a very pretty little spyglass, which she said she should call her Christmas present too.

We are now bound to the coast of California for mussel diggers, if we can find them, and for wood. After undergoing repairs it was too late to go on New Zealand [5] where we would like to have gone, but it may be all for the best for us to come here. Yesterday saw a ship supposed to be a merchantman from California, and today the island of Guadalupe is in sight at a distance. In a day or two we shall expect to see Cedros Island where Samuel hopes to find a sperm whale. How I wish that he might not be disappointed.

DECEMBER 29. Saw Cedros Island but nothing around there that had life of the fish kind. There was a ship laying at anchor on the back side of the island, probably after guano. We should have sent a boat inshore after fish, but it was very rough; and Samuel did not care to stop, as there were no whales to be seen.

DECEMBER 31. Yesterday we were following down the California coast. Today we made Magdalena Island.

P.M. As we were going up the bay saw four ships at anchor. We went as long as we could see, as Samuel wishes to go farther up the lagoon to get wood, and then probably we shall come down again. Anchored at dark in twenty-five fathoms of water.

1859

JANUARY 1. Oh, that I knew it was a happy new year to one and all of my friends at home. That it may be is my fervent wish and prayer. May our good Father have them all in his holy keeping. For the many mercies which were showered upon us during the past year, may we be truly thankful, and may we earnestly implore His guidance and blessing on this new year, which has just opened upon us so fresh and bright. If prosperity attend us, may we thank the Giver, and if adversity and trials shall be our portion, may we as truly thank Him, remembering that "what seemeth evil is for our highest good."

This morning we received a visit from Captain Chatfield of the *Massachusetts*. He informed us that the ships that were here were the *Rambler*, Captain Willis and family; the *Scotland*, Captain Weeks and family; *Majestic*, Captain Chester; and the *Dromo*, Captain May; also a potato schooner from San Francisco. After dinner Mr. Huntley went out in a boat to see what he could find in the eating line. Came home about dark with several bushels of very nice "quahogs" [6] and about a dozen mullet. Captain Allen and a Mr. Salter, the captain and owner of the schooner, came on board to tea with us; found their company very pleasant.

JANUARY 2. All the boats went out this morning. Samuel, Minnie, and myself went ashore, but as it was high tide, our excursion was a very unprofitable one. It is a very dreary, barren-looking country with nothing of vegetation except cactuses of the prickly-pear species, which almost entirely cover the ground, rendering it rather unsafe to walk without extreme care. Some of them were in bloom, the flowers being singularly bright and handsome. We took up several specimens and procured a box of earth to put them in, hoping we might preserve them. We saw while onshore what we supposed to be three graves with nothing to tell who they were or how they died. I thought as I stood looking at them that they probably had wives, mothers, or sisters who had not the privilege of weeping over their graves, and I gazed at them with tears in my eyes for their sakes. Those boats that stopped longer than we did better; at low tide they procured some clams, also brought home some nice fish and a large turtle.

JANUARY 4. We are endeavoring to get farther up the channel into the lagoon where the *Dromo* lays. The passage is very narrow, and it is only at low water that the banks may be seen. At every low tide we advance a little; shall get up in the course of time. The *Dromo* has taken two whales, the *Massachusetts* two, the *Rambler* one, and the *Scotland* one. Samuel wanted to get his wood before he commenced whaling, but as the whales have commenced coming in, he will probably get it as he can. Our boats today got a nice lot of fish and a heap of birds—snipe, curlew, and plover. The Spaniards came down the lagoon with a load of fresh beef, which they will continue to do through the season, so that we shall live on the fat of the land while here.[7] Had turtle soup and fried turtle steaks today, which was very nice indeed.

JANUARY 5. Got a little nearer our journey's end today. If it had not been cloudy, think we should have anchored by the *Dromo*. As it was we went to about a mile from her. Captain May came on board last night, and they decided that it would be advisable for the *Dromo* and the *Addison* to mate, that is, to divide the whales.[8] This morning two of our boats went in company with the *Dromo's* in pursuit of the monsters. On their way down struck one with a calf. Killed it about dark and anchored it fifteen miles from the ship.

JANUARY 6. The boats went up after the whale and got back to the ship about three o'clock. Afterward they cut him in. Captain May and his son came on board several times during the day.

JANUARY 7. The *Scotland,* Captain Weeks, and the *Oahu,* Captain Fehlber, came up here today. The *Oahu* is going farther up the lagoon; the *Scotland* has anchored near us. Captain Weeks came on board with his little Lulie. Minnie was delighted to see her, more especially as she is the first little girl that has visited her on board the *Addison.* Captain Fehlber also dined with us. The steward and steerage boy had gone ashore for wood, so I was obliged to get dinner for them with the help of the cook. We do not calculate much upon dinner now, as the officers are all away; nobody in the cabin but Samuel, Minnie, and myself. The boats usually get back at three or four o'clock, and then we have a good meal. We breakfast at half-past four. I did not get up so early first along, and Samuel and myself had our breakfasts afterwards; but as the steward would cook a separate one for us, I thought it best for us to eat with the rest, as Samuel always wanted to get up to see the boats off. We now get up to breakfast at half-past four, and then I go to bed again to pass away the time until sunrise, which is about seven. The weather here is delightful, just comfortably warm, having windows either open or shut. The nights are quite cool. I think it is just the weather that would suit my mother. It very seldom rains here, but occasionally there are heavy dews. Caught four turtle today.

JANUARY 8. Our boats went in one lagoon today, and the *Dromo's* in another. Our boats saw nothing, but the other ship had three boats stoven without getting fast. The boats got in between the whale and her calf—they push their calves up in the air at times to increase their speed—and she probably mistook the boats for her child. I am glad I don't go in the boats. Caught some very fine mackerel today from the ship.

JANUARY 9. The boats returned this P.M. with a whale, which they took to the *Dromo*. Mr. Parker, our third officer, got his boat stoven quite badly, but no one was hurt. Finished boiling today, as we only boil during the day, cool down at night, and all hands turn in except shipkeepers.

JANUARY 10. Boats took another whale today, which they were obliged to anchor, as there was a head tide. The boats go up the lagoon about thirty miles. Manuel, boatsteerer, attempted to strike a turtle yesterday and cut his hand so that he will not be able to go in a boat again at present. Our ship will be quite a hospital if they keep on coming down. Mr. Forsyth, our mate, has been laid up nearly ever since we left Oahu with rheumatism, the cook has been off duty for about two weeks, also one of the foremasthands, and Antone, boatsteerer, has been off duty several days with a cold, pain in his bones, lame back, etc., and tonight Heughan, another boatsteerer, has given up. It is bad to have boatsteerers give up now. They are needed so much now. Have been obliged to take two men from the forecastle to act in that capacity.[9] Since the *Oahu* left us, she has had several boats stoven and one man's leg broken, a bad beginning. The *Cynthia* has taken six whales and the *Carib* four. They are both a number of miles farther in the lagoon than we are or can get.

JANUARY 11. We were intending to go on board the *Scotland* to pass the day, but it rained some in the morning and was quite unpleasant, so we decided to postpone it until tomorrow.

JANUARY 12. A beautiful day for our visit. We left about 10 A.M. and returned in the evening. Had a delightful visit. I was very happy to go on my own account but doubly delighted that Minnie could enjoy the society of girls at sea, they being the first she has seen this voyage. Captain Weeks's oldest daughter is eleven years old, and she and Minnie enjoyed each other's society very much.[10] Samuel did not pass the day with us, as he was busy cutting and boiling, but he went early and took tea.

JANUARY 13. The *Scotland* took a whale today, being the second they have taken here.

JANUARY 14. Mrs. Weeks and children passed the day with us. Captain Weeks and Captain May came to tea; passed a very pleasant day. Captain Allen and Mr. Salters passed the eve with us.

JANUARY 15. Captain May and Samuel went fishing; got nothing except quahogs, as the tide was not right. Captain May's boats took a whale.

JANUARY 16. Samuel went on board the *Dromo* to help cut in the whale with a boat's crew, as Captain May was shorthanded.

JANUARY 17. Samuel is laid up today with a lame back in consequence of digging quahogs and cutting in whale. Captain Weeks came on board for me to go and see his wife, as they thought some of leaving at night. But while he was here, they decided to stop another day, so I put off my visit until tomorrow, as I was busy washing and I did not care to leave Samuel. Captain Weeks recommended new rum and saleratus to bathe his back, which I immediately applied. Got a whale today, which they were to bring to our ship, but Samuel sent for Captain May to take it to the *Dromo,* as he was not able to see to it.

JANUARY 18. Captain Weeks's boats took a whale yesterday, which sunk. They anchored him and went back for him today, when they had the misfortune to find that the sharks had almost entirely devoured him. Samuel's back being lame, I invited Mr. Crocker, our fourth officer, to take Minnie and myself on board the *Scotland,* which I presume he was very happy to do.

JANUARY 19. Captain Fish of the *Victoria,* fifty or sixty miles up the lagoon, was here this morning by daylight; came down for bomb lances. Passed the most of the day with us. Our steward set out to go ashore after wood this morning, fell in with a Spanish boat that had liquor, bought a good supply; then they went in the bushes and had a regular spree. After our boats came back from whaling, as he had not returned, Samuel sent Mr. Parker to look them up. He found them just arousing from their carousal. They came back looking quite crestfallen. We feared they had run, and it was quite a relief to me to have the steward to come back, although I have lost confidence in him. He is an excellent steward, and that is all you can say.[11]

JANUARY 20. As the captains were all going fishing today, I thought I would send for Mrs. Weeks and family to come and pass the day with me. We had a nice time today until, about noon, I saw one of the *Scotland's* boats coming back with a man lying down in the stern sheets, and presently the captain's boats went on board also. I knew something bad had happened, but I kept still, as I knew that it would make Mrs. Weeks feel very bad. She knew nothing of it until tonight when her husband came and said that one of their boatsteerers had his leg broken in two places by a whale. The whale escaped. When our boats returned at night, we found that one of the boats had been served in the same manner, but fortunately no one was injured. Mr. Forsyth has recovered so that he goes in the boats. The man that had his leg broken on board the *Oahu* has since died.

JANUARY 21. Today we went onshore and had a picnic: Captain Weeks, his wife, and two children; Samuel, Minnie, and myself; and Captain May and son. Started about nine o'clock in the morning. We took our steward with us, and Captain Weeks took his cook. Carried bread, crackers, cake, cookies, and pies with us. After we arrived there, kindled a fire and made a quahog chowder and stewed some birds for dinner. We had plenty of coffee and beer also. The captains went a little farther up the lagoon seining for fish. Their seine was too short so that most of the fish escaped. We had an abundance of oysters all around us growing on the trees, and the empty shells on all sides of us would show that we did them ample justice. We would have a tree cut down and thrown across the fire until the oysters were sufficiently roasted, then take the tree off and commence operations, each child having a separate fire and roasting her own oysters.[12] It was a pleasant day of their lives and one long to be remembered. It is a barren country, nothing growing except sand flowers, which were very pretty, and cactus plants. The children succeeded in making very pretty wreaths to adorn their heads, even in such a barren place.[13]

The tide went down about noon very suddenly in the lagoon where we were, leaving the boats high and dry about two miles [from] the channel, so that we made up our minds to have to stay very late, perhaps the most of the night. So we prepared ourselves accordingly; had a boat sail put up for a tent in the morning to protect us from the sun. We sent the men out to get a good supply of wood, and such a roaring fire as we had—it reminded us of the big logs and large fireplaces of old-fashioned days. We wrapped ourselves up in boat sails, colors, and table-cloths and were as comfortable as need be, though we thought our home friends would think it looked rather dubious, had they seen us, with no prospect of getting off until the rise of the tide, with those children, seven or eight miles from the ship.[14]

About 9 P.M. we found that the boats would float. Soon after, the moon rose and we started off; had a delightful sail by moonlight and arrived at the ship about half-past ten. On our arrival we were very happy to hear that our boats had taken a whale.[15] We all decided that after having such a pleasant time that we must try it again before we leave the bay.

JANUARY 22. We feared that the children might take cold last night, but our fears were unfounded, and we all feel better for our excursion. The whale that was taken yesterday was brought to our ship this afternoon, and the *Dromo*'s boats with one of the *Scotland*'s took another today. The whale carried them nearly down to the heads before they killed him. After being killed he sank. They anchored him, leaving one boat by him until they can get him up. Two Spanish boats were down today with beef, raisins, figs, oranges, and cheese. We bought some beef and some oranges, which were very nice.

JANUARY 23. They succeeded in pulling the whale up this afternoon. Got him alongside the *Scotland* a short time before dark. Another whale was taken in Clark's Lagoon today, which was taken to the *Dromo*, so we shall all make a smoke together. Captain Sherman of the bark *Cynthia*, laying about thirty miles above us, came down at night. Stopped to tea with us and went on board the *Dromo* to spend the night. I believe he wants to buy cotton cloth for trade.

JANUARY 24. Samuel went on board the *Scotland* to help Captain Weeks cut his whale; took Minnie with him [and] came home before dinner, leaving Minnie there to pass the day with the children. Captain May and Captain Sherman were here to dine with us. Captain Sherman took $140 worth of trade from the *Addison*. Captain Weeks came on board in the P.M. to invite us to pass the day on board the *Scotland*. He said we had better visit each other as often as possible, as we might not have another such nice time to gam for the voyage, and I for one do not expect to. It is so very smooth here. We both go up and down the ship's side; as there are so few men on board, we put them to as little trouble as possible.[16]

JANUARY 25. A bright and beautiful morning as usual. The days are all alike here. About nine o'clock Samuel and Captain May took us on board the *Scotland,* where we stopped until about 8 P.M. Their boatsteerer who had his leg broken continues very comfortable. His leg appears to be doing well. The mate of the *Scotland* came home about dark with his boat badly stoven. A whale came up under his boat, knocked them all in the water, but no one was injured. They afterwards fastened to the same whale, but he towed them so far out to sea they were obliged to cut from him. The brig *Antilla* from Oahu passed us today on her way up the lagoon. The captain came on board for a short time, and afterward Samuel went there. Our boats did not get home until eight o'clock in the evening. They took another whale and were obliged to anchor him on account of the tide.[17]

JANUARY 26. The boats went up the lagoon as usual this morning and will bring the whale down when they come. Samuel and Captain May went fishing and oystering this forenoon; were quite successful. Got over a hundred good-sized fish and as many oysters as they wished to bring down. Got the whale alongside about dark.

JANUARY 27. Captain May and Captain Weeks with their boats'

crews came on board this morning to assist Samuel in cutting in the whale, as we had only one boat's crew of our own to stop. Nothing was seen up the lagoons today. I believe I have not written down the loss of the bark *Black Warrior*, Captain Brown. She went ashore several weeks ago in what is called Seameron's Lagoon. Captain Brown came here without stopping to the Islands and had his oil on board that he took north, which fortunately was but 200 barrels.

JANUARY 28. Captain Weeks and family passed the day with us today. Set the signal for Captain May to come and dine with us, but he did not come. From the appearance of his ship we judged that he was stowing down.

JANUARY 30. Samuel and Captain Weeks thought it best to keep the boats on board today, not only to recruit the men but also give the whales a chance to come in, and they thought Captain May would do the same, as they were the majority; but he saw fit to send his boats alone, and the consequence was they got a whale. Rather an unfair piece of business, the rest of us thought. I suppose he claims it, as it was taken to his ship.

FEBRUARY 1. Samuel, Minnie, and myself went on board the *Scotland* and passed the day.[18] In the afternoon Captain Weeks, Captain May, and Captain Lawrence went after some oysters, which they found in abundance. Stowed down our oil yesterday; found that the four whales had yielded us 177 barrels of oil, a very good yield for mussel diggers.

FEBRUARY 2. Samuel went fishing today. Got about a hundred mullet and a few flounders. The boats took a whale in the main lagoon today, which was taken to the *Scotland*.

FEBRUARY 3. Samuel went fishing again today, as he wants to get some to save to carry north. Took the steward and steerage boy with him, so I had the cooking to do. I made four loaves of bread, six pies, six pans of cookies, and stuffed two fish for baking. We had five men left on board, three invalids. It seems very lonely to have them all gone from the cabin. The boats fastened to a whale again today but accidentally cut from him. I have mentioned about their getting oysters that grew on trees, but the story that they came home with today I think rather beats that. The most of the fish they took today they found inside of decayed logs of wood, splitting open the logs and taking the fish out, a strange kind of fishing, but nevertheless true.[19] Even the whales go up in the bushes, and the last one that was taken they killed on the flats.

FEBRUARY 5. Captain Weeks and family passed the day with us. Had a pleasant time, as we usually do.

FEBRUARY 6. Mary stopped on board last night with Minnie. I made up a bed on the cabin floor so that they might sleep together. She stopped on board through the day. They generally amuse themselves in cooking when they are together. Today they made cake and cookies, which were really quite nice, but I imagine they had a little of the steward's assistance. The boats chased a whale out of the lagoon today without getting fast.

FEBRUARY 7. Samuel went fishing today but had fisherman's luck: got no fish. The tides are low now, but little water in the lagoons where they want to fish. Mr. Parker brought home the largest turtle that I ever saw. Took several men to lift it.

FEBRUARY 8. Samuel, Minnie, and myself went on board the *Scotland* today. Samuel and Captain Weeks went fishing. Got a very few fish and a few birds. Captain Weeks told us that we must talk fast through the day, for he intended to move downstream the next day. I felt very bad to hear it, for we have taken much comfort together; but I suppose we shall all move very soon, as there are no whales taken now.

FEBRUARY 9. Captain Sherman of the *Cynthia* sent down for more goods today. He wants but one whale to fill his casks, which will make him a thousand barrels. The *Oahu* has taken sixteen whales and the *Antilla* six. It seems too bad that there should be so many whales thirty miles up the lagoon where a ship cannot go and so few down here; but the ships all draw too much water to cross the Divides, so the small craft has that whaling ground to themselves.

FEBRUARY 10. The *Scotland* did not get under way yesterday as she intended to. We were all calculating to go down to Man-of-War Bay today on a pleasure excursion. It was a strong breeze, but as we were afraid it would be our last chance, we decided to improve. We went on board the *Scotland* and went down in her seven or eight miles, then went ashore. The girls wanted to go in a boat by themselves, so I went with Captain and Mrs. Weeks, and Mary went with Minnie and Samuel. As the *Scotland* had no boats off, the officers and most of the crew were ashore with us. We had a nice quahog chowder, beer, coffee, three kinds of cake, white bread, cheese, figs, and oranges for the treat. The stewards made chowder three times in the course of the day.

When the time came for going home, as there was a strong breeze with the wind and tide both ahead, Samuel decided to pass the night on board the *Scotland,* which plan the ladies and children readily fell in with. We arrived safely on board about 5 P.M., had supper, had quite a nice sing in the course of the evening, played backgammon, etc. When it came bedtime, Minnie went to bed with Mary in her cot, which was hung in the after cabin. Mrs. Weeks, Lulie, and myself took her bed in her bedroom, Captain Weeks had a bed on the floor in the after cabin, and Samuel took the sofa.

FEBRUARY 11. This morning a ship went ashore on the flats in attempting to get across from the heads. She was supposed to be the *Euphrates,* Captain Heath. The *Rambler's* boats and the *Scotland's* went to her assistance. About 9 A.M. we started for our *Addison* home, reaching it about 1 P.M. We had a head wind and head tide so did not make very rapid progress. Found all well on board. The boats were all on board; as there was such a strong breeze in the morning, it was of no use to set off.

FEBRUARY 12. Samuel went fishing this morning, found that he could not get in the lagoons, so went to another place and filled his boat with oysters. He got a large kind called rock oysters, and had I been onshore in a starving condition, I should never have thought of their being any[thing] eatable in such unsightly-looking rocks. One oyster nearly fills a saucer. We had them fried in butter for supper, but they were rather too sweet for me, though they were nice. I like the tree oysters much better than those, however. In the afternoon Samuel and Captain May went seining. Stayed until about 9 P.M. Had a large fire on the beach, thinking it would attract the fish, but the water in the lagoons was too low. The ship that was ashore yesterday is off again, but we have not heard whether she received any damage.

FEBRUARY 13. Captain May came on board to dine with us today. It seems so lonesome not to see the *Scotland*. (She has gone down in the passage now.) We miss them very much.

P.M. Went ashore and walked around. Found quite a quantity of shells. Some quite pretty, but nothing very choice. The boats had the good fortune to capture a whale today, which was taken to the *Dromo*.

FEBRUARY 14. A Spanish boat came down today. Brought figs and cheese, but no beef. We bought four sacks of figs, some of which were very nice.

FEBRUARY 16. For the last three days I have been engaged in netting a bag for Samuel's seine. Finished it today. The schooner *Ella Fisher* came down today. Captain Allen came on board and passed the evening. Mr. Huntley went fishing today; took quite a quantity of them.

FEBRUARY 17. We have fish in abundance to eat now. Had one of the nicest, stuffed and baked, for supper that I ever tasted. Mr. Huntley and Mr. Crocker went fishing today. Samuel and Captain Allen went up in the afternoon. They did not take quite as many as they did yesterday. Mr. Forsyth went gunning; shot about a dozen curlew and ducks, which were very nice. Captain May came on board to tea with us.

FEBRUARY 18. Two of the boats went fishing today. Made a great haul; got nearly two boatloads. Captain Allen came on board in the afternoon and passed the night with us.

FEBRUARY 19. Commenced splitting and salting the fish immediately after breakfast. Samuel hopes to have some for sale at the Islands, as they will probably fetch eight or ten dollars per barrel.

FEBRUARY 20. Captain Allen left today for Man-of-War Bay, and as Samuel saw a ship going in there from below, he decided to take a boat in tow and go down in the schooner. A man whom we found on board after leaving the Islands by the name of John Jones, an assumed one probably, has asked and obtained leave to go to San Francisco with Captain Allen. He says he ran away from an English man-of-war then in port, the *Calypso,* and he dares not go back to the Islands again for fear of being apprehended. I sent several letters to San Francisco by Captain Allen. Wrote two sheets to my father and mother, one to Cynthia, one to George, a note to James, one to S. P. Bourne, one to Sarah, and one to Joseph and Harriet, which I hope they may all receive in due time.

Samuel arrived home about 8 P.M.; found that ship to be the *Scotland.* Saw Captain Weeks and family ashore. He has taken 19 barrels since he left here; was bound in for his wood and then going to leave. Ships are doing nothing below now. The *Paulina* took a whale a few days since. Had the second mate's and one man's legs broken and another man killed. The *Benjamin Rush's* cooper and one or more of his boatsteerers stole a boat, took another cooper and boatsteerer from the *Euphrates,* and cleared in the night for parts unknown. The following day the ships started in pursuit of them. Captain Allen sent Minnie by Samuel a fishline wound on a reel with a sinker and two hooks attached to it, which pleased her very much, as she employs herself a great deal in fishing from the stern. She has caught a number of fish herself.

We sent our boats around to tow the *Dromo* this morning out of Clark's into the main lagoon. After getting into the channel, he let go his anchor; and this afternoon when the tide turned, he got under way to come down and got ashore. He hopes to get off by tonight's tide if possible. Samuel went to his assistance soon after his arrival from below.

FEBRUARY 21. The *Dromo* got off last night without any trouble. Sent the boats up the lagoon today to see if there might not be a stray whale for us and had the good fortune to get one, which was taken on board the *Addison,* the last whale of the season probably.

FEBRUARY 22. Captain May went down to Man-of-War Bay in his boats today; reported eight ships as being there, but two, the *Paulina* and the *Scotland,* would leave today. We shall probably go down there as soon as we get our oil stowed down. Captain May will go tomorrow if it is a good time.

FEBRUARY 24. Took up our anchor this morning and got under way in company with the *Dromo,* as he did not go yesterday on account of there being a strong breeze. Stowed down our oil yesterday. The whole amount of oil belonging to the *Addison* taken on the coast of California is 213 barrels. We hope still to get a sperm whale on our way to the Islands. We anchored in the bay about noon. Saw a tent with flags flying onshore; concluded they were having a picnic. Soon after we were anchored, a boat came off to us with an invitation to us to unite with them, which invitation we cordially accepted. On our arrival there we found Captain Willis, wife, and three children; Captain Weeks, wife, and two children (he left the day before but came back on account of having bad weather outside); Captain Ashley, wife, and one child of the *Reindeer;* Captain May of the *Dromo;* Captain Chatfield of the *Massachusetts;* Captain Jernegan of the *Levi Starbuck;* Captain Chester of the *Majestic;* Captain Booker of the *Hibernia;* Captain Hathaway of the *L. C. Richmond;* and Captain Lawrence, wife, and one child of the *Addison.* Made ten captains, four ladies, and seven children. We could hardly realize that we were whaling. Had a nice chowder, coffee, cold ham, cake, bread, crackers, and cookies. We also roasted plenty of oysters.

FEBRUARY 25. As Captain Weeks expected to go to sea Monday, I invited him with his family to pass the day with us; and as I thought it would be very ·pleasant even though I had small accommodations, I invited all the ladies with their husbands and children to pass the day with us likewise, which invitation they cordially accepted. I should have been pleased to have invited all the captains in port, but our table could not be enlarged sufficiently to seat them all. We had for dinner oyster

soup, boiled ham, and stewed rabbit with dumplings, a goose-
berry pudding, and tarts made of bottled fruits; for tea we had
fried ham, fish balls, warm biscuit, preserves, pies, plum cake,
and plain cake. We had a very pleasant time, the children particularly.

FEBRUARY 26. Captain Weeks and family passed the night with
us, as they were smoking ship.[20] Mrs. Weeks, Lulie, and myself
took the bed; made a bed up on the floor in the stateroom for
Mary and Minnie. Captain Weeks took Minnie's berth, and
Samuel took the sofa. After dinner Captain Weeks felt as if he
wished to give his children one more run, so we all went ashore,
stopped two or three hours; then we went with them to tea on
board the *Scotland.*

FEBRUARY 27. Samuel went on board the *Scotland* this morning;
took Minnie with him. He also went on board the *L. C. Richmond.* They both went out in the forenoon, also the *Hibernia.*
Our boats are all engaged in getting wood. We keep a gang
ashore cutting all the time, and we find it very good wooding.
We had a call from several of the captains today. Captain Hathaway sent me a bag of oranges. The *Fortune,* Captain Lester, arrived today.

FEBRUARY 28. Another picnic today. Had a tent put up on a large
scale today with several American flags waving in the breeze,
which made it look very pleasant. The steward of the *Levi
Starbuck* and our steward were to make the chowders. The
steward of the *Rambler* was there also to superintend the tables.
Before the first two mentioned stewards went ashore, they went
on board the *Dromo,* where they were treated to liquor by the
steward of the *Dromo.* Our steward liked it and took a pretty
good supply, but the *Levi Starbuck's* did not care for much.
    They did very well in the forenoon, but as soon as the chowder
was served, they asked and obtained liberty to go on board one
of the ships to get more pork and potatoes for another chowder.
They came directly on board the *Addison.* Our steward broke
into our stateroom, helped himself to liquor, and when he got
back again, he was about drunk enough. He came to Samuel
soon after that, telling him he was tired of being steward and

wanted he should let him go. Samuel asked him where he got the liquor. He answered as independently as you please, "I got it from your wife's room." Samuel looked around for some of his crew that they might take him aboard, but as he could find none, he told him to go and not to show his face until he was sober. So he bid them all good-by, asked for a "chaw of tobacco," and off he went.

We had a very pleasant time with the exception of that. It made them all feel badly, but it mortified me very much. We considered that he was the best steward among all the ships and so had depended upon him. We had chowder, ham, coffee, beer, cake of all kinds, pies, bread, crackers, cookies, preserves, etc., etc. It was dark when we left, but no steward was to be found.

MARCH 1. I felt very badly about our steward last night. He must suffer greatly for the want of water after going off in the condition that he was in. We have no one on deck that can act as steward, and I don't know what we shall do if he does not come. I do not believe he could possibly live to get up where the Spanish settlements are with nothing to eat or drink. I hope he may live to get back.

We were invited to pass the day on board the *Rambler* today, so I made some cake for the cabin before leaving. Had a very pleasant time. There were eight captains there to tea. I carried Mrs. Willis some colored yarn to knit for her children, which she needed very much, and she gave me a pair of cotton stockings and a pair of thick shoes for Minnie, which were equally acceptable.

MARCH 2. As I was to be at home today, I thought it best to go to washing; but before doing so, made half a dozen pumpkin pies, which were quite nice. Sent two boats up the lagoon today fishing; will probably stop all night. I hope they may fall in with the steward and bring him back again. Captain Ashley [and] Captain Willis came on board in the forenoon and made us a call. Captain Willis brought us a piece of fresh pork, which was very nice. Captain Chatfield and Captain Jernegan passed the evening with us.

About dusk I was on the house with Samuel, and Mr. Forsyth

came and said there was a boat coming with the steward in it. He could hardly get up the side; he reeled like a drunken man. He came and asked Samuel's forgiveness; told him that he would be the most faithful servant to him that anyone ever had if he would take him back; said that he had nothing to eat except a small piece of bread that he took with him and not a drop to drink. He had traveled constantly; when he tried to come back, he lost his way and was about laying down to die when he saw fires. He followed the smoke until he arrived to where a boat's crew were from the *Levi Starbuck;* could just say, "For God's sake, give me a drop of water," and fell to the ground. In all human probability, if he had not found those men as he did, his bones would have been left there like many others who think to better themselves by leaving their ships. Captain Jernegan had three men to leave yesterday that have not yet been heard of. The *Dromo* and the *Majestic* left today.

MARCH 3. The steward is very lame and sore today. His feet and ankles are very much swollen, and he looks as if he had seen hard times. He seems very humble, and I can but hope that it will be a lesson to him. Went on board the *Reindeer* to pass the day. Had a very pleasant time as usual. How we shall miss these pleasant gatherings when we get to sea. It seems very much like home gatherings, only home friends are not with me.

MARCH 4. Our boats came back last evening, loaded with fish. Sent them around, or rather a supply of them, to all the ships. I thought we would have the captains here today that had no wives with them. I would like to have invited them all but thought the steward hardly able to attend to it. Captain Chatfield went out this forenoon, so that we only had two captains to dine with us, Captains Jernegan and Lester. Had a fish chowder, a large stuffed and baked fish, coffee, bread and butter and preserves, and a roll pudding. Had some huckleberry pies made for supper, but they did not stop. Captain Jernegan sent a boat in to look for his men. They saw a flag put up and their names written in the sand about twelve miles from the beach, but nothing more of them. They found the skeleton of a man which they supposed to have died this season. His name was also written in the sand near him, but they could not make it out. We are now painting the ship outside and in; expect she will look equal to a clipper when she gets on her new dress.

MARCH 6. As it is Sunday, we are not doing much. Let some of the foremasthands take a boat after dinner and go ashore. Captain Jernegan came here in the morning; he was going ashore to take one more look for his men, as he wants to go to sea. He would have gone yesterday had it not been for them.²¹ In the evening Samuel went on board the *Reindeer,* also on board the *Rambler.*

MARCH 7. Captain Jernegan and Captain Lester left today. Captain Jernegan did not succeed in finding his men. After dinner Samuel, Minnie, and myself went on board the *Reindeer,* stopped there about two hours, then went on board the *Rambler* to tea. Captain and Mrs. Ashley went also and passed the evening.

MARCH 9. Captain Willis came on board in the morning. He has decided to go to sea after dinner. He brought a man that he found secreted on board his ship after leaving the Islands. He wanted to get a passage to San Francisco, and as we were going to stop here a day or two longer and by that time the *Carib* might make her appearance and he could get passage in her, Samuel consented to take him, as he needed his services as boat-steerer should he remain on board. The *Victoria, Oahu,* and *Antilla* came down from the lagoon today. Captain Fish of the *Victoria* passed out; the other two anchored. The *Reindeer* and *Rambler* left this P.M. Captain Fehlber of the *Oahu* passed the afternoon with us.

MARCH 10. Samuel went on board the *Oahu,* also on board the *Antilla* today. Captain Molde of the *Antilla* is quite feeble; has a bad cough.

MARCH 11. Captain Molde of the *Antilla* sent a fine pig as a present to us this morning, also several tins of preserved meats put up in Germany, a nice present. Our boats that we sent up fishing arrived this morning. They were not very successful in getting fish but got four very large turtle and three small ones, also two boatloads of oysters. We shall try to keep some of them fresh as a treat to the good people of Maui. About 10 A.M. Samuel took us ashore that we might have one more run. We took a few oysters with us that we might have the pleasure of making a fire and roasting them. We went back a little way where the flowers grew; found a very pretty bouquet and some very handsome specimens of cactus flowers. Then we went on the beach, found a few shells, helped the boat's crew dig clams, filled a bag with shells for the benefit of our biddies. Ate our oysters. Minnie went in wading for a few minutes, and then we bid adieu to the shores of Margarita Bay for the present. After dinner we got under way with a nice breeze in company with the other two vessels.

MARCH 12. Saw nothing of the vessels this morning, as they were bound direct to the Islands and we are going down to Cape St. Lucas to see if there might not be a sperm whale waiting for us. Saw a grand sight this morning, one of the California steamers. She was about four miles from us. Consequently we could neither report ourselves nor get any late papers from her.

P.M. Saw another steamer, which was coming toward us. I had one letter written to Charles and Lizzie. I sealed and directed it, then hastily wrote a few lines to sister Celia. By that time the steamer was close upon us, so we lowered a boat and sent Mr. Parker off with the letters. The captain kindly slackened her speed; took the boat alongside long enough to take the letters and give us some papers. Such a crowd as there was on that steamer's deck I never saw. The gentlemen swung their hats, and the ladies waved their handkerchiefs, Samuel and myself following suit, although I imagine that I was looked upon by them as an object of pity, but I do not believe that I would exchange situations with any of them.

MARCH 13. Saw nothing but humpbacks, so decided to shape our course for the Islands, which we did accordingly. There was a head sea and quite a strong breeze, which made it very uncomfortable. A number on board were seasick, but it made no difference to Minnie and myself, although we had been laying at anchor over two months.

MARCH 20. Nothing of interest has occurred this past week. Moderate winds have prevailed. Have been expecting the trades daily, but they kept back until last night, when they made their appearance accompanied by squalls and some rain, the first we have had for nearly three months. Today there is a strong breeze, and the gallant *Addison* carries us on at the rate of eight knots towards our destined port.

MARCH 27. Have had the benefit of the trades more or less for the last week. Are now within three or four days sail of the Islands, where we expect to receive tidings, either good or bad, from the loved at home. God grant that we may have strength given us to bear up under whatever we may be called upon to hear.

MARCH 29. Saw a ship today steering in the same direction with ourselves. Made Maui this afternoon, but as the weather was unpleasant with a head wind, we made but little headway, laying off and on part of the night.

[MARCH 30–APRIL 21.] We arrived safely at anchor in the harbor of Lahaina about 4 P.M., March 30. Went ashore very soon afterward where we found accommodations as usual with our friend Gilman at Seaside Cottage. Found letters from home awaiting us containing the sad intelligence of the death of our beloved niece Celia M. Bourne. Of her parents, how can I speak? Those hearts that ache because the voice of their loved one is heard no more, of eyes that weep because eyes that were bright have grown dim. Her end was tranquil and peaceful, and her parents feel that though they have one less in their family circle, yet heaven has one spirit more. May they and we also live so that we may finally be united to the dear loved ones gone before. We also found two boxes there for us, one which my mother had sent nearly two years previous but which has just reached us, and the other was directly from home from our Falmouth friends.

We passed several days with Mr. and Mrs. Brayton. They have an infant son several months old. Mr. and Mrs. Bigelow have left since we were there last spring, and their place is filled by Captain and Mrs. Bailey, who arrived there last fall.

Two captains' ladies are stopping at Lahaina this season, ten at Hilo, and five at Honolulu. Mr. Bishop and family are at the States; his pulpit is supplied by Mr. Andrews, of Lahainaluna. We attended church two Sabbaths. The last was very rainy; there were but eleven persons present, I being the only female. I had been out in worse weather at home and felt as if I could not be denied the privilege of attending church, as opportunity occurs so seldom.

We left Maui the fifteenth April and arrived off Honolulu the next morning, where we went ashore and found "our room" vacant at Mr. Damon's and a place at Mr. Whitney's table. We took a passenger down, a poor sick man that came from California on account of his health and is now anxious to get back to die. He was probably too far advanced in his disease when he arrived at the Islands for the climate to be of any benefit to him.

Sunday, attended church at the Bethel; heard the Rev. Mr. Corwin, pastor of the Fort Street Church, preach in the morning, and Mr. Collins, who, I think, is an agent of the American Missionary Society, preach in the evening. Sunday night I watched with Mrs. Slocum. Poor woman, I think her days are nearly ended. She is a great sufferer and an uncommonly patient one. Saw Mrs. Weeks and her children. Her husband had been gone several weeks. She will stop there during the season.

Monday afternoon we left Oahu and went down to Kauai to procure fresh pigs, fowls, potatoes, etc. The *Tamerlane* was laying off and on when we arrived, and soon after, standing in too near, she went on the reef. They soon succeeded in getting her off without damage except the loss of her false keel. The *Rambler* also came in while we were there. Not being successful in obtaining what we wished for trade, the natives demanding money for payment, we left there and proceeded to Niihau, where we procured what we wanted on very reasonable terms. We left the island the twenty-first for Kodiak.

SIXTH CRUISE

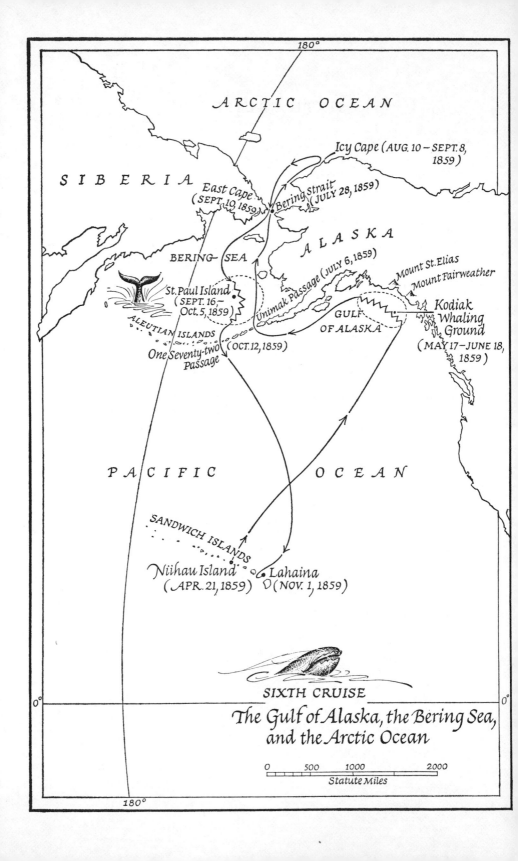

ARCTIC OCEAN

SIBERIA

Icy Cape (AUG. 10 – SEPT. 8, 1859)

East Cape (SEPT. 19, 1859)

Bering Strait (JULY 28, 1859)

ALASKA

BERING SEA

Unimak Passage (JULY 6, 1859)

Mount St. Elias
Mount Fairweather

St. Paul Island (SEPT. 16, – Oct. 5, 1859)

ALEUTIAN ISLANDS

One Seventy-two Passage

(OCT. 12, 1859)

GULF OF ALASKA

Kodiak Whaling Ground (MAY 17 – JUNE 18, 1859)

PACIFIC   OCEAN

SANDWICH ISLANDS

Niihau Island (APR. 21, 1859)

Lahaina (NOV. 1, 1859)

SIXTH CRUISE

The Gulf of Alaska, the Bering Sea, and the Arctic Ocean

0   500   1000   2000
Statute Miles

The Gulf of Alaska, the Bering Sea, and the Arctic Ocean

MAY–NOVEMBER 1859

———————◆‑◀◆▶‑◆———————

MAY 1. We have had quite moderate weather since we left. Some very warm pleasant days. Nothing has occurred of consequence to change the scene since we left. For several days we were in company with the *Rambler*. Captain Willis visited us once. He feels very lonely without his family; said he should feel still more homesick to enter his lonely cabin again after seeing us. We are now living upon fresh [meat], rather more of it sometimes than we care about: pork, chickens, ducks, turkeys, etc. As soon as it is a little cooler, shall have some of the pigs killed, baked up, and put down in barrels with lard. Also have an abundance of sausage meat, hog's-head cheese, etc. It takes too much for them all to eat. We had about forty when we left the last island.

MAY 3. Cloudy and quite a strong breeze through the day. About sunset it increased to a gale. As the wind was fair, we ran before it.

MAY 4. Moderated a little in the morning but soon came on again with increasing fury, a slight specimen of the weather we shall enjoy this season, with an occasional change of fogs. To pass away the time, as the deadlights were shut in the cabin making it dark and gloomy, I seated myself on my bed and commenced working Samuel a pair of slippers.

MAY 5. Not much change in the weather. A very heavy sea and

some very severe squalls. We have kept running. Samuel thought sometimes that he should be obliged to lay to, but we kept on.

MAY 6. The gale has abated, and I could go out to my meals today without fear of my dinner being thrown in my lap or under the table. For several days past we have been under the necessity of holding on our mugs with one hand and our plates with the other and occasionally snatching a mouthful between the rolls. Some very amusing scenes are enacted often at the table in a gale of wind. The sauce will somehow get on our meat, and the gravy in its turn will get upon the pudding.

MAY 9. I have been waiting for the last week for a good washing day. Today it made its appearance, and I have been very busily engaged.

MAY 11. Yesterday and today also we have experienced very fine weather. This morning soon after breakfast we heard the sound of "There blows!" "There goes flukes!" etc. We were all in quite a state of excitement, for it was supposed to be a right whale, which supposition turned out to be correct. The boats were very soon manned and lowered. Mr. Jackson, our second mate, had a chance to strike, but his boatsteerer missed him, to our great disappointment. He was a new boatsteerer that we shipped at Lahaina. I believe I have not mentioned that Samuel discharged Mr. Forsyth on account of sickness and promoted Mr. Huntley to first officer and shipped a Mr. Jackson to supply Mr. Huntley's place. We also left Antone and Manuel, two boatsteerers that we brought from home, in the hospital.

P.M. Saw whales again; four boats went in pursuit of them. Very soon I heard the cry of "A boat fast!" a joyful cry indeed; but our joy was of short duration, for when they were lancing the whale, they accidentally cut the line. Consequently, the whale was again at liberty. There will be a dead whale now for some fortunate one, for he could not in all probability live long, as there had been two bomb lances fired at him, one of which they heard explode inside of him. A sorry day's work, but I hope not a specimen of what we may expect through the season.

MAY 12. Damp and foggy weather through the day. Saw no whales.

1859

MAY 13. Another gale of wind; increased through the day. We lay to.

MAY 14. The gale still continues. At night moderated somewhat except in squalls. Laying to through the day. Rainy.

MAY 15. Moderated some. A strong breeze with rain occasionally at night. A calm with a heavy sea, which was more uncomfortable than a gale of wind. Foggy.

MAY 16. Rainy in the morning but cleared away by noon so that the remainder of the day was very pleasant. Looked sharp for whales but saw none.

MAY 17. Pleasant through the day.

P.M.   A strong breeze sprang up, which at night increased to a gale. Not a severe one by any means, but a heavy head sea which prevailed made the *Addison* pitch and rear quite furiously. Are in the vicinity of Cape Fairweather. Have seen the land along the coast, also Mount Fairweather. Saw four ships at a distance; they were neither chasing nor boiling.

In one of my boxes from home I had two tins of Quissett butter. Had one of them opened yesterday, and though not just from the churn, it tastes very nice to me. The butter we have now was very good when we left home, but in nearly three years time, of course, there would be a change, if not for the better.

We breakfast at six o'clock in the morning; as it makes a long day, I let Minnie sleep on and get her breakfast by herself. I make her milk porridge usually, as we have quite an abundance of milk. Our goat had kids while we were in port and now gives a quart or more milk a day. We have pumpkin pies, puddings, etc., which we all appreciate. When I put Minnie to bed at night, her last words are: "Good night, Mamma. Please make me some porridge in the morning."

MAY 18. The wind has left us. In the morning a calm with a thick fog. When June comes in, we hope for better weather. Foggy and rainy throughout the day.

MAY 19. A strong breeze with squalls of wind accompanied by

rain and hail. Saw two ships in the morning going on an opposite tack from ourselves.

MAY 20. A heavy sea with rain occasionally. Have seen neither ships nor whales. There is one consolation in knowing that if we should see whales, we could not take them in this weather. Consequently others more fortunate than ourselves are not taking them.

MAY 21. Squalls and calms with a heavy sea. Rainy through the day.

MAY 22. A fine pleasant day. Spoke the *Corinthian*. Captain Lewis came on board and passed the afternoon with us. He is just out from home; was mate of the *Tamerlane* last voyage. He has taken nothing and has heard of only one ship that had taken a whale. We gave him a pig, and he sent us a bushel of nice home corn and Minnie a bag of nuts—almonds, walnuts, and filberts—which are a great treat to her. We have a mill for grinding corn, so now we can enjoy hasty puddings, johnnycakes, etc., not forgetting the hulled corn,[1] for which we begged a few sticks of wood to make ashes, as ours is not suitable for that purpose.

MAY 23. Another fine, beautiful day. I improved it by doing a two weeks' washing. Several ships in sight, but no whales; land in sight along the coast from Cross Sound to Norfolk Sound.

MAY 24. Quite pleasant in the morning with a strong breeze. Several ships in sight. Saw the *Speedwell* ahead with her boats down chasing a whale without success. About 10 A.M. spoke the *Speedwell*, but as the wind was increasing and every prospect of a coming gale, we did not gam. Mrs. Gibbs and I shook handkerchiefs to our hearts' content. We were both much disappointed. After we left them, we saw the same whale that they had been chasing going to the windward, the first one we have seen for nearly three weeks.

MAY 25. The gale of yesterday lasted until about 12 P.M. last night. Seven ships in sight during the day. About 2 P.M. we lay aback for the *Speedwell* to come down to us, which she did. Captain and Mrs. Gibbs came on board, and we had a right good time. Captain and Mrs. Taber of the *Augusta* were in sight. After tea spoke the *Caroline*, of Greenport. Captain Pontus came on board and passed the evening. Mrs. Gibbs brought Minnie some lozenges and me some salt codfish, which was very acceptable. We gave them some pickled mullet and some figs, also a leg of pork, and some books. We heard from the captains that several small whales had been taken close in by the land. There is where they all expect to find them by and by. Consequently the ships are very plenty; it is supposed there are ninety ships here, but many of them will soon leave for the Arctic unless whales are seen more plenty than they have been. The gale of the fourth was felt very sensibly here. The *Arab*, of Fairhaven, was dismasted partially. Captain Grinnell has his lady on board.

MAY 26. This morning before we got up, they came down and told Samuel there was a bark hauled aback for us to speak. We ran down and found it to be the *William Gifford*, Captain Baker, of Falmouth, with his wife and two children. They wished Samuel to go on board and take me, but I was not very well, and Samuel thought it was coming thick, so he went alone for a short time. Found a box on board for us from Sarah, filled with bottled berries, originally, and a loaf of cake. The bottles were all broken except two and the contents had penetrated all the reading and the loaf of cake was nothing but powder. Minnie said they had sent me a nice lot of ginger. It was some time before we found out what it was. We went different ways after that; he went to the eastward where we had been, and we are going to the westward again on the ground where we saw those whales, if haply we might see them again. Saw one whale today going to the windward.

MAY 29. Have seen nothing but finbacks, humpbacks, and sulphur-bottoms for several days; not a ship to be seen. We are now bound in to the northeast to see what may be there.

7 P.M. Lowered for a right whale, but they could not get quite near enough to strike. He had previously been struck and injured; had an iron already in him, which one would suppose to be anything but comfortable.

MAY 30. Spoke the *Robert Edwards,* Captain Wood, in the morning. Thought it was too early to come on board, as he wanted to look out for whales. In the afternoon spoke the *Good Return,* Captain Fish. Both captains came on board, and we had a very pleasant time. Captain Fish is right from our home; consequently could tell us considerable news. He brought Minnie a large paper of candy and brought and sent me two tins of preserved pears, a bag of Indian meal, and three bottles of currant wine. Have neither of them taken anything, and they with others think the prospect rather gloomy. Captain Wood brought his wife out as far as Valparaiso, from which place she, being tired of the sea, left for home. Two other ships in sight at sunset.

MAY 31. Two ships in sight. Saw the *Good Return*'s boats down chasing whales without success. Pleasant weather with the exception of a little fog some part of the day.

JUNE 1.[2] Last night I was kept awake with the toothache and a violent pain in my head. Samuel gave me some laudanum to ease the pain, and it has made me feel very dull and stupid for the whole day. I was on the bed in the afternoon when they spoke a ship, and truth to say, I did not feel very glad to hear that it was the *Augusta* and that Captain and Mrs. Taber were coming on board. However, I got up and fixed up as much as possible at so short a notice, and it did me a great deal of good seeing them—cured me completely. I gave Mrs. Taber some of the Indian meal that Captain Fish gave me, some salt fish that we cured in the bay, and some figs. After tea Captain Fish lowered his boat and passed the evening with us. It was eleven o'clock when our company left, almost as light as day and calm as a lake. It was prophesied that one of the ships would get a whale tomorrow. I wish we might be the fortunate one, if any. Captain Taber has not done much this voyage. We saw one whale this afternoon; lowered the boats, but he disappeared very mysteriously. I cut Celia's loaf of cake for supper. It was just as fresh and nice as though it was just made; it was pronounced very nice.

JUNE 3. A thick fog. *Good Return* close by us. Captain Fish came on board in the afternoon. He brought me a jar of pickles and a jar of currant jelly; also brought us a few pickled codfish, which he procured of a Oahu brig, and a salmon. We in return for his many kindnesses gave him two pigs. Milton Fish also came on board. He is fourth mate and boatsteerer. I invited him into the cabin and had a nice talk with him. I never saw him before, but I knew his father and mother; indeed they are relatives of Samuel's.

JUNE 5. Quite a strong breeze the middle of the day, but in the afternoon it moderated again. I commenced a letter home this afternoon. I had previously thought that I would wait until we had got a whale before I commenced writing, but becoming almost discouraged, I thought I would wait no longer. It looks almost as dark to me now as it has any time this voyage because we want oil so much, but if patience has its perfect work,[3] we may do well yet.

JUNE 6. Quite pleasant in the morning. In the afternoon a strong breeze sprang up.

JUNE 7. During the night the wind increased to a moderate gale. Lay to in the afternoon.

JUNE 8. The gale remains about the same. One bark in sight.

JUNE 9. The gale remains the same, rather a moderate gale attended with considerable rain; gloomy, disagreeable weather. No whales to be seen, and all hands appear to be rather low in spirits.

JUNE 10. The gale has abated, and now by way of change we have a dead calm. For the last several days we have had a head wind so that we could not get where we wished to, and now we are delayed still longer. Oh, for patience. I took this day to wash, although it was Friday, as I had been waiting all the week for a pleasant day. On Kodiak we are under the necessity of taking a pleasant day for such purposes whenever it comes, whether Monday or Saturday.

JUNE 11. A pleasant day with a nice breeze. Made the land in the afternoon; saw Mount St. Elias rearing its lofty head far above the clouds. Two ships in sight, one close in by the land. In the afternoon raised, for a wonder, a right whale. The boats lowered very soon; chased several hours without success, although getting quite near several times. It was a very large whale, and how I did want them to get fast. However, it is encouraging to see one occasionally even if we are not to have them. We began to fear that they were all dead.

JUNE 12. Another dead calm. Land nearly covered in snow is visible all along the coast, some being very high.

JUNE 13. A strong breeze. A ship in sight at a distance. About 11 A.M. spoke the *General Scott,* Captain Huntting. Samuel went on board for a few minutes. They had taken nothing like many others, had been fast to a whale a few days previous that stove two boats, lost one man, etc.

P.M. The gale increasing so that after supper we lay to.

JUNE 14. The officer of the watch came below about four o'clock telling Samuel there was a ship five or six miles off that wanted to speak us, so we went down to her. She proved to be the *Julian,* of New Bedford, Captain Winegar, eight months out; nothing this season. Captain Winegar came on board about 5 A.M. and stopped until 9 P.M. He is very good company, and I enjoyed his visit very much. We heard of the *Montreal* having one whale, the *Corinthian* two, and the *Majestic* two. Raised whales, for a wonder, in the afternoon. Both ships' boats went down but did not succeed in striking them. There was a heavy long swell, which prevented their seeing the whales to good advantage from the boats. Yesterday we started south intending to go to Kamchatka ground, but in consequence of seeing these whales, we shall cruise over this ground tomorrow. Captain Winegar has his son, fourteen years old, on board with him. I sent him a couple of books and a paper of figs by his father.

JUNE 15. A pleasant day. The *Julian* in sight. Saw them chasing whales several times during the day, but we saw nothing. I forgot to mention that they had been fast to a whale which stove two boats and then went off taking a large quantity of line.

JUNE 16. A calm again. Two ships in sight. At half-past 9 P.M., just as we had retired for the night, the officer of the watch came running down saying a right whale just turned flukes close by the watch. It was rather late, but Samuel felt as if he could not let the chance escape, so sent the boats off to attempt a capture. The whale was about a mile to the windward. The boats, using their paddles, came almost up to him, the whale, meanwhile, laying on the water. Just as they got near him, he went down. The second mate's boat lay still and the whale came up in about two minutes close by the boat and the boatsteerer missed him, the same boatsteerer that missed before. He has had two chances now and failed each time, and Samuel feels that it would neither be doing justice to himself or others to give him another trial. A whale in these days is worth too much to lose recklessly. It makes us all feel very badly.

JUNE 17. A year today since we were stoven in the ice. How time flies, and here we are doing nothing even as we were then. Have been laying around today hoping we might see whales again but have seen nothing that looked like a right whale. A ship in sight which we suppose to be the *Julian*.

JUNE 18. We are again bound south, Samuel being satisfied there is nothing here for him. The other ship has got mad by her looks and is off with main royal and studding sails out. In the afternoon, she being quite near us, we luffed to, and Captain Winegar lowered his boats and came on board, bringing us a bag of corn and three bottles of port wine for my special benefit. His son came on board with him, a very interesting lad. Minnie enjoyed his visit very much. I don't think he enjoys a sea life very much. Poor boy, it made him think so much of his mother to see me. "Oh," he says, "I am so glad my mother used to give me such good counsel, for I don't think I shall grow to be so wicked as some of our boys are," referring to the sailors. I put up some little notions for him. After he had been on board a short time, we raised something which was thought to be a dead whale, but it proved to be a carcass of no value to anyone.

When Captain Winegar left, he invited us to pass the next day, which was Sunday, on board his ship. He felt that it would do him good to have a lady on board and insisted upon our coming. Finally Samuel told him if it was calm so that we could get nowhere, we would come.

JUNE 19. The morrow has come, and it is calm as a clock and as delightful a day as one often witnesses. I was glad, for I wanted to go, knowing that I should enjoy myself, the captain being excellent company. We started about 11 A.M. and arrived again on board the *Addison* at 10 P.M. We all passed a very pleasant day, Captain Winegar enjoying it very much; it reminded him so strongly of home. Minnie attracted much notice as usual. She is generally the center of attraction with company. She is not afraid to speak, and her replies are generally to the point and usually interspersed with some salt remarks. The captain gave me a couple of pounds of green tea, a couple of tins of preserved pineapple, and a few shells. I forgot to mention that we carried him a little pig and gave him a piece of fresh pork. The cook gave Minnie a little china cup and saucer, which pleased her very much. For dinner we had a roast duck, potatoes, onions, some very nice biscuit, coffee, mince pie, and for dessert preserved peaches, pineapples, and quinces. For supper we had oysters, cold duck, biscuit, preserved pears, mince pie, doughnuts, and cookies, Captain Winegar doing the honors very well. We arrived home delighted with our visit.

JUNE 20. Nearly calm. The ship *Julian* still in sight.

JUNE 21. Calm. Captain Winegar and Sammy came on board in the afternoon and stopped until 9 P.M.

JUNE 22. Samuel went on board the *Julian* to get some work done by his blacksmith, as we have none. Took Minnie with him, as he intended to stop the most of the day. Mr. Shepard, the mate, presented her with a little china doll, which she thinks of calling Emma Shepard. They returned home about 4 P.M., Captain Winegar accompanying them.

JUNE 23. A strong breeze with a head sea; rather uncomfortable weather, especially in the cabin.

JUNE 24. Samuel and Minnie went on board the *Julian* again, as Samuel had a gun which needed repairing in case we should ever see a whale again.

JUNE 27. Captain Winegar and Sammy came on board and passed the day by special invitation. We had a very pleasant time. After tea it became rough with a strong breeze, the barometer giving indications of a gale. Consequently he left early. We expect to part company now, after enjoying each other's society for nearly a fortnight, as he intends going through Unimak straits into Bristol Bay and we think of going farther to the westward through [One] Seventy-two Passage into the same bay, hoping to find whales before we go in. After Mr. Huntley came on board, we learned that there had been a stabbing affray on board the *Julian*. Two of the men, an Irishman and a Spaniard, got into a dispute, when the Irishman stabbed the other with his sheath knife quite badly in his shoulder. The mate had him put in irons immediately.

JUNE 28. Had quite a strong breeze through the night; more moderate today. All the strong breezes come from just the way that we wish to go, so that we do not make much.

JUNE 29. Saw a large right whale in the morning and another in the afternoon, but it was too rugged to lower.

JULY 2. We have decided to go through Unimak Passage, as we never shall get anywhere else with these winds, if luckily we may get there. Considerable rain has fallen this week, and fogs have prevailed. I have been almost sick the past week with a severe pain in my head and face brought on by a cold which settled in my teeth. Finbacks have been around the ship in great abundance today. Killed two from the ship. They turned up close by the ship, but before we could get a boat to them, they sank to the bottom.

JULY 3. A fine, pleasant day, but a head wind, the first day that we have had an hour of pleasant weather for a week. Tomorrow is the glorious Fourth, and what bright anticipations of the morrow are mingled with the religious exercises of today. If we could only get a whale on that day, our anticipation would be more than realized. We would ask no better celebration. I cannot give up the hope of getting something this season. I know there must be a little for us.

JULY 4. Minnie arose early this morning and hoisted our flag, which was all the celebration we could boast of, as we did not get that whale that we hoped to. A beautiful day, which I improved by washing, after waiting ten days for a clear day.

JULY 5. Clear and pleasant with a nice fair wind. Raised land this afternoon at the distance of sixty miles, a mountain on Unimak Island.

JULY 6. Quite thick with some fog. As we got hold of the land the day before, Samuel decided to run through into the bay, which we did with safety. Raised a ship in the afternoon. Saw the volcano on Unimak sending forth a perfect cloud of smoke.

JULY 7. Just after we got through last night, the wind left us entirely; but we were safely through, and all was well. Nearly calm in the morning, clear and pleasant, land visible.

JULY 13. Have had an abundance of fog ever since we have been in here. Occasionally the sun would shine through the fog so that we were enabled to get observations. Have been cruising around in all directions and seen neither ships nor whales and have not been able to catch even one codfish, after I had made so much dependence upon them. This is the anniversary of our wedding day. Twelve happy years have passed since that never-to-be-forgotten day. May we long be spared to gladden each other's hearts.

JULY 18. Have experienced almost constant fog ever since we entered the bay. Have seen no ships nor whales except finbacks. There appears to be plenty of feed here, and there may be whales by and by, but Samuel feels as if he could not stop. He must be moving, and now we are bound toward St. Paul and thence to the Arctic, for we are poor: the eighteenth of July and not a whale this season.

This is Minnie's birthday—eight years old. I told her a month ago that when it was her birthday, I would make a treat for her in the evening and she might invite all the officers to partake with her. So she has ever since been looking forward to it as a great event. Saturday I made preparation, and I was fortunate in doing so, for I suffered exceedingly Sunday night and the greater part of this day with a gathering at the roots of my tooth. I was able to get up, however, and prepare the treat for her. We set the table and called the officers down about half-past 7 P.M. Minnie was so happy she hardly knew what to do with herself, and I think we all enjoyed it pretty well. The officers all united in saying that they had not sat down to such a table since they left home. The treat consisted of a plate of sister Celia's fruit-cake, two loaves of cupcake frosted, two plates of currant jelly tarts, and a dish of preserved pineapple, also hot coffee, good and strong, with plenty of milk and white sugar. After we had finished, there was an ample supply left, which was sent into the steerage for boatsteerers, etc.

Minnie arose this morning about four o'clock to look at her presents. She had a box of little notions, a book, and a pocket handkerchief from Mrs. Brayton; a pair of china vases from Mary White; two packages of paper dolls, a book, and a package of drawing cards from Helen Whitney; an ivory shuttle and a half a dollar from her papa; and a bottle of cologne, a toothbrush, and a quarter of a dollar from her mamma. Not of much value, but they were all very pleasing to her.

JULY 21. The afternoon of this day the fog cleared up, and the sun came out bright and pleasant, after having a rainstorm of two days. We have been in the vicinity of Gore's Island for several days, but it was calm and so thick we could neither see it nor get observations. This morning Samuel thought he had cleared it and, as we had a good breeze, ventured to square the yards and make a fair wind of it. We got a latitude at noon and at 4 P.M. got good altitudes so that now we know just our position.

JULY 22. Made St. Lawrence Island this morning. Samuel intended going off Cape Bering first, but the wind hauled. We are headed now for King Island, where they have in times past made good cuts. I cannot think for a moment that Dame Fortune will permit us to leave the whaling grounds at the end of the season without one drop of oil. I exert all my powers to keep up the spirits of the captain and officers, and I really believe that they are in far better spirits than though Minnie and myself were not here. About 7 P.M. heard the cry of "There blows!" We were almost sure they were a school of bowheads, but they proved to be humpbacks.

JULY 23. Rainy for the most part of the day. About 6 P.M. came in thick and foggy, so that Samuel gave up his intention of going to King Island and squared away to go through the Strait. Saw a school of mussel diggers about sunset.

JULY 24. Quite thick. Saw St. Lawrence Bay and the land all along the coast in that vicinity.

JULY 25.[4] Saw the land. Rainy through the day. About 6 P.M. it set in very thick and foggy so that Samuel thought best to anchor, which we did at the mouth of Mechigmen Bay in fourteen fathoms of water.

JULY 26. Cleared up a few minutes in the morning so that Samuel obtained a glimpse of our position. About 10 A.M. a strong breeze came up, so that Samuel deemed it best to take up the anchor. Thick during the day, and our position anything but pleasant: land in every direction besides a current to contend with. We made short tacks.

JULY 27. Saw the land again this morning and found that we had kept about in the same place that we were yesterday, as Samuel hoped to do. Saw a ship this afternoon, which was a very welcome sight. Foggy more or less through the day.

JULY 28. Foggy through the night. In the morning cleared up a little so that we raised the ship close by. We have passed East Cape, and now if this breeze holds on for a few hours, we shall be in the Arctic, where I sincerely hope the fog will leave us. There has not been a day for the last month that we have not experienced more or less fog. About noon the wind left us, so we concluded that we would have a gam. We were almost afraid to, fearing that we should learn that they had been doing well in the Strait. We hauled up the mainsail and set the colors for the captain to come on board, when who should make his appearance but Captain Coffin, our last year's acquaintance of the *Champion.* I was very happy to see him. He has taken one right whale and picked up one finback this season. We did not grudge it at all, for he was one of the fleet that went into the Islands clean last fall, as it now looks we shall do the same this season.

Imagine our feelings when we were told there had been a grand cut taken off Cape Thaddeus by a few ships in June, where thirty or forty ships were hanging about for weeks in the ice last season and not a whale to be seen. Most of the ships that were there last season thought it of no use to go there so early this season, tearing their ships in pieces and getting nothing thereby, but would go to Kodiak the first part of the season and then come to the Arctic. The *Mary and Susan* took 1,600 barrels, the *Eliza Adams* 1,400, *Nassau* seven whales, *Omega* seven, *Mary* six, *William C. Nye* six. Those are all the ships we have heard of that were there. I never felt so heartsick in my life as when we were told that. Why couldn't we have been one of the number? Because it was not for us, I suppose.

Captain Coffin reports eight ships in sight of him yesterday. Came through Unimak straits in company with the *Julian,* [which] had taken nothing. Captain Coffin had been in Bering Strait ever since the eighteenth in company with a dozen or more ships trying to get through. The *Good Return* had taken nothing, the *Speedwell* nothing, the *William Gifford* nothing, *Cleone* nothing, *Robert Edwards* nothing, *Arab* nothing, *Christopher Mitchell* nothing, etc. Misery loves company, and it is comforting to know that we are not alone.

JULY 29. A thick fog in the morning, but it cleared away so that about noon it was quite pleasant. I regretted very much that I had not washed, for I have been waiting two weeks for a good day. Ships in sight in all directions. We were surprised to see ships coming from the vicinity of Cape Lisburne. Saw Captain Coffin speak a ship. Afterward we spoke the *Champion,* who informed us that it was the *Hibernia.* Captain Edwards had taken six right whales, two on Kodiak and two off Cape Thaddeus, where right whales were never heard of before. He reported that Cape Lisburne was full of ice and about forty ships there waiting for the ice to open. Oh, dear! Shall we get anything? That is my last thought when I go to sleep and my first when I wake and also the burden of my dreams. Captain Edwards reported the loss of the *William Tell* off East Cape; went ashore laying aback in a fog. Captain Austin was on board the *Hibernia,* and they were going down to take a look. He reported the *Saratoga* as having done very well on Kamchatka. Captain Coffin came on board to tea. After tea we spoke the *New England,* of New London. Captain Hempstead had taken two finbacks, which made him 11 barrels each, being all he had taken for a year and a half. When we hear of such poor ones, it ought to make us contented with our lot, for we have done very fair if we could only get a few hundred this season. Captain Hempstead felt bad, and I pitied him from my heart.

JULY 30. A wonderful circumstance. When we were called this morning, the sun was shining bright. "Now for a washing day," thought I, "if it is Saturday." So I went to work; had a large wash, it being four weeks since I had had one before. Just as I got about half through, the fog came thicker than I ever saw it before. I was obliged to put my white clothes in soak and dry the colored clothes in the cabin. Several ships in sight, also land. Saw Point Hope, a low point which makes out about fifteen miles. The land there is very deceiving, the water deep until you are close in. I was very glad we had an opportunity of seeing it before the fog came on. There is quite a settlement on the point. Saw the *Caravan,* another poor one. After dinner I made some cake to put away, for as we are in the midst of ships, it is likely that we shall have more or less company while there is no whaling to do.

JULY 31.[5] The last month of our dependence. When it is gone, we shall probably be able to tell whether there is anything for us. It does not look very promising today; it is blowing a gale of wind and quite thick. Several ships in sight. Passed the bark *Covington,* Captain Newman. Saw a bowhead today going like a shot to the windward, probably to the ice.

1859

AUGUST 1. Yesterday I found myself a little in advance of the true time. It goes rapidly enough of itself without hastening it. A gale of wind still. Several ships in sight.

AUGUST 2. A strong breeze, but they thought if I put my clothes out, they would dry in a short time, and I foolishly did. So the consequence was that I have old rags enough now to supply the whole ship. I found how they were going and took them in the cabin to dry, not, however, until several garments were torn past mending.

AUGUST 3. Quite pleasant in the morning. In the afternoon another gale sprang up, or the third edition of the former one. We have kept our position quite well off Point Hope. The wind is north so that we cannot go where we wish. Eight ships in sight during the day.

AUGUST 4. Thick a short time in the morning; afterwards cleared up fine, the pleasantest day of the season. Cape Lisburne in sight, but the wind is ahead, and we do not make much progress in beating. We are now forty miles from where we took our oil last season. Saw a whale after tea which we thought must be a bowhead, but it proved to be a finback, an unheard-of circumstance in this ocean. Fourteen ships in sight at 9 P.M. The barometer goes up slowly, which indicates pleasant weather.

AUGUST 5. A thick fog in the morning. Cleared up several times for a short time through the day. In the afternoon quite a strong breeze. About 8 P.M. we very nearly came in contact with the ship *Champion*. Saw her in the fog only just in time to escape her. I have feared land and ice in fogs before, but I never thought so much about ships. We spoke with Captain Coffin after passing him. He said that he thought he had seen three bowheads that day.

AUGUST 6. A strong breeze, which soon increased to a gale. Six ships in sight; the *Speedwell* close by us. Passed the *Robert Edwards*, the *Caravan*, and the *Champion*. After tea the gale increased and bade fair to be the most severe of the season.

AUGUST 7. The gale through the night and this forenoon was very severe, but about noon it moderated a little. The *Speedwell* still in sight. I wish it was good weather so that I might visit Mrs. Gibbs—if we could not see any whales, that is. I forgot the most important intelligence to note in my journal of yesterday. We saw a ship verily and truly cutting in a whale, the first we have seen this season. We have not even seen a smoke nor spoken but one ship that has taken a whale. Surely these are hard times indeed. We are supposed to be on the ground now where the whales were taken last year, but if the weather is to be as rough as it has been since August came in, there will be a small chance of taking oil, providing we see the whales. A thick fog every day in July and a gale of wind thus far every day in August. Who will say these are not hard times? About 9 P.M. saw what were supposed to be three right whales.

AUGUST 8. Foggy more or less throughout the day. Spoke the *John Howland*, Captain Whelden; picked up one dead whale this season. Thirteen ships in sight. Passed the *Eliza Adams;* saw the bark *Fortune.*

AUGUST 9. Quite clear with a strong breeze still from the north. We have been beating for the last ten days. Have seen considerable floating ice during the day. In the afternoon spoke the *Rebecca Sims.* Captain Hawes came on board and stopped until half-past 11 P.M. His wife remains at Hilo this season. He has taken nothing this season, twenty-one months out, 400 barrels. We heard by him that whale oil in April was down to forty-six cents per gallon. If that was the case, probably our oil that we sent home was sold much lower than we supposed it would be. I wish we had all on board that we have taken this voyage. Oh, how many poor souls there are around here just now, and we all bid fair to leave the ground in the same condition. These are trying times. Eight ships in sight. Land in sight all day.

AUGUST 10. Cold and blustering but quite clear. We are offshore quite a distance today and find a considerable ice, patches of it several miles in extent, also considerable loose floating ice. Sent the boats to the edge of the ice after dinner for walrus, which were in great numbers on the ice. They could not get in to the ice far enough to be successful. They took two which they brought to the ship. They are the worst-looking creatures that I ever saw, without exception.

Saw three ships gamming, one of which was the *Rebecca Sims.* After tea we went down to them, and Samuel went on board the *Rebecca Sims* where the captains had congregated. Very soon he came back, however, not meeting with a very cordial reception, for the captains wanted to come here where the lady was. They came back with him, and we passed a very pleasant evening. They were Captain Hawes of the *Rebecca Sims,* nothing this season; Captain Clark of the *Bartholomew Gosnold,* two whales; and Captain Thomas of the *Eliza Adams,* 1,600 barrels. He is the highest by far of anyone here except the *Mary and Susan.* She has 1,400. They took it off Thaddeus from the sixteenth May to the sixteenth June. Have seen no chance since. We made some coffee about ten o'clock and set out a small treat consisting of soda crackers, cheese, pie, and cake. Captain Thomas presented Minnie with a Japanese cricket, which he purchased at Hakodate. She was perfectly delighted with it. The captains left about twelve o'clock.

AUGUST 11. Cold and blustering with occasional snow squalls. Several ships in sight, also plenty of ice offshore, some of which appears to be very heavy. Sent two boats in to the ice for walrus in the afternoon, but it came in thick very soon after leaving so that they only took one, which they left behind. Nothing that looks like a whale is to be seen. Everyone almost despairs, but at the same time they do not dare to leave here, fearing the whales will make their appearance suddenly, as they did last year after so many of the ships had left the ground. We shot quite a number of ducks today; also had an addition to our family of eight little pigs. The wind has been northwest today, the first change from due north since we have been here; probably that has kept the ice down so late this season.

AUGUST 12. A southerly wind today. It is cloudy and snows occasionally, but there is quite an observable change in the atmosphere.

P.M. The wind soon after changed to the northwest again. Had boats in after walrus today. They towed nine to the ship and brought a number of heads on board. Several ships in sight.

AUGUST 13. A calm in the morning. We were several miles from the ice. Sent the boats in after more walrus, and if it breezed up, we were going to meet them; if not, they were to bring the heads only. The wind soon breezed a little. As we were standing off, we raised a bowhead and set the colors immediately for the boats to come on board.[6] The bowhead vanished immediately, and we have not seen him since. Eight or ten ships in sight.

After tea we lay aback for a bark to come down to us. Found it to be the *Tybee*, Captain Freeman, an old acquaintance. He very soon came on board, and we passed a very pleasant evening. We went down to the other ships, but they were gamming by themselves. Consequently we had no more addition to our party. Captain Freeman had been to Hakodate, and he wished Samuel to go on board and look at his wares which he purchased. Samuel returned with him about 10 P.M. and stopped until 1 A.M. He made a few purchases, and Captain Freeman sent me a pair of lacquered waiters and sent Minnie a cabinet, a very handsome present. He also brought a bucket of Hakodate apples and a jar of preserves. Quite a melancholy accident occurred to him while at that port. He smoked his ship for rats. The crew slept on deck. The steward and cabin boy went in the house aft to sleep and shut the door. In the morning they were both found dead.

Captain Freeman has taken four whales this season; was fortunate enough to be in the mob off Thaddeus. He reports ice in the Strait, which alarmed me a little, fearing that we might get caught in here and be obliged to stop all winter, but they say there is no danger of that. After we have a southerly gale, which we ought to expect now and which will drive the ice up north to the barrier, then we shall have good weather and in all probability find whales.

AUGUST 14. The French ship *Jason* ran off for us this morning wishing to speak us, which he did about nine o'clock. Captain Hache came on board. I had seen him before; he is a Frenchman but talks very good English. His boat's crew all wore heavy wooden shoes, which looked very queer to us. Before dinner Captain Freeman of the *Tybee* came on board; in the afternoon we had an addition of Captain Jenks of the *Mary* to our party, and after tea Captain Soule of the *William C. Nye* came on board. The *Jason* took two right whales on Kodiak; the *Mary* and the *William C. Nye* each took four off Cape Thaddeus. Captain Soule expects to find his wife and child in Honolulu when he arrives at that port in the fall.

Some ships within a few days found it quite difficult to get through the Strait, but it does not appear to give the fleet any alarm, so I will not let it trouble me. I think more of the whales now than anything else; it seems as if I should fly when I think it is the middle of August and not a whale yet. What shall we do? Where shall we go? Captain Soule says that he saw three bowheads today going very fast to the south. In consequence of that Samuel thinks he will lay aback tonight and he may see whales tomorrow. Eleven ships in sight.

AUGUST 15. About 11 A.M. raised two bowheads. Called the watch immediately; lowered four boats, two after each whale. Mr. Huntley soon had the good fortune to strike one and about half-past one o'clock had a large bowhead alongside. So the old *Addison* has saved skunk, as the saying is. Never was a whale more acceptable to a ship's company. May it be a precursor of several more. A dozen ships in sight and all chasing, but we were the only fortunate ones in this company. Saw a ship or bark boiling. They commenced cutting in about half-past 3 P.M.

AUGUST 16. Did not finish cutting in until half-past 1 A.M.; had considerable trouble. It was a very large whale, and inclining to sink, it caused them much trouble. Saw whales and lowered the boats several times without success. After tea spoke the *Henry Kneeland*. Captain Kelley came on board and passed the evening. He has taken nothing this season. He brought us two packages of papers that were sent us from Honolulu, one from J. S. Walker and the other from H. W. Severance. They were very acceptable. We learned that the vessel that we saw boiling yesterday was the bark *Fortune*, Captain Lester; his first whale also. We commenced boiling this afternoon. Plenty of ships in sight.

AUGUST 17. About half-past 4 A.M. raised whales but could not get near them. In the forenoon lowered again. The whales appear to be very wild, and no wonder when there are so many ships looking out for every whale that spouts. About half-past eleven the bark *William Gifford*, Captain Baker, ran down and spoke us. Mrs. Baker and myself passed the compliments of the day. Captain Baker wished Samuel to take Minnie and myself and bring us on board. Samuel did not want much to go, as he wanted to be on the lookout for whales, but finally consented to carry us and return immediately, which he did. Just as we were ready to start, Captain Earle of the *Jireh Swift* came on board for a few moments; he has taken five whales, one of the favored few. He accompanied us on board the *William Gifford*.

After dinner he and Samuel left, each for his own ship, and throughout the afternoon every ship had four boats down. The *Corinthian*, Captain Lewis, was the only fortunate one. He took a bowhead alongside about 4 P.M. Captain [Baker of the] *Gifford* has taken nothing this season and feels badly like the rest of us. They[7] have two children, a boy of five years and a girl of fifteen months. Little Charlie was delighted to see Minnie, the first child he had gammed with since leaving home. He shed tears when she left. I found a letter on board from sister Sarah which though old was very acceptable.

After tea we had an addition to our company of Captain Lawrence of the *Addison*, Captain Lowen of the *Gay Head*, and Captain Clark of the *Bartholomew Gosnold*. Captain Clark has taken nothing since we saw him: two whales. Captain Lowen has taken one whale this season. Mrs. Baker gave me a jar of honey, a tin of preserved quince, a bucket of Munganui potatoes, which are far before Sandwich Island potatoes, and gave Minnie some coconuts, which pleased her very much. We carried the children a couple of apples, a paper of figs, a few eggs for Mrs. Baker, and Minnie carried Charlie a picture and Mary a string of beads. Captain [and] Mrs. Baker and myself had a nice time talking about good old Falmouth. Our boats spoke the *Cleone* this afternoon; nothing this season.

AUGUST 18. I lay awake for the most of the night with the toothache. In the morning it left me, but I was confined to the bed for the most of the day with a violent sick headache. Lowered for whales with everybody else in the forenoon. Captain Earle of the *Jireh Swift* happened to be the fortunate one. A strong breeze from the south today.

P.M. Spoke the *Helen Mar*. Captain Worth came on board for a few minutes; nothing this season. He brought his pockets full of walnuts to Minnie. He also brought us letters from Thomas and Mercy at Talcahuano written in April. He saw them at that place. They were all well; had received my package that I sent by Captain Stewart in October. Thomas had not been very successful on Guafo the past season; taken 150 [barrels] sperm. He also brought us a package of papers from our Lahaina friends, also letters from Mr. and Mrs. Brayton as late as the fifteenth June. He left his wife and wife's sister at Lahaina; left them at Paita last season.

After tea we raised whales again; lowered the boats, and Samuel thinks they would have struck had it not been so rugged. It was almost too much so to lower. The weather looked bad, and as the ice was quite near us and we might be obliged to carry sail to keep off, and our ship being so light, Samuel thought it best to stow down some of our oil which we had on deck. So about nine o'clock they went to work. Samuel was on deck through the night, and Minnie slept with me.

AUGUST 19. A fine, pleasant morning. We need not have stowed down our oil last night, as it proved, but it was best to be on the safe side; oil is too scarce to be thrown overboard in these hard times. We stowed down 90 barrels; have not finished boiling yet. Lowered several times without success. Whales very wild; seek them once and then they vanish. Saw the ice today at a distance. It looks quite formidable. Twenty ships in sight.

AUGUST 20. Quite calm today, too much so to be successful in taking anything. Boats down for the most of the forenoon. Mr. Huntley spoke Mr. Whittens' boat. He said he had been wanting to see me all the season; thought I could tell him considerable news. They took a whale day before yesterday, which sank. They succeeded in pulling him up this morning.

As our boats were coming aboard, a ship signalized to one of them to come on board. Mr. Crocker went and returned with a letter and package of papers for us from Mr. Whitney. We have received our mails quite regularly for the last week. I wish they might continue, but it is probable that we have received the last, and much more than we expected. I was glad to see in one of the New Bedford papers the safe arrival of the United States supply schooner *Guthrie,* of which brother George is clerk. We also heard by letters received of the safe arrival of our bone and oil in New Bedford that we sent home last fall. Whale oil was quoted at fifty and fifty-five cents per gallon and Arctic bone eighty to ninety-five cents per pound. That is much better than we feared.

After tea we received a call from Captain Sanborn and Mr. Whittens of the *Omega,* and soon after Captain Newman of the bark *Covington* came on board. They were both in the Cape Thaddeus cut. Captain Newman has six whales and Captain Sanborn is now boiling his seventh. There is no one in the fleet (ourselves excepted) who I would rather have the oil than Mr. Whittens. I am truly glad for him. I could give him favorable intelligence of his wife up to February 18. Minnie gave him her wee bit of a note that she received from Lizzie to carry home, as he could not see to read it here. Thirty ships in sight within a few miles of Cape Lisburne. Is it any wonder that we do not get oil? Yet not one dares to leave for fear he might lose his chance of getting even one whale.

AUGUST 21. Samuel was called at two o'clock this morning to go aloft. He thought that if we could raise whales very early in the morning before they were stirred up, we should stand a better chance of getting one; but not a spout was to be seen. Forty-three ships in sight; not one of the lot had boats down, and out of the forty-three, three only were boiling. What a prospect! A strong southerly breeze today, but pleasant. The whales seem to have left the ground. Perhaps they have gone into the ice, as they were chased so much yesterday. Finished boiling this morning.

AUGUST 22. Samuel went aloft this morning about four o'clock; raised whales at half-past five. Sent two boats out and after breakfast sent the remaining two. There were plenty of whales all around us, and had there been a breeze, think we should have stood a good chance to strike, but it was a dead calm.[8] The wind died away in the night, and about 10 A.M. it came in thick; could hear the whales spout occasionally but saw nothing. We were obliged to call our boats on board with foghorns. After dinner a nice breeze sprang up, and the fog disappeared, also the whales. Chased one this afternoon, but he went very fast to the windward. Spoke the *Rambler,* Captain Willis. He was boiling a whale which he took night before last. Has taken two this season, one on Kodiak and this one. We did not gam, as both were busy. Saw a bark's boats strike a whale about 6 P.M. to the windward of us near the ice. Stowed down the remainder of our oil today; 168 barrels in all, a very good whale. About 10 P.M. spoke the *Magnolia.* Captain Pierce came on board for a short time, as he wished very much to see Samuel. They were formerly shipmates in the *Magnolia* with Captain Simmons. Captain Soule of the *William C. Nye* was mate, Captain Lawrence of the *Addison,* second mate, and Captain Pierce of the *Magnolia,* third mate. He is a Portuguese with, I should [say], considerable black blood in his veins, but a very likely man for all that.

AUGUST 23. Samuel was called at two o'clock this morning to go aloft. Raised whales standing towards the ice; sent the boats in and had the good fortune to get whale number two for the *Addison.* They killed him in the ice, and we went through the ice with the ship afterward to get the whale. I had thought, after my experience of last season in the ice, that I should be frightened if we should make the attempt to go through this season, but I was not frightened at all. Some of it appeared to be quite solid, but there was plenty of room to work the ship without coming in contact with the large pieces. While we were going through, I saw a sight that I hardly expected to see. Three boats from the bark *Lark,* of New London, were fast to a whale; the whale took them right alongside of our ship. He was spouting blood. Minnie and I watched with great interest until he turned up. After getting our whale alongside, we went out into clear water on the opposite side from where we came in. Six ships in sight boiling.

Saw the *Helen Mar* take a whale last night. Captain Willis came on board this morning; was very glad to see us, only it reminded him almost too much of his own family. He has taken two whales; picked up a dead whale on Kodiak and taken one

bowhead here. His two are just equal to our one. In the afternoon saw the *William Gifford* with a whale alongside and after
supper saw the boats towing a second one to the ship, a famous
beginning. I am really glad for them.

AUGUST 24. Samuel got up at three o'clock and went aloft. Saw
no whales but called all hands at four o'clock to breakfast them.
Sent four boats in the ice to see if there might be another whale
for us. About nine o'clock saw the *Rambler* with a whale alongside; before noon saw three more taken. Passed the *Lark,* boiling.
We have not commenced, as all our boats are off. At noon set
the signals for the boats to come aboard. They had seen a number of whales but could not get near them. After they had eaten
their dinner, they started off again. I was on deck when they
went and took off both of my shoes and threw after them for
luck.

I took this day to wash, as it was so pleasant. We are having
a delightful spell of weather, and it seems to me that it is too
good to last. It is getting quite late in the season, but it may be
that the last part will be better than the first. Ships in sight in
all directions as far as the eye can see. If there were a few ships
here, it would be capital whaling, but as it is, I suppose no one
will do first rate.

Captain Pierce of the *Magnolia* came on board about teatime.
He is getting quite desperate because he can get nothing here.
I tell him it is all right; he ought not to get any more. There are
plenty of poor ships that need this cut. He got 800 [barrels] off
Thaddeus. We passed close by the *Rambler* while she was
cutting. He thought he should send his boats in again to stop
all night, but I hardly think he will, as there is quite a strong
breeze and ships will all prefer to stand off from the ice.

AUGUST 25. A strong breeze and rugged. Lowered twice for
whales. Mr. Huntley got almost within darting distance of one.
Had he spouted once more, I think he would have been ours.
Passed close by the *William C. Nye.* Captain Soule performed
some curious capers on his house for our benefit, probably showing his indignation because we were boiling and he was not.
Spoke the *Covington;* nothing since we saw him. We heard of
the *America, Speedwell,* and *William Gifford* gamming several

nights since. I wish the *Addison* had been amongst them. Saw one ship take a whale today.

AUGUST 26 [and 27]. Samuel thought last night he would try to work one side a little out of the fleet, and if the whales were not as plenty, he might stand a better chance of striking one. So we ran off the first part of the night and then lay aback with only one ship in sight of us. In the morning we were among a fleet of thirty. Lowered the boats after breakfast. There were several whales in sight, but it was a dead calm and the whales were going quick.

After our boats came on board, our old consort the *Julian* ran down to us. Captain Winegar and Sammy came on board for a short time, and right glad were we to see them. He has taken nothing yet and feels very badly. He lost an anchor and chain in the Strait. He said when he was with us before that Old Hagar had had his foot on him all the voyage. I asked him now if he had yet taken it off. He replied that he was bearing him down now harder than ever. I sincerely hope he may do well yet. After dinner he left us and went into the ice with his boats.

After tea spoke the *Sharon,* Captain Swift. As it was foggy, he came on board. Soon afterward Captain Winegar came; he could not see his ship. We blew foghorns all the evening and fired several guns but heard no answering signals. We had some coffee made and got supper for Captain Winegar. We all sat down and enjoyed it very much. Minnie begged the privilege of waiting with Sammy. She thought it would be very nice for them to sit down together, for she says, "It is age before young." Sammy says, "Age before beauty, you mean, Minnie." "Well," she says, "I don't think we are either of us very beautiful, so I think age before young does better." She loves Sammy dearly, and every time he comes on board she asks me if I don't wish he was her brother. They left for the *Sharon* about 10 P.M., and I presume the captain found his ship, as we saw them both in the morning of the twenty-seventh going in the ice, or rather standing near the ice along the edge of it.

The ice looks heavy today. It is different from when we went in the other day. Saw a ship take a whale today, which we suppose to be the *George and Susan.* He was boiling also. Samuel got a latitude today and found we were in 70 degrees 12 minutes off Icy Cape, much farther north than we supposed, too far north for the whales, we think, as there were but a very few in the ice. Our boats saw but two, and they were among the heavy ice where a boat could not get. In the afternoon we stowed down about 50 barrels of oil. We want to go south a little now, but the wind is from that quarter, and we cannot go as we wish. Came in foggy about teatime as it did the night before; quite a swell also.

AUGUST 28. Light wind from the northeast and rainy. About noon a strong breeze sprang up. After dinner Captain Clark of the *Bartholomew Gosnold* came on board to learn the news. He had been off on an exploring expedition for the last ten days on the compass ground, off Point Hope, etc. Had seen nothing. He felt badly when he heard there had been a number of whales taken in the ice since he had been gone and was almost ready to exclaim with some of the rest of us, "Is there anything good for me?" He stayed on board but a short time, and then we both worked in towards the ice.

AUGUST 29. A strong breeze with a very heavy head sea. Stowed down the remainder of our oil today, which with what we have in the cooler will make 302 barrels, the product of two whales, our season's work thus far.

AUGUST 30. Strong breezes from the south and rainy, also thick with a heavy swell. Chased a whale for a short time in the afternoon, but it was of not much use, it was so rugged. The bad weather seems to be coming on early this season.

AUGUST 31. Very rugged, but the gale has abated. Lowered for whales after breakfast; chased until 2 P.M. in a pouring rainstorm without success. Mr. Crocker's boatsteerer, a green Kanaka, missed one. (Oh, how vexatious!) There were an abundance of whales in sight. They would come up and spout once, then disappear from public view, the wildest set of whales that were ever seen, I do believe. About a dozen ships in sight chasing with the same success as ourselves. After tea passed the bark *Martha*, the *Rebecca Sims*, and the *Henry Kneeland*, having a gam. A strong breeze through the night.

SEPTEMBER 1. A gale of wind from the south; too rugged to lower the boats. Saw whales several times during the day. We are standing off and on from the ice, as we suppose, not knowing where we are except by soundings, as we have not seen our position for several days. Passed the brig *Victoria* in the morning and the *Arab* in the afternoon. I went on deck to look at the last-named ship because there was a lady on board. I have been wishing to see Mrs. Grinnell all the season, but that is the nearest I have come to it as yet.

It is grand to see the ships as they rise and fall with the gigantic waves in a gale of wind, but it causes us to feel our weakness and the strength of Omnipotence more than anything of which I can conceive. "They that go down to the sea in ships do see the wonders of the Lord" [9] and must at times feel the need of a higher power than man—insignificant man, compared with Him who holds the waters in the hollow of His hand and commands the stormy waves.

There has been a strong current generally in this ocean that it has been necessary to guard against, but this season there has been none noticed, probably on account of the abundance of ice. It is not very pleasant here in thick weather and especially now as we begin to have some night. There is the current to contend with if there be any, the ice, some of which is very heavy, the land, and the great number of ships which are constantly going back and forth. But we have been safely kept thus far, and He can still keep us from all harm.

SEPTEMBER 2. Last night for the first part of the night the wind blew very hard from the westward. Afterward it moderated. This morning we found ourselves, as it was clear, almost surrounded by ice with land about eight miles distant. If the gale had continued much longer, we should have found ourselves with a number of others in rather a bad fix; but as it is, we are all right. Had a few snow squalls this morning, but afterward it cleared up bright with the wind from the north. Lowered two boats for a whale after breakfast, but he was not seen afterwards. After tea spoke the *Cleone,* cutting in a whale which, Captain Simmons said, made them three. He also reported the *Fabius* with four. They all seem to be beating us, and I know none can try more than we do. Saw another ship cutting. A strong breeze sprang up after tea. By observation we found our-selves latitude 70 degrees 30 minutes.

SEPTEMBER 3. A strong breeze which almost amounts to a gale through the night and continued through the forenoon. Several ships in sight. About 3 P.M. raised a whale. The weather had moderated sufficiently to lower the boats, although it was pretty rugged. Called the watch and sent off all four boats. How little we thought that the death angel was hovering over us and that one of our number was then leaving us, never more to return. It was even so. Poor Frank's days are numbered, and he is now in the world of spirits. Oh, these sad events are the worst of whaling.

Not much time had elapsed after the boats had left before we heard the joyful sound of "A boat fast!" Joyful at all times, but more especially to us now after being so unfortunate this season. Mr. Huntley fastened to him and fired a bomb lance into him. Afterward Mr. Jackson fastened and then went on the whale to lance him. While he was rolling over from the effects of a bomb lance, the whale capsized the boat, throwing all hands into the water instantly. They had all regained and were clinging to the overturned boat when the whale made a second attack, perhaps to see what it might be. Whatever might have been his motives, he made a dash at the boat and stove it almost to atoms. The men, when they saw him coming, jumped again into the water, and poor Frank was not seen afterward. He could not swim, and he might have got injured in some way.

Mr. Jackson was brought on board immediately with his crew by Mr. Parker. He was hurt, he thinks, by the whale's flukes. His knee is badly swollen but otherwise not seriously injured. And after all this chapter of accidents, when the whale was killed, what were our feelings to see him sink to the bottom. The boats stayed by him for some time and would probably have succeed-ed in pulling him up had there not been such a heavy sea. As it was, the irons came out, and the boats came on board, sad, weary, and discouraged. Samuel sent Mr. Parker to find the re-mains of the boat, if it was possible, as all the craft, bomb gun, etc., belonging to her was there, but it could not be found.

The wind breezed up as usual towards night, and we who could retired to rest, weary and sick at heart. Frank was a Por-

tuguese about twenty years old, one that we brought from home
with us and a very good man; but he is gone, making the third
body we have committed to the sea this voyage. Oh, that it
might be the last! May it be a warning to us all to be prepared
so that when the angel of death draws near, be it sooner or
later, we may be found ready, one and all.

SEPTEMBER 4. A regular northerly gale. Just the weather to go
out, clear and bright, if we only had a good season's work; but
as it is, we must try to stop a little longer and see if we cannot
get one more whale. We have endeavored to stay around near
the place where the whale sank yesterday to see if he would not
come up for us, but he has not made his appearance. Ten ships
in sight today. If we could only get three or four more whales
before we leave, how thankful we would be. I suppose our
company received a shock yesterday that it will take them some
time to overcome. The wind continued through the day, towards
night becoming a regular gale. Just before dark passed the *Mary
Frazier;* the *Cleone* near by.

SEPTEMBER 5. The gale increased through the night, and this
morning it blows with redoubled fury. A gale so severe and so
long as this we have not seen before this voyage. About noon it
commenced moderating; the *Polar Star* close by us in the afternoon. There has been and is quite a heavy sea, but it is so short
that it does not much affect the motion of a ship. She lay to very
nicely. Saw one bowhead today.

SEPTEMBER 6. Spoke the *Cleone* this morning. Captain Simmons
informed us that he picked up our boat. Samuel went on board to
see about it; found that he picked it up, found it stoven very
badly, attempted to tow it, and it broke in two. He took the
other part in, but Samuel did not think it worth taking, so left
it with Captain Simmons for firewood. There was no gun in it
when he found it. Probably it was loose in the boat and was
lost when she capsized. Captain Simmons returned with Samuel
and passed the day with us, as it was calm so that we could go
nowhere to look for whales. After dinner Captain Jones of the
George and Susan came on board, and before supper we had
an addition to our company of Captain Tinker of the *Mocte-*

zuma. He is a cousin of Mercy's and has visited Falmouth since we left home. They left about 9 P.M. Captain Tinker sent us some pickled halibut and some onions, which were very acceptable. Captain Simmons has taken three whales; the other captains, two each.

SEPTEMBER 7. Cruised around all day without seeing anything. Wind very light, almost a calm. After tea spoke the *Majestic,* Captain Chester, and soon after Captain Tinker of the *Moctezuma* lowered his boat and came on board. Captain Chester has taken two whales this season, one on Kodiak and one here. While they were here, the wind blew up quite strong from the north; and Samuel has almost concluded to leave if we have another northerly gale tomorrow, thinking, as the bad weather appears to have come on in earnest, that we shall stand a better chance to get another whale in Bristol Bay than we shall in the Arctic. I wish we knew what was best for us, but to do the best that we know how under existing circumstances ought to be all that is required of us.

SEPTEMBER 8. A strong northerly gale through the night. About 9 A.M. squared the yards to go as far down as Cape Lisburne and farther still if we saw nothing. The consequence was that we saw nothing. About 3 P.M. raised two ships laying to. One of them kept off with us, and before night we raised another which we spoke just before dark. She proved to be the bark *Emerald,* Captain Pierce; nothing the season. That will hardly pay the expenses of a wife and two children in Honolulu.

SEPTEMBER 9. Two ships in sight of us through the day. About noon the wind left us, a dead calm with a heavy swell. Made no headway at all through the afternoon. After tea one of the ships set a signal for gamming. Samuel did not go, but the other captains went. By one of the ship's signals we found her to be the *Christopher Mitchell.* Saw East Cape before sunset.

SEPTEMBER 10. Dead calm and thick for most of the night. Towards morning a slight breeze sprang up. Samuel did not sleep much. About 4 A.M. heard a sound as of breakers very near; could not tell whether it was land or ice. Thick throughout the day. Heard foghorns once from another ship. About 4 P.M. it lighted up so that we saw what we supposed to be East Cape and found that during the calm we were carried to the northeast by a very strong current.

SEPTEMBER 11. Saw land astern of us this morning which we suppose to be St. Lawrence Bay. A bark on our lee beam about 10 A.M. She set her signal, and we went down and spoke her. She proved to be the bark *George*. Captain Silva came on board and stopped until about 2 P.M. He has taken two whales this season. Was stove in the ice several weeks ago and leaks quite badly. Light airs for most of the day so that we make but little headway. Captain Silva went on board again about 2 P.M., and just before dark we spoke again to see if it was advisable to run. They decided to do so, and Samuel was up through the night. It was quite a dangerous route to attempt in the night in a thick fog, as Indian Point, a very low neck of land, runs out for a long distance; and on the other hand there is a strong current setting you in to St. Lawrence Island, which lies at the entrance of the Strait.

SEPTEMBER 12. We went through safely last night by soundings. I went to bed last night and slept soundly through the night. When Samuel is on deck, I have no fears. I am thoroughly glad, however, that we are through, and so is Samuel. Bering Strait is a very dangerous place, and I greatly wonder there are no more ships lost there than there are, although I have heard that a number of years since there were eleven lost in one season. The *George* nearby through the day. Foggy for the most part through the day.

SEPTEMBER 13. Spoke the *George* in the morning. Captain Silva came on board and passed the day. Another bark in sight in the afternoon. We lay aback for her to come down to us. Found her to be the *Pioneer*. Captain Barker came on board and passed the afternoon. Learned from him that Mrs. Bryant of the *America* was quite seriously injured by the hog house fetching way and pressing her up against the side of the ship while they were cutting in a whale. Mrs. Baker went on board and stopped a day or two with her, and then Captain Bryant put away for the

Islands, so that I fear it was a serious injury. We were also sorry to learn by him that the *Julian* had been quite badly stoven in the ice; had taken nothing. Captain Barker hails one mussel digger as his season's work. We had before learned that the *Neva* was badly stoven. He confirms the report. She is two years out without a drop of oil. What are we all coming to? And what are the owners going to do? They must sink an enormous amount of money from the catchings of the last two seasons. The *Good Return* was ashore a day or two before we left Cape Lisburne but got off without injury.

SEPTEMBER 14. A gale of wind and thick for the most part of the day. We are now on our way towards St. Paul, having seen nothing in the vicinity of Gore's Island. Spoke the *George* in the forenoon. Captain Silva told us that he saw a right whale in the morning close by his ship, so near that they gallied him. That is encouraging if we could only have decent weather; but as it has been, we could do nothing were there plenty of whales here.

SEPTEMBER 15. The gale still continues. Spoke the *George* in the morning. Captain Silva has got tired of the weather here and is now bound off. Samuel will try it here a little longer. I felt sorry to have him leave us, as he was the only one in sight and we have been among ships so long that it seems rather lonely to be left alone. In the afternoon raised two ships. One lay aback for us. We went down and were pleased to find it the *Speedwell*. Mrs. Gibbs and myself had another flourish of pocket handkerchiefs. As it was blowing a gale, we could do nothing else. Captain Gibbs left the Arctic the eighth and reports whales plenty where we are and plenty of bad weather. We had experienced the truth of his last statement and were very happy to hear the first. We immediately took in sail and lay to and before dark had the pleasure of seeing five or six whales.

SEPTEMBER 16. Moderated some in the morning; continued to do so until it was nearly calm. Then a thick fog set in. After tea raised four whales very near the ships; lowered the boats. They had not been down fifteen minutes when the starboard boat struck. They had just got two irons nicely into him when he sounded, taking the whole of the line, about 300 fathoms, with him. Had it been clear, they might possibly have fastened to him again; but it was just as thick as it could be, and the boats came on board again after being absent about half an hour. This makes the fifth whale we have struck this season and succeeded in saving two of them. If we only had the weather, think we should stand a chance of making a good season's work yet.

I am very sorry to be obliged to record the death of Minnie's white hen (Minnie). She was the one that we brought from home with us. Minnie claimed her, so we did not kill her with the rest, and she became quite a pet on board. We hoped to carry her home again. She has had bunches in her throat. Several operations have been performed on her, but as fast as one was taken out, another would grow. She could eat nothing, and we thought it best to have her killed and put out of misery, which was done today. It made us feel very badly to lose her. We become exceedingly attached to such pets on shipboard. Three ships in sight today.

SEPTEMBER 17. A thick fog as usual today. Lowered for whales about 5 P.M. but without success.

SEPTEMBER 18. Thick for the most part of the day with a strong breeze. Lowered for whales about 10 A.M.; fastened to one. He appeared quite still, the other boats were drawing near, and we were beginning to hope that the prize might be ours, when lo! here he was close to the ship, loose. What a change in our feelings. The boats chased him for a while but soon gave up in despair, as he was going very fast to windward. When the boats returned, we learned that they were obliged to cut from him in consequence of having a foul line. Out of six whales that we have been fast to, we have saved two. The *Benjamin Morgan* has struck seven and saved five, which makes quite a difference in a season's work. Saw the *Rambler's* boats fast to a whale for a few minutes this afternoon, but they soon lost him.

SEPTEMBER 19. Spoke the *Rambler* this morning. We did not gam, as both hoped to see whales and the wind breezed on quite strong. After dinner, however, not seeing any whales, Captain

Willis ran down to us, lowered his boat, and came on board. He said I must see how much he wanted to see us to come on board in such a strong breeze, almost too much for whaling. He left the Arctic the fifteenth; had taken nothing since we saw him. He hopes to get a whale or two here, and I hope he may, providing we can do the same. He brought me a box of eggs, which I was pleased with. He did not stop to tea, as it was getting to be very rugged, and I was very glad to see him safely landed on board the *Rambler*. At such times I always think of the sad fate of Captain Lamphier and his boat's crew, who were lost on returning to their ship.[10] Saw no whales during the day.

SEPTEMBER 21. More like good weather than anything we have seen, although the sea has not yet gone down. Spoke the *William Rotch* in the afternoon. Captain Ellison said that he had seen several whales through the day; but we saw nothing, although we cruised over a great deal of ground. After tea raised the *Rambler* with a whale alongside. We did not really envy him, but we wanted one too.

SEPTEMBER 22. Pleasant weather, so much so that it seems as if we must have a whale to cut in. Have been cruising all around today and saw nothing that looked like a whale. Minnie has a very strong desire to go to Asia. She wishes to see where the ark was, also to visit Shiloh and see the Tabernacle, to go to Jerusalem and see if she could not obtain a piece of the Cross; and today while she was conversing on the subject, she seemed to think that if she ever went, she should take a shovel with her and see if she could not find where Moses was buried on the mountain. She thinks that as he was such a good man that his body would not turn to clay as they do now. She has a great many strange and original thoughts, I think, for a child of her years. Three ships in sight, the *Rambler* boiling.

SEPTEMBER 23. Good weather. Saw no whales except one in the afternoon that a ship's boats were fast to, which we supposed to be the *Good Return*. They did not succeed in capturing him.

SEPTEMBER 24. A dead calm. Samuel lowered a boat about 9 A.M. and went on board the *Rambler*, Captain Willis having set a signal for him. While there they spoke the *Good Return,* and Captain Fish went on board. He has taken one small bowhead and picked up two, making him in all about 200 barrels. He reported the *Julian* as having been in St. Lawrence Bay to repair and took one bowhead while there. Reports a great many whales in that bay, but it was blowing a gale of wind so that their anchors would not hold. Captain Willis sent Minnie and myself a lot of books to read, which were indeed a treat. Sent Minnie a bottle of lemon syrup and me a fowl. After Samuel came on board, the ships to windward raised a whale, which was missed by one of the *Rambler's* boatsteerers. Shall we have another chance? I fear not, as we have seen only this one for the last four days. If we could but get one or two more, how grateful we would be.

SEPTEMBER 25. A strong breeze, almost a gale, and quite rugged. Raised a whale about 9 A.M. Hesitated whether or not to lower the boats but finally did so, as we could not resist the temptation. Had the good fortune to strike. The whale did not take the line, no line was parted, neither did any get foul. All things worked right, and about one o'clock P.M. had him alongside. It was very rugged, and Samuel feared that we should not be able to get him in, but they finally succeeded after many hindrances, taking them thirteen hours to cut him in.   159 barrels.

SEPTEMBER 26. A strong breeze. Towards noon rather moderated. After dinner lowered for a whale and got fast to him. The boats could not get near him, he being inclined to run; and as there was but one iron in him, that soon came out, making the eighth whale that we have been fast to this season.

SEPTEMBER 27. Commenced boiling today. Two ships in sight. Almost or quite a dead calm. Saw whales in the afternoon; chased for some time, but as there was no wind, the boats could not near them.

SEPTEMBER 28. Fine, pleasant weather. Saw one whale, but he came too near the ship before we saw him and gallied, or frightened, him.

SEPTEMBER 29. A strong breeze from the north; clear, bright weather. Plenty of finbacks in sight. They have probably driven the right whales farther north where we cannot go, as the wind is from that direction.

SEPTEMBER 30. A strong breeze with a heavy head sea. Saw the islands of St. Paul and St. George today. Have seen the former several times before this. The *Good Return* in sight. In the afternoon had several boats down. We saw no whales; even if we had, Samuel thought it would have been impossible to get a boat down our ship's side without swamping. We were engaged for the most of the day in stowing down our oil: 159 barrels, a very good whale. We lost about 20 barrels in cutting in.

OCTOBER 1. Last night it moderated even to a calm. The wind commenced breezing up again about 10 A.M. and continued until it amounted to a gale. The *Good Return* in sight; commenced boiling this morning. Suppose he must have taken a whale the day before we saw him, as he was unsuccessful in his attempts yesterday. Moderated towards night, and the rain poured almost in torrents.

OCTOBER 2. Moderate breezes from the south today. Raised whales immediately after breakfast, lowered the boats, and gave chase to them. In the course of the forenoon about a dozen whales had made their appearance, but they were exceedingly wild, and not a boat could get near them. We send but three boats out now, as our second mate is off duty and has been for nearly two weeks. Cause: a disturbance between him and the mate. Nearly calm throughout the day.

OCTOBER 3. A strong breeze from the north. Spoke the *Good Return* in the forenoon cutting in a dead whale which she picked up in the morning. Our olfactory nerves assured us that it was so some time before we spoke him. The gale increased throughout the day. I think Samuel would have started to go out today had we not so many whales yesterday. Two ships in sight besides the *Good Return*.

OCTOBER 4. The gale still continues; blows rather stronger than it did yesterday. Samuel is almost ready to start before it. Have had very heavy squalls of wind and hail through the day.

OCTOBER 5. The weather continues the same. After breakfast we made sail for the One Seventy-two Passage. A heavy sea and squalls the same as yesterday.

OCTOBER 6. Last night the *Addison* barely managed to head her course, and now we can run no farther, for we have a strong breeze from the south. Laying to.

OCTOBER 7. The wind from the south the same as yesterday. At 6 P.M. the wind suddenly changed to the southeast and blew very hard from that quarter.

OCTOBER 8. The wind blew very hard through the night and considerable rain fell. Towards morning it moderated some. After breakfast the wind hauled to the westward, and we had the benefit of what I think may be called a violent gale from that quarter. Carried away our main topsail in a squall.

OCTOBER 9. The gale has abated a little since yesterday, but it still blows very fresh. We have a heavy sea from all directions, and our good ship pitches, plunges, and rolls about in a way that would almost frighten a looker-on, especially in the squalls, which come very often today. I think this may be called the line gale, although it is rather late for it. At any rate it is the hardest gale we have experienced this voyage.

OCTOBER 10. The weather the same as yesterday. We are looking forward now for tomorrow night to bring a change, as the moon fulls then.

OCTOBER 11. About the same in the forenoon. About noon the wind hauled a little so that we could run. If the weather improves this afternoon and the wind is favorable, we shall be off the passage in the morning.

OCTOBER 12. The wind blew very strong through the night with very severe squalls. We ran through the night until about three o'clock, when the squalls were so severe and not being very clear, Samuel thought it advisable to luff to until daylight. At daylight we commenced running again and in about two hours raised the land. Found our chronometer about ten miles out of the way. We went through the One Seventy-two Passage. Saw three islands. Had a strong breeze through, which with the heavy sea and immense tide rips occasioned some knocking about. Raised a ship five or six miles ahead of us in the passage. Towards night we came to the conclusion that the weather had considerably improved.

OCTOBER 13. We are nicely through and have fairly commenced our passage to the Islands with 460 barrels of oil and 6,000 or 7,000 pounds of bone, the product of our season. It is very small, but I feel that we ought to be thankful even for that. It is so much better than we feared almost to the close of the season, although it is by no means what we hoped for. In consequence of our partial failure of this season, we shall be obliged to extend our cruise, before going home, several months longer than we intended and hope yet to have 3,000 barrels for the voyage.[11]

OCTOBER 14. Fine weather today with light winds; making not much progress. I spent some time on deck after dinner. The weather seems much warmer today than it has done for some time.

OCTOBER 15. Cloudy and some rain with a head wind. Some part of the day we could nearly head our course.

OCTOBER 16. The wind variable, the same as yesterday, mostly ahead; some rainy. About 6 P.M. the wind breezed up from the north.

OCTOBER 17. A strong breeze through the night; everything alive with motion so that it was impossible to sleep. The gale continued until about 4 P.M., when it moderated. Before dark made more sail.

OCTOBER 18. A strong breeze from the southwest for most of the day. Towards night the wind changed to the north, and we are now, 7 P.M., going along at a fine rate toward our destined haven. We have now on board a Kanaka (John Adams) who is very sick and has been for some time with consumption or some kindred disease, and I very much fear that he will never see his home again. I earnestly hope for his sake that he may reach it. Have been employed today in trying on Minnie's port clothes, every garment of which is under the necessity of being lengthened. No slight job when so many suits are needed in these warm weather ports.

OCTOBER 19. A fair wind with a strong breeze and a heavy sea.

OCTOBER 20. The same as yesterday, except that it grows warmer.

OCTOBER 21. Almost a calm, bright, warm, and pleasant. Had the stove taken down the first thing. I went to washing after breakfast, having a four weeks' wash of ship clothing besides a great many port clothes to wash. Minnie took her little tub and washed her dog's bedclothes, for Jip has had a bed all the season that had to be made up like anybody's bed. Samuel commenced cleaning the after cabin for his share of the day's work, while the steward took the forward cabin. The men on deck were employed in washing whalebone. I took Susie the bird on deck today for the first time, and the air resounded with a perfect gush of melody.

OCTOBER 22. Pleasant as yesterday with a nice breeze. All hands been variously employed. I stood at my ironing table nearly all day doing up skirts, dresses, shirts, spencers, collars, drawers, etc., etc. They helped John Adams on deck after dinner to bask in the sunshine for a little while. He seemed to enjoy it very much and thought he felt better for it. Took Susie on deck again.

OCTOBER 23. A strong breeze with occasional squalls. The work is laid aside today except work of necessity, as it is the Sabbath. For the last twenty-four hours have made quite rapid progress in our voyage.

OCTOBER 24. A nice breeze. Samuel and myself cleaned our bedroom, while Minnie took hers in her own hands and succeeded very well, needing but very little help from me.

OCTOBER 25. A head wind and not much of it. I spent the day in letting down clothes for Minnie, preparatory to washing.

OCTOBER 26. Pleasant weather but a head wind carrying us out to the westward. Washed again today for the last time probably before going in port. In the afternoon a Portuguese, Manuel by name, got badly hurt by a marlinespike falling on his head from aloft. It cut a large place in his head, and it is a wonder that he had not been killed instantly. They sang out from aloft to look out. He lifted his head to look up as it fell, and it glanced off. Probably to that he owes his life.

OCTOBER 30. A strong breeze, and we are going very nearly as we would wish, the first time for several days that we have headed within a couple of points as we would wish. It is doubtful now if we fetch Maui. We shall probably see land tomorrow night if this breeze continues.

OCTOBER 31. Saw land today. Have been heading a very good course and shall fetch Maui without doubt.

NOVEMBER 1 [through 30]. Arrived at Lahaina about three o'clock P.M.[12] Had a visit from the customhouse officer, soon after which we went ashore. John Adams has seemed low for several days past, and we very much feared that he would never reach Maui. On our arrival he was carried ashore to his friends and bore the change as well as could be expected. We went immediately after landing to Mr. Gilman's, where we were very cordially received; found all friends well, bade them an affectionate *aloha*, and left for Honolulu the afternoon of the next day.

The king and suite were to leave the same time in the schooner *Maria*, and as her accommodations were so small, Samuel was asked to take a few, the governor and some of his attendants, on board the *Addison*, which he consented to do on condition that they should pay the steamer for towing us in.[13] They accepted the terms.

When we arrived on board, we found hardly room for the

soles of our feet on deck. The governor and Princess Victoria, father and sister of the present king, were on board with their train of attendants numbering in all about ninety souls! Each one with a trunk, chest, box, or canny-pail, his dishes of poi, and a huge pile of sugar cane beside him. On either side of the deck were two large lounges with canopies for the governor and princess with velvet coverings, velvet pillows, and embroidered pillowcases. Each one was furnished with a calabash containing some fragrant herb, which was used for a spittoon, and almost every female was furnished with a white, earthen vessel, the name and nature of which modesty forbids me to mention.

The princess declined taking tea with us in the cabin but partook of her poi and chickens on deck with several of her attendants, each one dipping her fingers in the dish according to custom. She bears rather a disreputable character. She converses very well in English. When she left the next morning, she gave us a very polite invitation to stop at her house; but I declined, thinking it would be far pleasanter to stop at Mr. Whitney's, where we had stopped several times before.

Arrived at Honolulu the next morning. Mr. Richmond, a nephew of our agent who is clerk with Wilcox and Richards, came on board and kindly offered to procure a boarding place for us, which he did at Mr. Whitney's. We found several letters at Lahaina and a number more awaiting us at Honolulu. Letters from Sandwich informed us that my dear father's health had been very poor throughout the summer, but that it had been improving for the last few weeks, and they thought as the weather became cooler he would continue to improve. How anxious I shall be on his account for the remainder of the voyage. Not one word more shall I hear, unless we should receive letters by the next mail, which I do not expect, until we arrive home. Oh, that he may live until our return. Our other friends were all well. Received Willie's daguerreotype in a letter. He has grown very much and changed much in his looks since I saw him. From his picture I should judge that he was a fine-looking young man.

On our arrival at Mr. Whitney's found that Mrs. Whitney's niece Emmie Cutts, who arrived while we were there last fall, was married two nights previous to Charles Judd, a resident of Baker Island. They left for that place on the next week after our arrival.

We were pained to hear of the death of Captain Palmer of the *Kingfisher*.[14] Mrs. Palmer arrived from Hilo a few days after our arrival, where she had been stopping through the season with her two children (one born since her husband left her), on her way home by way of California, a poor broken-hearted widow. My heart aches for her as it has seldom ached for anyone. It is hard to be thus bereft when one is at home, surrounded by loving friends, but to a stranger in a strange land it is desolate indeed. Oh, what a sad going home was that from what she had been fondly anticipating. May He who kindly tempers the wind to the shorn lamb deal so gently with her.[15]

It was my painful duty to attend her on board the *Kingfisher*, then to overlook and pack up the clothing of her dear departed husband, and a trying duty it was to me. What must it have been for her.

Two other captains died in the Okhotsk Sea this last season, Captain Tallman of the *Midas* and Captain Waterman of the *J. D. Thompson,* both of them leaving families at home. Reports came by the Okhotsk fleet confirming the loss of the *Ocean Wave* and the *Phoenix,* about which there had been so much anxiety. The *Ocean Wave* was lost, and all on board found a watery grave. The *Phoenix* was lost at the same time within a very short distance, and all were saved. We were also pained to hear of the death of Mr. Baxter, who came out with us as second officer. He left us a year out, then went a short cruise south in the *Ocean Wave,* procured his discharge from that ship, went to Fraser River, returned again to the Islands, sailed for home in the *Trident,* and was washed overboard in a gale of wind off the River La Plata.[16]

We passed the time of our sojourn in port very pleasantly for the most part. Went to the theater building one evening to see Professor Anderson perform and again to hear the Swiss bell ringers.[17] Saw many acquaintances while in port, some being home friends and others acquaintances of the voyage, especially captains and their wives, of whom there were many in port. We would generally meet at some boarding place, five or six couple, and after spending an hour or two very pleasantly, would adjourn to an ice-cream saloon.

The last of November the *Yankee* arrived from California, and I with many others was anticipating news from home, although I did not really expect letters. We received one, however, from sister Sarah written from the first to the tenth of September. The only sad news it contained was the death of our minister, who has been settled since we left home. That evening we went out to make calls. On our way home called at Captain Wilcox' to get some New Bedford papers. After we arrived home I sat down, as I usually do on the receipt of home papers, to look over the deaths and marriages. Samuel had stepped out, and I was left alone. Shall I ever forget my sensations when the first paragraph on which my eyes rested was the death of my dear father. What a shock and how unexpected! Can it be that I have seen him for the last time? Oh, how fondly I have anticipated meeting Father, Mother, brothers, and sisters once more. It has been the great wish of my heart. Oh, it is so hard that I could not have heard one word in connection with his death. It seems as if it could not be, the thought that he is no more, that he died when I his eldest daughter was far away, that I never more shall see him. Oh, it almost overpowers me, and my poor mother, I fear that the blow was too heavy for her to bear. With what a sad heart shall I return home. I feel as if his vacant place would be more than I can bear.

SEVENTH CRUISE

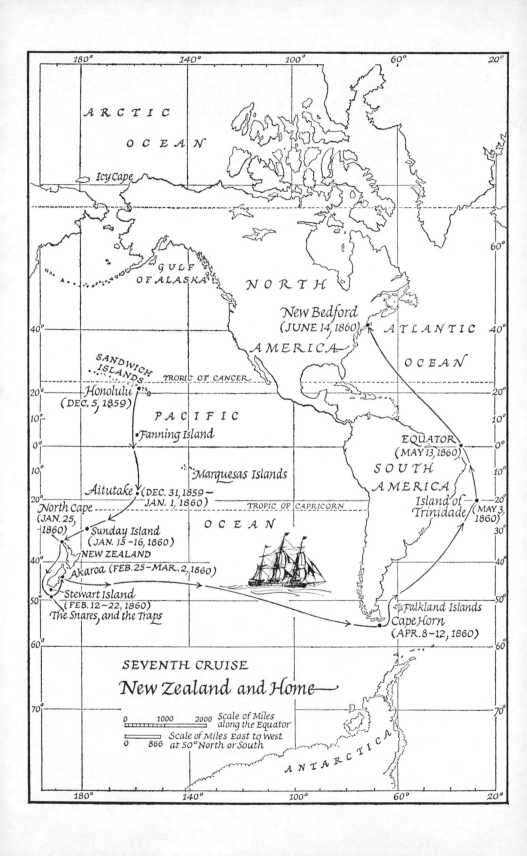

ARCTIC
OCEAN

Icy Cape

GULF
OF ALASKA

NORTH

New Bedford
(JUNE 14, 1860)

ATLANTIC

AMERICA

OCEAN

SANDWICH
ISLANDS

TROPIC OF CANCER

Honolulu
(DEC. 5, 1859)

PACIFIC

EQUATOR
(MAY 13, 1860)

Fanning Island

SOUTH

Marquesas Islands

AMERICA

Aitutake (DEC. 31, 1859 –
JAN. 1, 1860)

TROPIC OF CAPRICORN

Island of
Trinidade

(MAY 3,
1860)

North Cape
(JAN. 25,
1860)

OCEAN

Sunday Island
(JAN. 15 –16, 1860)
NEW ZEALAND

Akaroa (FEB. 25–MAR. 2, 1860)

Stewart Island
(FEB. 12–22, 1860)
The Snares, and the Traps

Falkland Islands
Cape Horn
(APR. 8–12, 1860)

SEVENTH CRUISE
New Zealand and Home

0   1000   2000   Scale of Miles
along the Equator

0   866   Scale of Miles East to West
at 50° North or South

ANTARCTICA

New Zealand and Home

DECEMBER 1859–JUNE 1860

[DECEMBER 2–20.] We left Honolulu for the last time, on this voyage at least, the second day of December.[1] I have always fondly anticipated the day when we would leave for "a cruise and home," but I left with a sad heart. Home will hardly be home—that vacant chair. How my heart aches to think of it, and I shall not realize it fully until I get home. It will be a sad meeting should we live to reach home. Several ships came out on that day, as there had been bad weather for three or four days previous so that the pilot declined taking any out. We kept in company with the bark *Behring,* for Boston with a cargo of oil, for several days. Nothing of interest occurred until we saw a school of sperm whales December 20. It was a dead calm, and the boats pulled nearly all day after them without success. We were then in the vicinity of Jarvis Island. We have almost a new crew on board now. We have ten or twelve that came out from home with us; the remainder are a new set with the exception of Mr. Parker, who was our third mate last season and is now promoted to second mate, and a boatsteerer.

DECEMBER 23. Raised a bark today, the first sail we have seen since we lost sight of the *Behring.* A fever has prevailed to quite an extent on board for a number of days. The second mate, a boatsteerer, cooper, steerage boy, five or six men forward, and now Minnie is down with it. It does not run very high and is similar, I think, to the boohoo.

DECEMBER 24. Spoke the bark this morning, the *Lagoda.*[2] Captain Willard came on board and passed the day. Minnie sat up a little today after tea. As it was the night before Christmas, Minnie hung up her stocking. Samuel went on board the *Lagoda* with Captain Willard on his return to look at his chart. When he came back, he brought a very handsome portmanteau to

Minnie and a cake of soap as a Christmas present from the captain.

DECEMBER 25. Minnie awoke bright and early this morning to examine the contents of her stocking. With Captain Willard's presents she was very much pleased. Her father made her a pair of ivory candlesticks with little candles of the same material, which were very cunning, and I presented her with a book. Those with candies made up the supply. The captain made us a short visit in the afternoon.

DECEMBER 26. The *Lagoda* nearby. Captain Willard lowered his boat and came on board in the afternoon.

DECEMBER 27. Captain Willard came on board today with his carpenter, that he might use our turning lathe; but he was not at all successful. Samuel turned two ivory lamp picks for him.

DECEMBER 28. As we can sail a little faster than the *Lagoda*, Samuel has decided to go on and not stop any longer for him. At night the *Lagoda* is just discernible astern.

DECEMBER 31. We are very near Aitutaki now, and according to the east longitude reckoning, our Saturday is their Sunday, so we decided to keep this day. If not, it would be necessary for us to lay by two days.[3] Our sick people have about all recovered. Afternoon, about 4 P.M. Mr. Baird, mate, went ashore with a boat's crew. One ship laying off and on, which we spoke after tea. We found her to be the French ship *General Teste*, Captain Le Mercier. Samuel went on board for a short time. Mr. Baird returned about 8 P.M., loaded with pineapples, bananas, coconuts, etc., from the missionary's family, bringing a cordial invitation from them to us to come on board early in the morning and stop with them as long as possible. They also sent me a bottle of milk.

1860

JANUARY 1. A new year has opened again upon us, but one with whom I hoped once more to take sweet counsel is no more. A sad new year is this for my mother, but how little I can realize the loss as yet. This New Year's Day we spent at Aitutaki, one of the Hervey, or Cook, Islands, in the family of Mr. Royle, the English missionary, the only white family on the island. They appeared delighted to see us and did everything for our comfort that it was in their power. They have six daughters; the two eldest have been in England for the last three years. The youngest is six years old, a very pleasant playmate for Minnie. They have been residents on the island and engaged in their benevolent work for twenty-one years, and the natives are all under their influence. They seem much better than any that I have before met with. I visited their schoolhouse and chapel, which were both neat and commodious.

There were five ships lying off and on during the day: the *General Teste;* the *Covington,* Captain Newman; the *Minerva,* Captain Crowell; and the *Louisa,* Captain Hathaway, all bound home. The captains all dined at the missionary's. We carried a few things ashore for them and received several presents: some pieces of tapa matting, a fan, some juice, and some straw braid for a bonnet for Minnie and myself.[4] We returned on board about 8 P.M. after having had a delightful visit. It is a beautiful island, a perfect garden as regards vegetation. Pineapples grow in great abundance and, in great perfection, oranges, limes, bananas, plantains, breadfruit, yams, custard apples, etc., etc., all of which we procured a quantity. I had written a letter which I wished to send home by some ship bound direct. As Captain Crowell was going directly home, he kindly came on board to get it. Hope both he and it may arrive in due time.

JANUARY 2. We have been busily engaged in putting up pineapples in jars to take home, providing they will keep. Not a ship in sight today. We all left Aitutaki last night. I think Mr. Royle's family must feel rather lonely today. They appear to enjoy society very much, and no wonder, for there is only a few weeks in the year that they have the pleasure of beholding a white face, out of their own family. They all look forward to the shipping season with great anticipations. I never had the pleasure of eating as much pineapple as I wished before. Oh, how luscious they are! It would be a mockery to put sugar upon them to eat as we do at home. I am very fond of all the tropical fruits.

JANUARY 7. We have been pursuing the even tenor of our way[5] for several days. Have been engaged in washing, ironing, and putting up pineapples, besides my regular routine of work. We have been saving our white sugar nearly all the voyage for this occasion and have put up a famous lot in jars, bottles, etc. Have had a hard rainstorm today, almost without intermission. A ship in sight which we signalized this forenoon and found to be the *Rambler*. If it was good weather, probably we should have a gam.

JANUARY 8. The rain still continues. The *Rambler* in sight. Luxuriated today in roast chickens for the cabin and a pork sea pie for the forecastle, with occasional lunches of pineapple, bananas, and coconuts. It cleared up a little in the afternoon, and the *Rambler* ran down to speak us; but just as we were within hailing distance, the rain came down in torrents. Captain Willis wished Samuel to take Minnie and myself and come on board. (He said he had but one.) He could take her in a monkey jacket, but Samuel thought it was too rainy. We had the pleasure of looking at Mrs. Willis and the children, and possibly we may have a gam yet, as we are bound in the same direction. I should like much to have a visit from them.

JANUARY 9. Found the *Rambler* in sight this morning. About 9 A.M. Captain Willis set his signal, and soon after Samuel, Minnie, and myself went on board and passed the day very pleasantly. This meeting with families at sea is very pleasant for all concerned, particularly so for the children.

JANUARY 14. We have had almost a dead calm ever since the ninth. Have gone but a few hundred miles. Today we had a little breeze. The weather has been very warm and uncomfortable. In the afternoon the *Rambler* ran down to us, and Captain and Mrs. Willis, Henry P., Jennie, and Jimmie came on board and stopped until 9 P.M.

JANUARY 15. Sunday, or Raoul, Island in sight. About noon we came round to the landing place on the opposite side of the island, and Mr. Baird went in with his boat to get some onions, cabbages, etc. Just before he reached the shore, we raised whales and set the signal for him to return to the ship. Consequently we got no vegetables. Three ships in sight, the *Belle, Northern Light,* and *E. L. B. Jenney.* We spoke the *Belle.* Mrs. Brown and myself exchanged compliments. They report the *William Thompson* with 175 [barrels] sperm since leaving Oahu. He is making a grand voyage. We made the discovery some time after the boats lowered that they were schools of grampus that we were in pursuit of instead of sperm whales, which they very much resemble. After the boats had all returned to their respective ships and it was nearly dark, Samuel thought to run for them and have a gam, as they all appeared to be gamming; but before we reached them, they all braced forward as if about their own business, so we gave up our intention.

JANUARY 16. We lay off and on the island through the night. In the forenoon Mr. Baird went in with his boat's crew. It is a small and rather a desolate-looking island, inhabited only by two families, although one of the men has two or three wives and a dozen or two children. The bark *Belle* is in sight. In the afternoon experienced quite a severe thundershower. It rained very hard and was so thick that we could not see a ship's length for several hours, in consequence of which the boat did not get back until about 7 P.M. We procured some onions, cabbages, and green corn, which was a great treat to us, being the first we have had since we left home. After the shower was over, the *Belle* tacked for us and about 7 P.M. lowered a boat, and Captain and Mrs. Brown and their little Lyman came on board. They stopped until about 10 P.M., and we had a very pleasant call from them. They have taken 100 barrels sperm since they left Oahu.

JANUARY 17. Saw Macauley, or Goat, Island in the morning. We approached near it after dinner and sent in two boats for fish and goats. The island is uninhabited. For dinner today we had succotash, or corn and beans, and we did them ample justice. The boats returned about sunset with three or four dozen fish, two goats they had killed and one live one, and four parakeets.

JANUARY 18. We have been standing today from Curtis Island to Hope, or French, Rock. About noon we raised a school of sperm whales, sure enough. Lowered all four boats, but they were going to the windward three times as fast as a boat could pull, so were reluctantly obliged to give up the chase and return to the ship.

JANUARY 19. We lay around the rock through the night hoping to see whales waiting to be caught, but nothing of the kind greeted our eyes. About 11 A.M. experienced quite a severe shock of an earthquake, which jarred us considerably.[6]

JANUARY 20. We are now on our way toward the North Cape of New Zealand and where we do hope to get a whale. About noon raised a ship. Just before dark she hauled aback, and we ran down to her. Before she reached us, I saw a lady on the house. As we drew near, we found her to be the *James Arnold*, of New Bedford, a sperm whaler. Captain and Mrs. Sullivan came on board and brought with them their cooper, Frederic Read (Anna's brother).[7] I was very glad to see him, although he had grown out of my knowledge. They brought us some apples and peaches, which were a great treat. They procured them from a ship just from New Zealand. I gave them some late papers, which are always acceptable, and some peanuts. They are twenty-nine months out with 1,500 barrels sperm oil. They have seen Thomas and wife this voyage and Lewis and his wife, and now they have seen Samuel and wife.[8] They left us about 9 P.M. I feel as if I had been peculiarly favored to have a visit from three different ladies in less than a week.

JANUARY 21. A strong breeze, but almost ahead. We have very fine weather now, just cool enough for comfort. We have experienced very warm, trying weather since we left Honolulu. Minnie and myself are fully agreed that we prefer going north to sperm whaling in warm latitudes.

About a week ago the steward throwed all the teaspoons we used for breakfast overboard in his dishwater. Samuel reproved him for his carelessness, but as he had not been at sea for some years, thought not much about it. We managed to find just enough to set the table with, and this morning he did the same thing again! So now we have one teaspoon left, and that does execution for us all as a public stirrer, Samuel using it first, then I take it, then the mate, and so on down. It caused us a great deal of merriment at the table, but really I think it is no laughing matter. What we shall do when we have company is what troubles me.

JANUARY 23. Rugged and blowing fresh, so much so that it was not suitable to wash. Raised a ship in the morning to the windward. As he wished to speak to us, we hauled aback. About noon we spoke; found her to be the *Sea Gull,* Captain and Mrs. Nichols, sperm whaler. It was too rugged to gam, which disappointed us very much, as we were acquainted at home. They were bound up to French Rock. Mrs. Nichols and myself almost wore out our pocket handkerchiefs waving them.

JANUARY 24. A pleasant day, but a head wind. Improved the day by washing.

JANUARY 25. A fair wind. Made land today, the North Cape of New Zealand. About sunset raised a ship astern. In the evening saw a light on the shore which we supposed to proceed from a volcano or burning mountain.

JANUARY 26. A gale of wind and ahead, which makes Samuel look sober, as we have had a long passage and he is in great haste to get on whale ground. In the afternoon our three pigeons which the Damon boys gave Minnie flew from the ship, and the wind was so strong that they could not get back. We thought they were lost, but Samuel wore ship, and we fetched them. Right glad were they to get on board again, being much fatigued with their journey.

JANUARY 27. Raised a ship this morning, but as we were bound in opposite directions, we soon lost sight of her. Still rugged and a head wind.

JANUARY 28. The wind is not very strong today, but it is still ahead and quite rugged.

JANUARY 29. A fine day. The ship nearly heads her course for the first time in almost a week. Yesterday we had a large hog killed, and we all, fore and aft, have been indulging today in fresh pork.[9]

FEBRUARY 5. Nothing of note occurred during the week now past. We are having a long passage. When there is a breeze, we have always been favored with a head wind. Saw a brig several days since supposed to be bound into one of the New Zealand ports. The weather has been pleasant for the last week. Today we have a strong breeze amounting almost to a gale.

FEBRUARY 6. The gale still continues with squalls of rain at intervals. Mr. Baird has been confined to his room through the day with a cold. Spoke an English ship but could not make out her name; bound up to Cape Farewell. Had not seen a whale for some time. We had our stove put up once more, as the weather has become quite cool and uncomfortable.

FEBRUARY 9. The wind has blown strong through the week, first from one direction and then from another. Saw a ship this morning. Passed a carcass in the afternoon. Raised a ship just before dark. We were laying to; he was running before the wind. Spoke us as he passed; proved to be a large merchant ship, probably from Hobart Town or Sydney. A very strong breeze.

FEBRUARY 11. A furious gale from the westward about equal to those we experienced in Bristol Bay. If we can get our victuals to our mouths, we are fortunate. Before that we are not sure of them. Our cook was obliged to get two suppers tonight. In shipping a sea, everything was taken from the stove by the roll of the ship, fish, potatoes, meat, and coppers all rolling around the deck together. Such terrible times are not very common.

FEBRUARY 12. The gale still continues. It comes in squalls of wind and hail with great violence. Saw a sperm whale playing around the ship in the morning; nothing seemed to disturb him. Query: Would he have been so still had it been good weather? About noon it moderated a little. Raised land to the leeward, the Snares, as they are called, two small islands around which it is very good whale ground if we can only have the weather.

FEBRUARY 13. More moderate today but very rugged. Spoke the *Mary and Susan,* Captain Stewart; understood him to say that he had taken four whales and that his casks were full. He was here, I suppose, as much as a month before us. She was bound direct for New Bedford. Saw Mrs. Stewart and her little boy on deck. Captain Stewart said the whales were to the southwest of us.

FEBRUARY 14. Tried to get to the southwest today, but the wind not being fair, we made but little. Too rugged to lower even if we had seen whales. Had seven little pigs today.

FEBRUARY 15. Strong breezes today. We have gale upon gale in rapid succession. The mother pig ate up five of her children and the other two died, so we are as well off as we were before in that respect.

FEBRUARY 17. Raised a ship in the morning; spoke her about noon. She proved to be the *Eliza F. Mason,* Captain Smith; said he took two whales ten days since about here but had seen nothing since. He did very well here last season. He wanted Samuel to go on board, but he said he would lower for nothing short of a whale while it was so rugged. Mrs. Smith and child were on board.

FEBRUARY 18. We have been heading in towards the Snares to-day. Saw the *Eliza F. Mason* in company with another ship, gamming. If they had not been so far to the windward, Samuel would like to have joined them to gain what information he could in regard to whales. We have not seen a right whale yet and have been all over the ground. A fine, pleasant day, and a great pity that we could not have improved it by getting a whale; the pleasant days are so few. About sunset it commenced blowing again quite strong.

FEBRUARY 19. The wind blowing a gale. Saw the *Eliza F. Mason* in the morning. The gale continued to increase until, about noon, it blew furiously, the sea being a feather white. I believe it blew harder than anything we have had this voyage. Towards night it moderated some but continued to blow quite a hard gale.

FEBRUARY 20. More moderate. Made a little sail in the morning. Samuel would like to go in near the land to see if he can find a sperm whale. As the moon changes tomorrow, it is a good time. Raised the Snares in the afternoon. After tea witnessed a whirlwind, which appeared to be forming into a waterspout. It passed across our bows very rapidly. Heavy squalls of wind and rain during the day. Saw a ship in the morning.

FEBRUARY 21. Fine, clear weather; rugged, but would do to lower a boat in case we saw whales. Passed the Snares in the forenoon. Signalized a ship about noon, with Jonathan Bourne's signal;[10] supposed to be the *Washington*. Raised Stewart Island about noon. At 4 P.M. the ship hauled aback for us. She proved to be the *Marengo*, seven months from home with 400 barrels oil, Captain Weld, commander. He came on board and stopped to tea with us. Gave us several letters to take home in case he should not see us again.

FEBRUARY 22. Passed between Stewart Island and the Traps, a ledge of rocks seven or eight miles from shore. Spoke the *Marengo* in the afternoon. Samuel went on board and Mr. Eldredge, the mate, came here. He brought Minnie some lozenges that his little daughter Minnie put up for him. Captain Weld sent me some teaspoons, as he thought it was too bad that one solitary spoon should perform such a round of duty. He also sent us some reading matter. Saw one of our Falmouth men, John Green, fourth officer, from whom I gathered considerable information.[11]

FEBRUARY 23. Fine weather in the forenoon. A strong breeze after dinner which soon amounted to a gale. About 4 P.M. spoke the *Rambler;* had taken nothing since we saw him. Saw Mrs. Willis and the children. Afterward spoke the *Marengo* again. Minnie's pigeons flew on board the *Rambler* and did not return, as there was such a strong breeze. We saw them fly but thought nothing of it, as they had frequently flown on board other ships while we were speaking and immediately returned.

Minnie regretted the loss of them very much, but her papa tells
her that he will get her some more in Akaroa where we are now
bound.[12]

FEBRUARY 24. Raised the land in the vicinity of Akaroa about
3 P.M. A strong breeze in the morning, but moderated down in
the afternoon. After tea spoke the *Marengo*. Captain Weld came
on board and passed the evening.

FEBRUARY 25. We were within ten miles of Akaroa heads this
morning when the wind died away. *Marengo* near us and a
sloop in sight. About noon the wind breezed up, and we anchored in Akaroa Harbor about 4 P.M. The bay makes up eight
or ten miles so that the harbor is perfectly landlocked. It was
Saturday with us, but as we knew it was the Sabbath on New
Zealand, we took this day for our Sabbath. Quite a number of
boats came off to us, and I have had a very polite invitation
from the harbor master, Mr. Greaves, to go onshore tomorrow,
which I needed no urging to accept. One of the gentlemen
brought off a basket of peaches, which he presented us, and
several brought off apples, which were a great treat to us.[13]

FEBRUARY 26. This morning there was quite a row on deck. We
have been pumping oil for some days, and Samuel wished to
ascertain whether it was a general leak or whether a cask had
been stoven, so he told them to break out a little. The boatsteerer and eight or ten men that we shipped at the Islands
thought it was not their business to do it, as they had no share
in the oil, so refused duty. Samuel called them all aft, and after
some confusion and considerable noise, they all agreed to go to
work.[14]

About 10 A.M. we went onshore. Instead of Captain Greaves
taking us to his own house as we anticipated, he took us to the
house of Mr. White, the merchant of the place, where we were
very pleasantly received by Mrs. White. His is "the house" of
the place, adorned with lawns, walks, arbors, waterfalls, brooks,
caves, etc. Although it is but two years since he has lived there,
he has made many improvements. They have three children,
Mildred, Florence, and Constance, whose society Minnie enjoyed very much. She dined with the children in the nursery at

1 P.M. while we took a lunch. As their dinner hour was 6 P.M., we did not dine with them but returned on board about 3 P.M., as Samuel was anxious to be on board again. We visited their garden and orchard, ate our fill of peaches, which were very abundant, and brought a basket filled with them on board.

FEBRUARY 27. Samuel and Minnie went onshore early in the morning. I did not accompany them. Minnie took some peanuts and some little toys to the children, which pleased them very much. Whilst they were absent, a number of natives, Maoris as they are called, came on board. Some of them were frightfully tattooed, but I have seen natives who look much worse than the New Zealanders. A boy by the name of Willie Adams, who was off Sunday, came off today and brought me a basket of apples and peaches, a bouquet of flowers, and a bottle of milk. I gave him in return for his kindness some peanuts, oranges, and a book.

Samuel and Minnie returned about 3 P.M., bringing with them Captain Greaves and a Dr. Catling, who is quite a proficient in music, as Captain Greaves asked it of me as a privilege that he might bring him off—it would be such a treat to him to play on our melodeon, the only one they have onshore in the church being a very poor affair. The doctor played for the most of the afternoon and appeared to be much delighted with it, and we enjoyed the music much. They stopped with us until evening. I was quite well pleased with the appearance of the doctor. He is not long from England, belongs to the navy, and was engaged in the war of the Crimea. I should judge that he was a very talented man.

FEBRUARY 28. Samuel went onshore early in the morning for Captain Greaves, as he was going up the bay with him for potatoes. They returned before noon; stopped on board to dine. Then Samuel, Minnie, and myself accompanied him to his house, where we were very cordially received by Mrs. Greaves. She is a native of the West Indies, a Creole, but resided in New York for two years when a child. They have two children, Everett and Adele. We had a very pleasant visit at their house. Dr. Catling was there also.

Mrs. Greaves took us to the house of a French lady.[15] She

made considerable of me because I was acquainted with all the French whaling captains. We went there more particularly to visit their orchard, which consists of four hundred peach trees all borne down with fruit. Such a sight I never saw before. It looked wicked to see them lying upon the ground. We were feasted with peaches, currants, raspberries, and strawberries. They were engaged in making peach wine, which I was told was very nice. She kindly gave me some peaches to take on board.

Samuel visited another orchard with the gentlemen, where he bought some plums and gave the owner of the orchard five dollars to let his men go in and pick up as many peaches as they could carry away, which he agreed to do. We went on board about dark, well laden with fruit.

FEBRUARY 29. Went onshore quite early in the morning according to a previous agreement with Mrs. Greaves, as she was to walk out with me. Visited two orchards laden down with fruit. Nature has bestowed her gifts with a lavish hand in Akaroa. Every view is delightful. Ferns of every variety are abundant and grow to an enormous size.

The French lady whom we visited yesterday wished to get a pair of American shoes. I told her I had none to spare, but on looking over my shoes on my return, I found a pair that were too large, so I took them onshore and presented them to her. She was delighted with them and hardly knew what to do for me, so she told me that I must send three men up before I went on board. Then she went privately and got me a bottle of cherry wine, not wishing her husband to know it. When we returned, I found she had sent me a box of nice large peaches which she had gathered from the tree, a geranium and a fuchsia in boxes, both in bloom, and a bunch of herbs of various kinds. Many thanks to Madame Rosello and "Marmora." [16] We will drink her health in a bottle of cherry wine.

Mrs. Greaves had a very fine flock of fowls, and on Samuel's admiring the breed, she kindly gave him a flock[17] of them. We carried onshore some peanuts, oranges, books, papers, etc., as a present to them, and Mrs. Greaves in return gave Minnie a brooch of Parian marble and gave me a sack of lady's cloth which was made in England. We called during the day on Mrs. White. She gave me a cordial invitation to pass the day with her; said she wished very much to come on board but had not been well.

We returned to the ship about 5 P.M. Dr. Catling came with us. He appears to be a very pleasant man and a man of talent. I was sorry to learn his history. It seems that he has not much independence of character and has been led away by wild companions. On coming out to New Zealand, in a fit of intoxication, he married one of the steerage passengers on board the ship, a servant girl without education or refinement. When he came to himself, he was utterly overwhelmed and ever since until within a month or two has sought to drown his sorrows in the intoxicating bowl. Recently Captain Greaves has taken him in hand, and he has promised to reform. Oh, when I heard his history I was so thankful that he had not been tempted on board the *Addison*. He favored us with music for most of the evening, and after he had left, Samuel informed me that our melodeon was sold and he was to take it onshore tomorrow. It cost $71 and he has sold it for $125, a very good bargain. It seems like parting with an old friend, and I can hardly have the heart to tell Minnie; she has taken so much comfort with it. I gave the doctor some little curiosities, which pleased him very much.[18]

MARCH 1. This morning we sent a boat off for Mr. White, as he was coming to look at the slops.[19] When the boat returned, Minnie was delighted to find that he had brought Millie with him. She brought Minnie a basket of peaches and apples. We got a lunch about 10 A.M. for them, as they do not breakfast until that time, the two girls having a tea party by themselves in the stateroom. I find they all like our Yankee cooking, but they cannot understand how we can breakfast so early in the morning.

We then sent a boat onshore for Captain Greaves and family, who were coming to pass the day with us. They came in the return boat and brought a Miss Blackby with them; also, their servant girl. They appeared to enjoy their visit very much, and I tried hard to make it agreeable to them. Our folks had been fishing the day before, so we had a fish chowder for the first course, which was a new dish entirely to them all. I had to give them full instruction in the art of making chowders. The nicest way that they ever ate fish before, said they all. Then we had stewed pigeons with dumplings, gravy, etc., another Yankee affair, then a bread plum pudding. When we are among Romans we must do as the Romans do, so I did not have my tea made until we had got through dinner, then had it carried on deck and sipped it at our leisure. Captain Greaves brought a book, *Judah's Lion,* to Minnie; Mrs. Greaves brought one entitled *The Book and Its Story* to me.[20] I sold several articles to her that I could spare and gave her some little things which could not be obtained here.

In the afternoon Samuel and Captain Greaves went onshore with the melodeon. Minnie felt badly, but she had children on board to take up her mind. Her papa told her that he would take it ashore, and if they did not want it, he would bring it back again. When he returned and told her they wanted it, the tears started; but he told her we would soon be home and then he would buy her a new one, which soon pacified her. They were very much pleased with the instrument in the church; it is a far better-sounding instrument than they have had in Akaroa ever before.

MARCH 2. Samuel went ashore early in the morning to see if it was a good wind to go to sea. It requires a very good wind to go out. Some said they would not venture, but Captain Greaves said it was a good time; and as he is considered a very good pilot, he volunteered his services to go outside the heads with us, which Samuel very gladly accepted. They came on board about 9 A.M. The anchor was already up, and we soon started off, leaving the *Marengo* alone. Our crew gave three cheers as we were starting off.

I have said nothing about the *Marengo* for several days. When we first came in, Captain Weld came on board two or three times a day, but since that time I am sorry to record that he has taken to drinking so that he has not been himself for several days. Mr. Eldredge and Mr. Green [have] come aboard often. Mr. Eldredge brought me a tin of very nice huckleberries and some more lozenges for Minnie, and Mr. Green brought her a very pretty Western Islands basket. The doctor sent a box of peaches on board, a small sketch of Akaroa, and a jar of peach jam. Captain Greaves brought her a jar of prunes and brought a fancy shirt, or jacket, for me to present to Samuel from him when we were in warm weather, so now I hector Samuel with a very momentous secret I have entrusted to me, which will do to go with his Masonic secrets. We left Captain Greaves about 11 A.M. and thus bid farewell to Akaroa after a very pleasant sojourn of several days.

MARCH 3. A strong breeze nearly amounting to a gale. Moderated towards night.

MARCH 4. Nearly calm, beautiful weather; improved it by washing.

MARCH 6. A moderate breeze. Was employed during the morning in ironing. In the afternoon spoke the bark *Nimrod,* of Sag Harbor, Captain Green, fifteen months out with one sperm whale and one right whale, making in all 120 barrels. I felt that he was just sent to us that our murmurings might be quelled. We are very anxious and beginning to be discontented. We had hopes of doing something down here, and we have only seen one whale and that in a severe gale of wind. We have cruised all over good whale ground and have done all that we could do, but thus far it has been a failure. Samuel feels as if he could not stop here much longer but get around Cape Horn as speedily as possible and see if there may not be a barrel or two for us on the other side. Captain Green reported having spoke the *William Gifford* four days previous. Captain Baker took four whales on the northern New Zealand ground in November; has taken nothing since.

MARCH 7. Raised the Chatham Islands today. Saw Chatham, Pitt, and Round islands, also Solitary Rock, but saw no whales.

MARCH 8. A strong breeze with considerable rain. Caught several gonies today for their feet, which were very curious.

MARCH 9. Fair weather. Cruised in towards the land but saw nothing. About sunset, as we had a strong breeze with prospects of another gale, Samuel decided to give her sheet and let her go, so now we are in reality homeward bound. With what delight would I have hailed the sound had we taken three or four hundred barrels of oil and were I sure of meeting all whom I left behind; but that vacant chair rises before me, and my joy is changed to a flood of tears.

MARCH 10. A strong breeze, and we are on our way before it with all sail out, studding sails, etc., as if our good ship realized that we are going home.

MARCH 11. A gale of wind, but we are off before it almost flying through the waters. Made 224 miles the last twenty-four hours.

MARCH 12. A strong breeze with a heavy sea. Made 180 miles.

MARCH 13. A strong breeze as yesterday; fine, pleasant weather, being quite warm. Made 200 miles.

MARCH 14. A strong breeze and rugged with considerable rain; double-reefed the topsails and went before it.

MARCH 15. Pleasant weather with the wind nearly ahead. Found by observations that we had made 240 miles the last forty-eight hours. Jip the dog was taken vomiting this afternoon. Minnie administered a remedy in the form of two peppermint lozenges, which she believes had the desired effect.

MARCH 17. Quite moderate, cloudy weather. Made 240 miles in forty-eight hours.

MARCH 18. A strong breeze with a sea running mountain-high. Everything is on the move. The old *Addison* understands pitching, rolling, and all that sort of thing first rate. In such times our dishes particularly fare hard. Well, no matter, if we have enough to last us home. Made 200 miles the last twenty-four hours.

MARCH 19. Rugged with a strong breeze and a heavy, irregular sea; everything in commotion. Went 200 miles the last twenty-four hours.

MARCH 21. Rugged yesterday and cloudy with a strong breeze. Clear today but still rugged; 395 miles in forty-eight hours.

MARCH 22. Rainy but more moderate. Were unable to get observations.

MARCH 23. Clear and moderate. Embraced the opportunity of washing. Made 320 miles in forty-eight hours.

MARCH 24. Moderate with occasional rain squalls through the day. Having had a hog killed, we had a quantity of the meat chopped; and today I have been making it into sausage meat, filling eight good-sized bags. Made 140 miles the last twenty-four hours.

MARCH 25. Strong breezes with a heavy sea, the usual accompaniment here. From New Zealand to Cape Horn is a long tedious route, especially at this season of the year. As we were to have roast pork for dinner, I thought I would have a luxury in the shape of stewed apple for sauce, as we had a few apples left. So I prepared them, sent and borrowed a saucepan of the cook, stewed them very nicely, sweetened them, and was just preparing to take them up when there came an extra roll which was a little more than I could manage; and my applesauce was spattered all around on the cabin floor, and the saucepan went into the pantry. Consequently our dinner was eaten minus the apple. Made 194 miles the last twenty-four hours.

MARCH 26. Fine weather, but a heavy swell from the southward. They must have had a hard gale farther south than we are. Made 180 miles the last twenty-four hours.

MARCH 27. Quite moderate. Made 180 miles in twenty-four hours.

MARCH 28. Thick and rainy with a moderate breeze. Obtained no observations.

MARCH 29. Calm in the forenoon, dark weather with the barometer down very low. In the afternoon a severe gale sprang up very suddenly. We lay to twelve hours. No observations.[21]

MARCH 30. Good weather with a heavy sea, the effects of yes-

terday's gale. Found by observations we had made 480 miles
the last three days.

MARCH 31. Variable head winds and calms for the most of the
day. Pleasant with the exception of a snow squall just before
dark.[22]

APRIL 1. Minnie had been making great dependence upon this
day and was bitterly disappointed that it came on Sunday, but
she has made arrangements with some of the officers to postpone
it until tomorrow. Fine weather in the morning with a head
wind. One or two snow and hail squalls in the afternoon; head
winds and calms during the day. Made 100 miles on our course
for the last forty-eight hours.

APRIL 2. Fine weather but calm for the most of the day. Towards
night a slight breeze sprang up from the north. Had a very nice
day for washing, much finer than we could reasonably expect in
this region. Made 44 miles the last twenty-four hours.

APRIL 3. Weather the same as yesterday. Raised a ship on our
weather bow apparently steering to the north, a welcome sight.
We have been alone on the deep, as it were, for several weeks.
Made 86 miles in twenty-four hours.

APRIL 4. A fair wind once more; quite a strong breeze until
noon, when it moderated. Squalls of rain quite common during
the day. Made 150 in twenty-four hours. Saw another ship
today going as we are.[23]

APRIL 5. Fine weather in the morning. Saw a ship steering to
the northward. Towards night a strong breeze sprang up from
the south, which soon amounted to a gale, so that we were
obliged to lie to through the night. Made 56 miles the last
twenty-four hours.

APRIL 6. Very changeable weather. Calms, snow squalls, and
winds—or puffs, rather—from every point in the compass, not
more than ten minutes from any one direction. Saw three ships
in the morning, two headed to the north and one as we are.

Towards night we drew near enough to signalize and found it to be an Englishman. Made 38 miles the last twenty-four hours.

APRIL 7. The same weather as yesterday, very disagreeable, cold, snowy, and icy. Every hour or two during the day the decks have been covered with snow. Minnie enjoys it exceedingly in pelting with snowballs, though she always gets the worst of it. After dinner I went on deck during one of the squalls, and we all engaged in the amusement, both fore and aft. Our consort of yesterday was in sight for most of the day, but towards night we lost sight of him, as we took advantage of every minute of fair wind, which he did not. Made 70 miles in twenty-four hours.

APRIL 8. The same weather. Samuel is almost beside himself to be detained here, off Cape Horn of all places. Fortunately we have moonlight nights, which we hoped to have until we were out of danger from ice, but at this rate we shall hardly so do. We have very long nights here requiring lights below before five o'clock. The last remaining parakeet died today. We were sorry to lose him. The snow has fallen to quite a depth several times today. This morning it was over shoe. Made 48 miles the last forty-eight hours. Saw two ships this morning bound to the north in an opposite direction from ourselves.

APRIL 9. Calms and light winds from all directions during the day. Just before dark a strong breeze sprang up from the right direction for us, and we vainly thought it a commencement of better things, but it lasted only a few hours.

APRIL 10. Light winds and calms as usual. Very little snow has fallen for the last two days, but we have occasionally squalls of wind. Two ships in sight bound in opposite directions from ourselves. Made 220 miles in forty-eight hours.

APRIL 11. Light winds again. We suppose ourselves to be today off the Diegos, a group of islands to the southwest of Cape Horn. Made 70 miles the last twenty-four hours.

APRIL 12. A strong, delightful breeze sprang up last night, and we are flying through the water with all sail set as we have not done for the last two weeks. By observations today we have passed Cape Horn and are now in the broad Atlantic, whose waters wash the shores of our beloved home, which now seems very near. Saw one ship today under short sail trying to get to the southwest. That wind that is fair for us is ahead for him. Made 210 miles the last twenty-four hours.

APRIL 13. Light winds through the night, but a nice breeze during the day. Raised two ships in the morning bound in an opposite direction from ourselves, and about noon raised one bound as we are. Made 135 miles the last twenty-four hours.

APRIL 14. Fine weather with occasionally a snow squall. Raised three ships bound as we are. One of them outsails us. We keep up with the second and beat the third. Made 180 miles in twenty-four hours.

APRIL 15. A strong breeze with squalls through the night. The wind being aft, we went through the water at a very brisk rate. One ship in sight in the morning; passed her and was very soon out of sight. Made 235 miles the last twenty-four hours.

APRIL 16. A nice breeze, but cloudy the most of the day. Quite a heavy sea, and we are all sufficiently exercised by rolling. No observations today.

APRIL 17. Light winds, but fine, pleasant weather. There is quite a perceivable change in the atmosphere within a week. Made 330 miles the last forty-eight hours.

APRIL 18. A head wind from the northeast, which soon amounted to a moderate gale. Were under short sail or laying to the most of the day.

APRIL 19. A hard rainstorm part of the night; fine weather in the morning with a strong breeze. About noon it moderated. Afternoon calm with a heavy sea. Made 145 miles to the northward the last forty-eight hours.

APRIL 20. Quite a strong head wind with a heavy head sea. Samuel has been laid up today with a catch in his side which he has felt coming on for some days.

APRIL 21. Heavy squalls of wind and rain in the morning, accompanied by thunder and lightning. Mr. Baird prophesied a bad time, but fortunately the sun soon came out, dispersing the clouds, and the wind moderated, but the heavy sea continued through the day. Made 240 miles to the eastward the last forty-eight hours. Samuel has been flat on his back all day. Could not rise in bed without a severe catch. I have been applying hot cloths today.

APRIL 22. Pleasant the first part of the day. In the afternoon frequent squalls of wind, rain, and hail, accompanied by quite a severe thundershower, which lasted about two hours. Made 155 miles the last twenty-four hours.

APRIL 23. Quite a strong breeze through the night, but more moderate in the morning. Occasional squalls of rain through the day. Towards night a strong breeze sprang up from the southwest, which soon amounted to a gale; but as it was fair, we took in some sail and ran before it. Made 160 miles the last twenty-four hours.

APRIL 24. A hard gale through the night, and the old *Addison* rolled as hardly ever a ship rolled before. Every dish or article of furniture that could by any manner of means get out of place did so. Moderated towards morning and has remained so through the day, but there is still quite a sea. Made 180 miles the last twenty-four hours. Samuel has entirely recovered from his lameness and has been on deck the most of the day. The weather begins to feel quite warm again. Had our stove removed from the cabin today and have bid farewell to stoves and fires below for the remainder of the voyage.

APRIL 25. Fine weather with a moderate breeze. Sat on deck several hours with my work in the afternoon, the first time for a number of weeks.

APRIL 26. Quite a strong breeze. Samuel sat down last night to disadvantage, which brought on the catch in his side again so that he has been up but little today. Made 310 miles the last forty-eight hours.

APRIL 27. Nice weather, warm and pleasant. Sat on deck with my work most of the afternoon. One of our hens flew overboard while I was on deck and was very soon eaten by the birds. The wind has not been very fair today; the ship has hardly headed her course.

APRIL 28. Nice weather with quite a light breeze. After breakfast I had a general cleaning in the after cabin, which brought to my mind scenes of home, house cleaning. I do the cleaning in our own rooms usually myself, as I have thought that stewards and cabin boys generally make the paint and varnish look worse than before they commenced. Our dog Jip had a sort of a fit in the afternoon. We suppose it was caused by the change of weather. Minnie felt very badly for fear he would die. They showered him plentifully with cold water. At night he appeared rather better but was wild and easily frightened.[24] Made 197 miles the last forty-eight hours.

APRIL 29. In a few Sabbaths more, Providence permitting, we shall be in our own home, attend public worship in our own church, and enjoy many privileges from which we have been for so long deprived. May we enjoy them with thankful hearts. Some with whom we have passed many pleasant Sabbaths and many happy hours have gone before us to the spirit land. How we shall miss them.

We have very fine weather today—a nice breeze which Samuel thinks may be the trades. We are almost to the line, and home seems to be very near. Jip is better today; seems to have nearly recovered. Samuel's side is better also, but he cannot sit but a very few minutes at a time. Made 112 miles.

APRIL 30. Saw a ship in the morning bound in an opposite direction from ourselves. Fine weather with strong trade winds. About noon saw another ship coming towards us. After dinner we passed. Samuel chalked our longitude on our waist, hoping she would notice it and do likewise, but she took no notice of it. We signalized and found her to be the *Grimsbok* (bark), of Boston, a very pretty craft. Made 188 miles the last twenty-four hours. About sunset passed within two miles of a large merchant ship bound through the Indian Ocean.

MAY 1. Passed within two miles of a large ship in the night. Pleasant weather with moderate winds. Saw two ships during the day. Made 130 miles in twenty-four hours.

MAY 2. Saw a ship in the middle watch last night. Moderate winds, but fine weather. Made 123 miles in twenty-four hours.

MAY 3. Saw a ship in the morning. About noon raised the island of Trinidade, which Samuel wishes to make to prove his chronometer. Found her out of the way considerably. In the afternoon signalized an English ship and exchanged longitudes. Made 192 miles in twenty-four hours.

MAY 4. Fine weather as usual. Samuel commenced scrimshawing again for the first time after having a lame side. His work today was turning a bedstead for Minnie. The men are all engaged in fixing up the ship. They are now at work on the rigging. I made about twenty-five caps today for them to put on. I expect she will look quite nicely when she gets painted. The owners take a great deal of pride in having their ships to look well when they arrive. Made 215 miles the last twenty-four hours.

MAY 5.[25] Moderate winds. We get along very slowly. Still I can hardly realize that we are so near home. I am nightly with my friends in dreams and nightly see and converse with my dear father. I tremble when I think what other changes there may be in store for us. But the divine promise that "as our day is so shall our strength be" [26] is as true now as when first uttered if we will trust in Him "who doeth all things well." [27] Made 120 miles the last twenty-four hours. Raised a ship in the afternoon a long way ahead bound in the same direction as ourselves, which was thought might be a whaler.

MAY 6. Passed the ship about three o'clock A.M., which proved to be a merchantman. We left him in the distance a long time before noon. He must be a very dull sailer. Made 130 miles in twenty-four hours.

MAY 7. Fine weather as usual. Passed a ship last night in the first watch. I looked out the cabin window to see her by moonlight. A ship under full sail is a very grand sight, particularly by moonlight. Made 140 miles the last twenty-four hours.

MAY 8. Two ships in sight in the morning. Fine weather but very warm. Made 130 miles in twenty-four hours.

MAY 9. Saw a ship at a distance in the forenoon. The wind very moderate, making only 130 miles in twenty-four hours.

MAY 10.[28] Fine weather, but a very light wind and very warm. Made only 100 miles in twenty-four hours.

MAY 11. Made 108 miles in twenty-four hours. It takes us a long time to get to the line. At this rate we shall not be home before the middle of June.

MAY 12. This has been a very busy day. They have all been engaged in washing ship on deck, and the steward and cabin (or steerage) boy have been cleaning the forward cabin. I wiped up a little in my apartments, as I do every Saturday, but do not wish to clean for good until we get nearer home. I shall feel badly, after all, to give up my *Addison* home. It would be folly to think of spending four years less happily than the last have been spent, had it not been for the last sad home news that causes me to dread the thoughts of going home. Made 140 miles in twenty-four hours. Caught two porpoises in the afternoon and saw a few blackfish in the morning.

MAY 13. Crossed the line at noon today for the last time, making the sixth time on this voyage, twice in the Atlantic and four times in the Pacific.[29] Made 140 miles in twenty-four hours. Samuel sets today the twelfth June for us to arrive home. Mr. Baird sets the eleventh, Mr. Bowman the thirteenth, and Mr. Van Dorus the fifteenth.

MAY 14. Everybody has been engaged in washing ship outside today. I have been washing. Very warm in the forenoon, but in the afternoon it was some squally, and the wind hauled ahead.

MAY 20. For the last week all have been very busy washing and painting ship.[30] Have had fine breezes since the fourteenth, except that we could not head just as we wished for three or four days. The wind is more free now, so that we have studding sails out and going along finely. Made 190 miles the last twenty-four hours and 920 miles the last week.

MAY 21. Fine weather, but very warm, especially while washing. My washhouse adjoins the galley, so that I have the full benefit of the cook's fire. Made 175 miles in twenty-four hours.[31]

MAY 22. Employed in ironing today, doing up the shirts, collars, skirts, etc., and considered that I had very good success. Made 160 miles the last twenty-four hours.[32]

MAY 23. Today I have been engaged in cleaning Minnie's little room, the blue waters receiving many of her treasures which we thought of not sufficient value to take home. Although it is in the midst of house cleaning at home, I do not believe any of them had a warmer time than I had or that they perspired more than I. I need not do any of the cleaning, except that I do it from choice, as then I know it is clean. Made 110 miles this twenty-four hours.[33]

MAY 24. Saw a ship today supposed to be an Englishman. Fine weather as usual and moderate. Made 140 miles in twenty-four hours.

MAY 25. Saw a bark today (or brig, I should have written) bound probably to the West Indies. Very moderate, almost a dead calm, making only 85 miles in twenty-four hours. Weather extremely warm, the sun being directly overhead.[34]

MAY 26. Very moderate. Our good ship "just moving her slow length along." [35] Caught one fish today. Minnie raised three of them. They caught one and gave her for raising it. The cook fried it for her supper, and it was very nice. Made 108 miles in twenty-four hours. Lightning during the night.

MAY 27. A dead calm for the most of the day. Caught about two dozen fish of the kind called pall-fish,[36] the same as was caught yesterday. Got no latitude today owing to an error in time. Cleaned my room yesterday, probably for the last time except a few finishing touches.

MAY 28. Saw two schooners in the morning. Sent a boat on board one, hoping it might be a Yankee and we might get some late papers; but it proved to be the *Elizabeth*, of New Brunswick, bound to Barbados with a cargo of lumber. The captain said in reply to the question "Have you any late papers?" that they had neither a book nor a paper of any kind on board except one or two Bibles. The other schooner was several miles off. Made 170 miles in forty-eight hours.

MAY 29. The air close in the morning with some thunder. In the evening there were several clouds from which lightning proceeded incessantly with occasional peals of thunder, apparently at a great distance. The lightning was very sharp and lasted through the night. Made 75 miles the last twenty-four hours.

MAY 30. Commenced packing for home today. Packed a basket of books and three boxes of books and clothing. Home seems very near; it excites me very much to think of it. If I could only meet all of the dear family circle that I left behind, how joyful would be my anticipations. The weather is some cooler than it has been for a few weeks past. Made 148 miles the last twenty-four hours.

MAY 31. Last night we had thunder and lightning with occasional showers of rain through the night, the lightning very sharp and the thunder deep, but the clouds passed off without coming very near. Today the air is very pure and clear. Packed a box of preserved pineapple today. The wind is not as we would like to have it. We do not get to the westward as we would wish, but perhaps there will be a change by and by. Made 82 miles the last twenty-four hours.

JUNE 1. The first day of summer at home, but we have had summer for some time. I think we shall have no warmer weather at home than we have had here. Packed two large baskets today and filled the commode with light articles to take home in it. Passed a ship last night. Made 75 miles in twenty-four hours.

JUNE 2. Cleaned the after cabin and the water closet today, so that now my cleaning is completed. Also put the medicine chest in shipshape order. Saw a schooner and a ship in the afternoon. The ship was bound in an opposite direction from ourselves, the schooner the same as we were; but at sunset she took in sail, so we decided that she was a whaler cruising on this ground, but it appears to be a very dry spot just now. Nothing to be seen except gulfweed, of which there is an enormous quantity. Occasionally we get a few pieces for the hogs, hens, and ducks and often find them filled with crabs and very small fish. Made 90 miles in twenty-four hours.

JUNE 3. Cloudy in the morning with occasional peals of thunder. Commenced raining about 10 A.M. and continued in showers throughout the day. Consequently could get no observations.

JUNE 4. Pleasant weather. Washed today, probably for the last time on board the *Addison*. We have all set Saturday night or Sunday morning to get in, and I hope we may not be mistaken. In the afternoon I repaired a coat for Mr. Baird and mended one ensign which I think is a disgrace to our country. I have spent a good many hours in mending it on this voyage, but it is now almost past mending. Had plenty of thunder and lightning through the night. Made 165 miles in forty-eight hours.

JUNE 5. Ironed today and afterward had my ironing board taken on deck to the carpenter, as I considered that I had no further use for it. Had very sharp lightning through the night. Once the cloud was very near. Made 154 miles in twenty-four hours.

JUNE 6. Some rainy and quite cool today. Saw two ships and a schooner. Spent most of the day in sewing. Made 180 miles today. A strong breeze and quite rugged.

JUNE 7. A strong breeze and rugged. The wind is not very fair, the ship hardly heading her course. We have not gone as much to the westward lately as Samuel would like to have gone. Thunder and lightning again last night. I am very glad that it all comes in the night. Packed five trunks, a barrel, and two boxes today and in the afternoon washed all the dishes in the pantry, or rather scoured them. They are all white and get stained by use and not being properly washed. They look very badly. I have taken them in hand occasionally all the voyage. I also rubbed up all the spoons. I think I felt about as much fatigued when it came night as though I had been house cleaning at home. Made 178 miles in twenty-four hours.

JUNE 8. Today I have been cleaning lockers, drawers, etc., putting up the slops that we had below, etc. I have got everything about ready in my department, but the other rooms try me sorely. Our steward is no hand to clean and takes no interest in making things look nice. He goes through the ceremony of cleaning and that is all. Saw a brig in the morning, and a ship passed close to us in the afternoon. About 2 P.M. a strong breeze sprang up from the right direction, and we now feel as if we were going right into New Bedford. We are now in the Gulf Stream. Made 90 miles in twenty-four hours.

JUNE 9. A gale of wind from the northwest, directly ahead, sprang up about 6 A.M. after being calm all night. We had a great deal of lightning last night, but a little thunder. We were very much favored in that respect, as they often have very severe tempests in the Gulf Stream. I never saw such lightning before. The flashes would extend almost entirely around the horizon. This wind puts us all down. It changes the course of our proceedings altogether. Instead of being in New Bedford Saturday or Sunday, we are likely to be here some time longer. This is a time to cultivate the virtue of patience. Made 55 miles on our course in twenty-four hours.

JUNE 10. The gale still continues. We are under short sail and go first on one tack and then on the other but cannot carry sail enough to make much. We saw several outward bound ships yesterday going before it, and today we saw two like ourselves. This is real discouraging. It makes us all feel very badly to be so near home and making no headway, but probably it will all come out right at last. This is the Sabbath that we anticipated being at home. My books are all packed except my Bible, and even if they were not, I have read and reread them. It is unpleasant on deck, and I do not know what to do with myself. I lay down this forenoon to try to get a nap, but sleep would not come. After dinner I tried it again and was more successful, but I awoke with a headache and felt so stupid that I wished I had not attempted it. We have made 16 miles on our course the last twenty-four hours.

JUNE 11. The weather the same as yesterday, and our folks are all quite downhearted. Have been tacking all day in company with one bark, one brig, one schooner, and three ships. About noon spoke the bark, which we found to be the *Andes,* of Harpswell, bound to Boston. Made 35 miles on our course these twenty-four hours, having been able to carry a little more sail than the day previous.

JUNE 12. The wind fair in the morning but almost a dead calm. However, that is better than a head wind. Samuel set the thirteenth a long time ago to get in, and I will hold on to that a few hours longer. In the afternoon towards night the wind breezed up from the right direction, which gladdened us all. Saw several vessels during the day. Samuel thinks if this wind holds we shall make Block Island in the morning and get in by afternoon.

JUNE 13. Had a fine breeze through the night until about 4 A.M., when just as we made Montauk it died away calm. About 9 A.M. the pilot came on board. By that time we had given up all hopes of getting in today. This day drags very heavily.[37]

At 1 P.M. a slight breeze sprang up. Passed the schooner *B. C. Babcock,* of Egg Harbor. Saw a propeller and ships and small crafts too numerous to mention. The pilot could give us but very little news. Had not a paper on board and did not even know who were the candidates for the presidency.[38]

EPILOGUE

After the Voyage

The *Addison* anchored off New Bedford in the Acushnet River near Palmer Island at daylight on June 14, having followed the returning bark *Eliza* by a few hours and passed the outbound *Syren Queen*. The sails were furled for the last time, and the crew and cargo[1] were discharged. George Bowman left the ship at six that morning in one of the sharks' boats which met the ship, taking Minnie's dog Jip to Falmouth with him. Mrs. Lawrence and Minnie left the ship soon afterward and went directly to the home of George Chipman, the Lawrences' closest relative in New Bedford.[2]

Many changes had occurred in their absence. Hoop skirts were no longer the fashion, and probably Mary Lawrence's hoops were summarily discarded. As a defense against the critical eyes of passers-by she bought a stylish new hat on the evening of her arrival, but for girls of Minnie's age store clothes could not then be purchased, and the child in her old-fashioned dress was the object of many curious stares.[3] When the family reached Falmouth, they found that the First Congregational Church, with its Paul Revere bell, had been enlarged and moved intact across the village green. But other less obvious changes were occurring which were destined to bring to an end the New England whaling industry.

The Barnstable *Patriot* failed to report the return of the Lawrences, although it did contain a news item about Mrs. Lawrence's brother, Charles Chipman, who, as Captain of the Sandwich Guards, had had a prominent position in the 1860 Fourth of July parade. The same issue of the *Patriot* also answered the question implicit in the last entry of Mrs. Lawrence's journal. Abraham Lincoln and Hannibal Hamlin were the Republican nominees, opposing the Douglas, Breckinridge, and Bell tickets in the critical November election. The *Patriot* warned that the election of Lincoln would be fatal to the Union.[4]

This electoral campaign reflected a national conflict of economic, social, and political forces of which Samuel and Mary

Lawrence seem to have been hardly aware. The Dred Scott case had been decided by the Supreme Court in 1857. In 1858 the Lincoln-Douglas debates had taken place. In 1859 John Brown had attempted to seize the United States arsenal at Harper's Ferry and had been hanged. Shortly after the *Addison's* return the election of Lincoln precipitated Southern secession and confederation in 1861, and war followed.

Whalemen's newspapers took little notice of this succession of events, but they reported with understandable interest the drilling of the first oil well at Titusville, Pennsylvania, in 1859 and were confident that petroleum posed no competitive threat to the producers of the sweeter, nonexplosive whale oil.[5] War arrived almost unheralded by the Honolulu *Friend* and the New Bedford *Shipping List.*

"We left Honolulu for the last time, on this voyage at least," Mary Lawrence had written at the beginning of the seventh and last cruise of the voyage. But there would be no next time. In 1861 she was collecting stockings, blankets, and quilts for the ill-equipped men who had gone south in Captain Charles Chipman's company of Massachusetts Volunteers. In 1862, too old and perhaps too set in the ways of a ship's captain to begin again as a naval officer, Samuel Lawrence made a will and took command of the government steam transport *Tillie.* For the rest of the Civil War he carried men and supplies south to the embattled Union Army. On one such trip he met his brother-in-law, now Major Chipman, some time before Chipman was killed by a stray ball before Petersburg. Samuel had become a steamship captain and never again sailed tall ships.[6]

The Civil War dealt several severe blows to the whaling fleet. In 1861 the federal government purchased dozens of whaleships to sink at the entrances of the Confederate harbors of Charleston and Savannah. Manned by whaling captains and crews, the stripped ships were sailed south heavily ballasted with stone. The first "stone fleet" included many ships the Lawrences had known, among them the *Fortune, Contest, South America, L. C. Richmond, Harvest, Rebecca Sims,* and *Corea,* the last a venerable ship captured from the British fleet during the Revolutionary War. The *America, New England, Majestic,* and *Montezuma* were among the ships in the second stone fleet. Forty whalers perished in that operation.

In 1861, too, the first whalers were lost to Confederate privateers, and before the war was over, great columns of flame and the sooty smoke of burning whale oil marked the end of many New England investments. Confederate Navy cruisers operated mainly in the Atlantic Ocean, where departing and returning Pacific Ocean whalers had to run under their guns. The *Levi Starbuck* and the *Ocmulgee* were taken by the C. S. S. *Alabama* in 1862, and the *Golconda* was captured in 1864 by the C. S. S. *Florida*. But it was ruinous to the whaleship owners to keep the fleet in port.

The killing blow was struck by the C. S. S. *Shenandoah* in the Bering Sea in June, 1865, after the war had ended. Captain Waddell had not received the news of General Lee's surrender when he came upon the Arctic whaling fleet becalmed, and having placed the captains and crews aboard four bonded whalers (among them the *General Pike* and the *Milo*) and dispatched the four to San Francisco, he burned the dozens of unmanned ships. The *Congress 2nd, Covington, Euphrates, Jireh Swift, Nassau,* and *William C. Nye* were among them.

After the Civil War attempts were made to revive tall ship whaling from New England ports, despite the diminished fleet and growing competition from petroleum. Many of the surviving whalemen and whaleships sailed again for the old grounds, and frequently wives and children went along. Often these voyages were profitable, but bad fortune dogged the fleet.

During the summer season of 1871 the Bering Sea ice seemed unusually thick. The whalers, however, confident of their knowledge of Arctic conditions, followed the receding ice field closely through Bering Strait and on toward Icy Cape. Around Point Belcher the fleet anchored and commenced whaling. When the ice pack advanced toward their ships, they paid little attention to it, certain that it would retreat again. But it did not, and soon the fleet was trapped. When the ice pressed harder and the wooden hulls began to crumple, the whalers abandoned all thirty-four ships and rowed their whaleboats desperately for the few free ships far to the south. All of the crews and the women and children aboard were saved, but the ships were lost, among them the *Awashonks* (formerly Augustus Lawrence's ship), *Champion, Gay Head, George, J. D. Thompson, Reindeer,* and *William Rotch.* As if this catastrophe had not been enough, twelve more whalers, including the *Marengo* and *Onward,* were lost in a similar disaster in 1876.

New England whaling was all but at an end, but whalers, many of them steamships, continued operations from San Francisco, learning finally how to winter over in Arctic bays and inlets. Many of these ships were manned by New England crews. But the growing use of petroleum drove the whalemen from even this last outpost.[7]

In 1860, soon after the Lawrences' return, the *Addison* was rerigged as a bark, an arrangement of sails which allowed her to perform as effectively as before with fewer seamen. She was sent back to sea under a new captain the same year. By whaling carefully in the Pacific and Indian Oceans and shipping her bone and oil to England for sale, she was able to survive the wartime hazards with some profit. After this extraordinarily long voyage ended in 1867, she whaled twice more, once for only a year, and was then transferred back to the merchant trade from which she had originally come. She was lost off Fayal, the Azores, in 1875.[8]

The Lawrence brothers drifted rapidly away from whaling. In 1862 Thomas Lawrence completed the voyage mentioned in his sister-in-law's journal and gave up the sea to operate a general store and post office. Lewis Lawrence and his family made a last voyage aboard the *Ohio* in 1866, with his brother George as mate. On his return in 1871 Lewis entered the ice business. Both Lewis and Thomas became respected elder citizens of Falmouth, while George entered the merchant service and moved to New York. Samuel also continued to live by the sea but never again went whaling. After the Civil War he became a merchant captain for the Old Dominion Steamship Line and moved his family to Jersey City. He commanded in turn the *Hatteras, Albemarle, George W. Elder, Richmond,* and *Isaac Bell;* ultimately he became a senior captain of the line. In 1882 he retired from the sea to the company office ashore and moved his family to Brooklyn, New York.[9]

Samuel Lawrence died of asthma in Brooklyn on September

11, 1892, and Mary Lawrence followed him on March 3, 1906. She is remembered in those last years as a small, sweet, devout old lady with unshakable Christian principles and a ready wit. Electric lights and automobiles were common in Brooklyn, and gasoline could be purchased from pumps along the city streets when the aged Will Chipman arrived to help Minnie bring Mary Lawrence's body back to Falmouth.[10]

Minnie never married. She lived alone for several years after her mother's death before taking a position as a housekeeper to an elderly man in Mohawk, New York. A tall, dignified woman, she was remembered locally as a poet, author, raconteur, and friend of the writer Joseph Crosby Lincoln. She frequently held a landlocked audience entranced with her memories of adventure at sea and her descriptions of the strange sights and sounds and smells when the tryworks fires flickered in the night and the sailors sang hymns and chanteys on the decks of tall ships.

In 1920 George Bowman, haunted by the fear that he was the sole survivor of the whalers on which he had sailed, remembered Minnie and attempted to locate her, but whether or not he succeeded we do not know.[11] By this time the age of mass-produced automobiles had come, a world war had been fought, and the Jazz Age was in progress.

On April 9, 1923, Minnie died and was buried a few days later in Oak Grove Cemetery in Falmouth.[12] She lies there now among the other whaling Lawrences under a four-sided obelisk. On the four sides are carved these names: Augustus, Thomas, Lewis, and Samuel.

The last whaler, the bark *Wanderer,* sailed from New Bedford in 1924, and on the following day she was wrecked in a gale. The age of New England whaling had ended.

APPENDIXES

THE *ADDISON'S* TAKE

————————◆·◀◆▶·◆————————

The total quantities of oil taken during the voyage, compiled from Mary Lawrence's figures, were as follows: whale oil, 2,396 barrels; sperm oil, 60 barrels. Alexander Starbuck (in his *History of the American Whale Fishery from its Earliest Inception to the Year 1876* [2 vols.; New York: Argosy-Antiquarian, Ltd., 1964], I, 275) gives the following figures for this voyage: whale oil, 2,382 barrels; sperm oil, 60 barrels. Several factors may explain the small discrepancy between the figures for whale oil. Some oil was used during this voyage for trade and for shipboard illumination. Some may have been lost by leakage or evaporation. Aside from actual decreases in the quantity, an apparent loss might have occurred if Mrs. Lawrence rounded off her figures. Also, the sizes of the barrels may have varied so as to fit the curvature of the hold more compactly, whereas the figures used by Starbuck were determined by a gauger in port. He sounded the barrels to determine their actual content using a figure of 31.5 gallons per standard barrel (see "Gauges of Oil" in Stuart C. Sherman's *The Voice of the Whaleman with an Account of the Nicholson Whaling Collection* [Providence: Providence Public Library, 1965], pp. 54–55). The amount of bone shipped home, according to the available bills of lading, was 27,187 pounds.

The *Addison* account book in the Deacon Isaac Bailey Richmond Papers, property of Carleton R. Richmond, Little Compton, Rhode Island, gives $50,532.79 as the profit figure used in computing the lays of the crew, the latter amounting to 35 3/4 per cent of the profit. The total cost of fitting out the *Addison* for the voyage was $27,654.02

The *Addison's* take, compared with the figures for the average 1860 importations to New Bedford (derived from Volume II, Appendixes J and K of Starbuck) seems to have been about average or slightly above average. However, it is clear from the text that the Lawrences were disappointed with it. The agent's account book in the Richmond Papers shows that the *Addison's* profits were significantly lower than those of other I. B. Richmond ships, including the ship of Thomas Lawrence, the *Alto.*

CREW LIST OF THE *ADDISON*

———————————————

[This list was compiled from the following sources: one copy of the whalemen's shipping paper of the *Addison* in the Melville Whaling Room of the New Bedford Free Public Library, New Bedford, Massachusetts; the *Addison* account book, the agent's account book, bills of lading, and another copy of the whalemen's shipping paper, to which were attached certificates of discharge and engagement executed in the Sandwich Islands, from the Deacon Isaac Bailey Richmond Papers, property of Carleton R. Richmond, Little Compton, Rhode Island; the New Bedford whalemen's weekly newspaper, *Whalemen's Shipping List, and Merchant's Transcript;* Captain Samuel Lawrence's slop book, Falmouth Historical Society, Falmouth, Massachusetts; and the George Bowman Journal, Nicholson Collection, Providence Public Library, Providence, Rhode Island. Many crewmen, especially the Portuguese, shipped under assumed names. Their actual or alternate names and places of origin are given in parentheses. The salary figures in parentheses represent the actual money received after voyage expenses had been subtracted from the lay.]

APPENDIX B

INITIAL CREW

Name	Origin	Quality
Samuel Lawrence	Falmouth, Mass.	Master
Ebenezer Nickerson	Sandwich, Mass.	Mate
Robert D. Baxter	Falmouth, Mass.	Second Mate
William St. John	Burlington, Vt.	Third Mate Second Mate
James Gifford	Falmouth, Mass.	Boatsteerer
Narcisco Manuel (or Manuel Francis)	(Azores?)	Boatsteerer
Antone Jacinto	São Jorge, Azores	Boatsteerer
William F. Heughan	Calais, Me.	Boatsteerer
Thomas Conroy	New York, N.Y. (Ireland)	Cooper
Charles B. Beecher	Milton, Conn.	Second Cooper
Antone Lewis	———	Steward
Andrew Brinnell	———	Carpenter
John Gadson	New York, N.Y.	Cook
John White	———	Carpenter
William Johnson	Albany, N.Y.	Seaman
Willie Dermont	Copley, Ohio	Seaman
John Martin	———	Blacksmith
William Harding (Paul Joseph da Sylveira, or "Joe Portuguee")	(Pico, Azores)	Ordinary Seaman

Lay or Salary	Date Signed	Disposition
1/14 lay 2/16 owner	Nov. 24, 1856	Returned with ship
1/18 lay ($845.00)	Oct. 30, 1856	Discharged Oct. 1858
1/35 lay ($554.83)	Oct. 21, 1856	Discharged Nov. 1857
1/55 lay	Oct. 29, 1856 Nov. 3, 1857	Discharged Mar. 1858, sick
1/90 lay	Nov. 20, 1856	Discharged Mar. 1858
1/90 lay ($376.56)	Nov. 18, 1856	Discharged Apr. 1859, sick
1/90 lay ($376.84)	Oct. 8, 1856	Discharged Apr. 1859, sick
1/90 lay ($642.37)	Nov. 8, 1856	Returned with ship
1/55 lay ($918.61)	Oct. 30, 1856	Returned with ship
1/160 lay	Oct. 31, 1856	Discharged Nov. 1857, sick
1/135 lay	Oct. 25, 1856	Discharged Nov. 1858
1/175 lay	Oct. 29, 1856	Deserted prior to sailing
1/175 lay ($31.85)	Oct. 30, 1856	Discharged Apr. 1857, sick; died in Sandwich Isls.
1/175 lay	Nov. 25, 1856	Deserted Nov. 1857
1/150 lay	Nov. 4, 1856	Discharged Nov. 1858
1/150 lay	Nov. 20, 1856	Discharged Oct. 1857, sick
1/175 lay ($31.85)	Nov. 6, 1856	Discharged Apr. 1857, sick
1/175 lay ($288.71)	Nov. 3, 1856	Returned with ship

APPENDIX B

INITIAL CREW

Name	Origin	Quality
Walter A. Seals	Alexandria, Va.	Ordinary Seaman
Edward Leighton	St. Johnsbury, Vt. (London, Eng.)	Green Hand Boatsteerer
James Wilson (John Joseph, or "Cisco")	Newark, N.J. (Azores?)	Green Hand
Francis Finley (Antone Jacinto, or "Boy Antone")	Lewiston, Me. (Azores?)	Green Hand
James Haight (Francis Lavarez, or Vara)	Exeter, N.Y. (São Jorge, Azores)	Green Hand
Richard Greene (Manuel Joachim)	Flushing, N.Y. (Santa Maria, Azores)	Green Hand
William S. Weeks (John Cardosa de Leamas)	Tisbury, Mass. (Flores, Azores)	Green Hand
Joseph C. Avery (John Sylvia?)	New York, N.Y.	Green Hand
Joseph Whitman	Greene, N.Y.	Green Hand
Bernard Fallon	Salem, Mass.	Green Hand
Charles W. Brown	Calais, Me.	Green Hand
James McElwee	Calais, Me.	Green Hand
Thomas C. Weeks	Concord, N.H.	Green Hand Cook
William Maxon	Scruple, N.Y.	Green Hand
George F. Cornell	New Bedford, Mass.	Boy

ADDED APRIL 1857

James Smith	——	Cook

Lay or Salary	Date Signed	Disposition
1/175 lay	Nov. 17, 1856	Deserted Nov. 1857
1/200 lay 1/90 lay ($252.61)	Nov. 4, 1856 Dec. 1859	Returned with ship— "good man"
1/225 lay ($224.55)	Nov. 3, 1856	Discharged Nov. 1859— "good man"
1/225 lay ($82.08)	Nov. 3, 1856	Drowned Dec. 28, 1857
1/225 lay ($175.00)	Nov. 3, 1856	Drowned Sept. 2, 1859
1/215 lay ($234.99)	Nov. 3, 1856	Returned with ship
1/250 lay ($202.09)	Nov. 3, 1856	Returned with ship
1/200 lay	Nov. 4, 1856	Deserted Apr. 1857
1/200 lay	Nov. 6, 1856	Deserted Nov. 1857
1/200 lay ($252.61)	Nov. 17, 1856	Returned with ship— "good man"
1/200 lay	Nov. 20, 1856	Deserted Nov. 1857
1/215 lay	Nov. 20, 1856	Deserted Nov. 1857
1/200 lay slush added ($252.61)	Nov. 20, 1856	Returned with ship— "good for nothing"
1/200 lay	Nov. 24, 1856	Discharged Nov. 1857
1/300 lay ($175.90)	Nov. 19, 1856	Returned with ship— "good boy"
1/100 lay 1.5 seasons 1/80 lay	Apr. 1857 Oct. 1857	Discharged Nov. 1858

APPENDIX B

Name	Origin	Quality
Kupihi (Kepuhi?)	Sandwich Isls.	Seaman
Miro Kanaka	Sandwich Isls.	Seaman

ADDED OCTOBER 1857

Michael Chappell	——	Third Mate Second Mate
Andrew Sylva	——	Cook
Joseph Brador	——	Seaman
William Makapapa (Makapuu?)	Sandwich Isls.	Seaman
Bill Kaoao (Kauai?)	Sandwich Isls.	Seaman
Harry Kaiewa (Kaiwi?)	Sandwich Isls.	Seaman
Samuel Pahukula (Pohakuloa?)	Sandwich Isls.	Boy
John Boy Kama (Kaimu?)	Sandwich Isls.	Seaman
William Kalama	Sandwich Isls.	——
Charlie Kema (Kaimu?)	Sandwich Isls.	——
Jack Kanialama	Sandwich Isls.	——

ADDED MARCH 1858

James N. Brown	——	Third Mate

APPENDIX B

Lay or Salary	Date Signed	Disposition
1/130 lay 1 year	Apr. 1857	Discharged Oct. 1857
1/130 lay 1 year	Apr. 1857	Discharged Oct. 1857
1/30 lay season	Oct. 1857	
1/25 lay season	Mar. 1858	Discharged Nov. 1858
1/100 lay ½ slush	Oct. 1857	Did not sail
1/120 lay 1 year	Oct. 1857	Discharged Mar. 1858, sick
1/140 lay 1 year	Oct. 1857	Discharged Oct. 1858
1/140 lay 1 year	Oct. 1857	Oct. 1858
1/140 lay 1 year	Oct. 1857	Discharged Oct. 1858
1/150 lay 1 year	Oct. 1857	Discharged Oct. 1858
1/140 lay 1 year	Oct. 1857	Deserted Feb. 19, 1858, Marquesas
———	Oct. 1857	Died Oct. 11, 1858
———	Oct. 1857	Discharged Oct. 1858
———	Oct. 1857	Discharged Oct. 1858
1/35 lay season	Mar. 1858	Discharged Nov. 1858

APPENDIX B

Name	Origin	Quality
John Scott	Ireland	Seaman
Robert Harrigan	———	Seaman
Matthew (Nathan?) Hart	———	Seaman
Johnny Maui Kaava	Sandwich Isls.	———
George Kamimi	Sandwich Isls.	———
Ropeyarn Nawiliwili	Sandwich Isls.	———
Abraham Kawaihau	Sandwich Isls.	———
Johnny Teapot Kaiwi	Sandwich Isls.	———

ADDED OCTOBER/NOVEMBER 1858

Name	Origin	Quality
Henry Franklin Forsyth	———	Mate
Adrastus (E. B.) Huntley	———	Second Mate First Mate
John H. Parker	Sandwich, Mass.	Third Mate Second Mate
Thomas Crocker	———	Fourth Mate
Old Jack Boatsteerer	———	Boatsteerer
John Jones	———	Seaman/Boatsteerer
John Brown	———	Cook
Henry Drew	———	Steward

Lay or Salary	Date Signed	Disposition
1/130 lay season	Mar. 1858	Discharged Nov. 1858
1/130 lay season	Mar. 1858	Discharged Oct. 1858
1/130 lay season	Mar. 1858	Discharged Nov. 1858
————	Mar. 1858	Discharged Oct. 1858
————	Mar. 1858	Oct. 1858
————	Mar. 1858	Discharged Oct. 1858
————	Mar. 1858	Discharged Oct. 1858
————	Mar. 1858	Discharged Oct. 1858
1/18 lay and other considerations	Oct. 1858	Discharged Apr. 1859
1/25 lay season	Oct. 1858	
1/18 lay	Apr. 1859	Discharged Dec. 1859
1/35 lay season	Oct. 1858	
1/28 lay ($384.12)	Dec. 1859	Returned with ship—"good second mate but sickly"
1/55 lay season	Nov. 1858	Discharged Dec. 1859
1/60 lay season	Nov. 1858	Discharged Dec. 1859
————	Dec. 1858	Discharged Mar. 1859
1/90 lay season	Oct. 1858	Discharged Apr. 1859, sick
1/90 lay voyage	Nov. 1858	Discharged Dec. 1859

APPENDIX B

Name	Origin	Quality
John Davy	Bathurst, N.B.	Carpenter
George C. Adams Kama (Kaimu?)	Sandwich Isls.	Seaman
Thomas Gonzales	———	Seaman
Jack Malay	———	Seaman
George Hall Makalapa	Sandwich Isls.	Seaman
Long Bill Puuloa	Sandwich Isls.	Seaman
Jack Kanekolohi (Kauno-o-Kaleioohie?)	Sandwich Isls.	Seaman
John Kou (Kau or Koa?)	Sandwich Isls.	Seaman
Ben Pencamimi	Sandwich Isls.	Seaman
John Coffin Kahiokii (Keokea or Kauiki?)	Sandwich Isls.	Seaman
George Kahului	Sandwich Isls.	Seaman
Tom Waihalulu (Wailuku?)	Sandwich Isls.	Seaman
Jack Keliikomu	Sandwich Isls.	Steerage Boy
Johnny Boy	Sandwich Isls.	———

ADDED APRIL 1859

Alonzo Jackson	———	Second Mate

APPENDIX B

Lay or Salary	Date Signed	Disposition
1/120 lay voyage	Nov. 1858	Returned with ship— "not good for much"
1/140 lay season	Nov. 1858	Discharged Nov. 1859
1/130 lay season	Nov. 1858	Discharged Dec. 1859
1/145 lay season	Nov. 1858	Discharged Dec. 1859
1/140 lay season	Nov. 1858	Discharged Dec. 1859
1/140 lay season	Nov. 1858	Discharged Dec. 1859
1/140 lay season	Nov. 1858	Dec. 1859
1/140 lay season	Nov. 1858	Discharged Dec. 1859
1/140 lay season	Nov. 1858	Discharged Dec. 1859
1/140 lay season	Nov. 1858	Discharged Dec. 1859
1/140 lay season	Nov. 1858	Discharged Dec. 1859
1/140 lay season	Nov. 1858	Discharged Dec. 1859
1/150 lay season	Nov. 1858	Discharged Dec. 1859
———	Nov. 1858	Oct. 1859
1/25 lay season	Apr. 1859	Discharged Nov. 1859

APPENDIX B

Name	Origin	Quality
Joseph Enos	———	Boatsteerer
Jack Boatsteerer	———	Boatsteerer
Manuel Tiscara	———	Seaman
Joe Sylvia	———	Seaman

ADDED NOVEMBER/DECEMBER 1859

Marcus Baird	Brooklyn, N.Y.	Mate
George L. Bowman	Falmouth, Mass.	Third Mate
William Van Dorus	New London, Conn.	Fourth Mate
Harrison Green	Vermont	Boatsteerer
Daniel Crilly	Lowell, Mass.	Steward
Hiram John Neal	Vienna, Me.	Seaman
Michael Killeen	Philadelphia, Pa.	Seaman
Abram McFarlane	Saratoga, N.Y.	Seaman

Lay or Salary	Date Signed	Disposition
1/90 lay voyage ($124.85)	Apr. 1859	Returned with ship
1/80 lay season	Apr. 1859	Discharged Oct. 1859
1/135 lay season	Apr. 1859	Discharged Dec. 1859
1/135 lay season	Apr. 1859	Discharged Dec. 1859
1/20 lay, $30 per month ($211.00)	Nov. 1859	Returned with ship— "good first mate"
1/45 lay, $5 per month ($32.33)	Nov. 1859	Returned with ship— "a good third mate"
1/50 lay (none)	Dec. 1859	Returned with ship— "make a good third mate"
1/80 lay, $10 per month ($66.30)	Nov. 1859	Returned with ship— "don't want him"
$12 per month ($86.00)	Nov. 1859	Returned with ship
1/150 lay, $5 per month ($32.50)	Nov. 1859	Returned with ship— "good boy"
1/150 lay, $5 per month ($34.33)	Nov. 1859	Returned with ship— "bad"
1/150 lay, $5 per month ($34.33)	Nov. 1859	Returned with ship— "rascal"

APPENDIX B

Name	Origin	Quality
Charles Granger (John H. Noya?)	(Flores, Azores?)	Seaman
Thomas Addison (Davis?)	(Philadelphia, Pa.?)	Seaman
Jonathan H. Northrop	——	Seaman
William King	——	Seaman
Daniel Jourdon	——	Seaman
Charles H. Arnold	——	Seaman
G. S. Codington	——	Seaman
James Doane	Providence, R.I.	Seaman
Alfred Maxwell	Rio de Janiero, Brazil	Seaman
John de Freitas	Pico, Azores	Seaman
Cornelius Relyea	New York	Seaman

APPENDIX B

Lay or Salary	Date Signed	Disposition
1/150 lay, $5 per month ($34.33)	Nov. 1859	Returned with ship— "good man"
1/150 lay, $5 per month ($34.17)	Nov. 1859	Returned with ship— "fair"
1/150 lay, $5 per month ($33.50)	Nov. 1859	Returned with ship— "fair"
1/150 lay, $5 per month ($33.50)	Nov. 1859	Returned with ship— "troublesome"
1/150 lay, $5 per month ($33.50)	Nov. 1859	Returned with ship— "good man"
1/150 lay, $5 per month ($33.50)	Nov. 1859	Returned with ship— "good man"
1/150 lay, $5 per month	Dec. 1859	Did not sail
1/150 lay, $5 per month ($33.50)	Nov. 1859	Returned with ship— "fair'
1/140 lay, $5 per month ($33.50)	Nov. 1859	Returned with ship— "good man"
1/140 lay, $5 per month ($34.33)	Nov. 1859	Returned with ship— "good man"
1/140 lay, $5 per month ($33.50)	Nov. 1859	Returned with ship— "good man"

LIST OF SLOPS AND TRADE ITEMS
CARRIED ON THE *ADDISON*

———————◆ ◄◆► ◆———————

[This list was taken from the *Addison* account book in Deacon Isaac Bailey Richmond Papers, property of Carleton R. Richmond, Little Compton, Rhode Island.]

SLOPS FOR SALE TO THE CREW AND OTHERS

Quantity	Item	Cost Per Item	Sale Price Per Item
50 pairs	Extra brogans	$1.15	$1.75
100 pairs	Thick pumps	.93	1.50
100 pairs	Denim pants	.45	.88
50 pairs	Duck pants	.65	1.12
36 pairs	Duck frocks	.63	1.12
12 pairs	Denim frocks	.45	.88
100	Striped cotton shirts	.45	.88
48	Calico shirts	.50	1.12
12	Calico shirts, extra, done up, in box	1.25	2.00
12	Extra heavy wool frocks	.92	1.50
36	Heavy wool frocks	.79	1.50
24	Russia caps wool lined	.79	1.50
24 pairs	Double mittens	.21	.38
96 pairs	Heavy yarn socks	.29	.50
24	Neck comforters	.21	.38
12	Shields caps	.15	.38
5 pounds	Yarn	.95 (pound)	.33 (skein)
18 pairs	Blankets	1.92 (pair)	1.92 (each)
20	Monkey jackets	3.60	6.50
20	Reefing jackets	3.20	5.75
60 pairs	Satinet pants, assorted	1.40	2.50
20 pairs	Vermont pants	1.60	3.00
20	Kersey wide stripe heavy shirts	1.10	2.00
72	Kersey dark and light stripe shirts	1.05	2.00
12	Striped kersey undershirts	.70	1.25
75 pairs	Striped kersey drawers	.70	1.25
24	Palms	.12	.25

24		Belts and sheaths	.12	.25
12		Coarse combs	.08	.20
12		Fine combs	.08	.20
12 pairs	Braces	.11	.25
24		Iron spoons	.04	.10
24		Coconut handle sheath knives	.13	.33
72		Jack knives	.23	.38
6 pounds	Linen thread	.75	1.50
12 pairs	Shears	.23	.50
12		Cotton kerchiefs	.11	.25
250		Needles	.12½ (per hundred)	.12 (paper)
1 paper	Darners	.25	.02 (each)
24 pairs	Thick boots	2.42	3.75
24		Tar hats	.29	.62
36		Palm hats	.15	.33
12		Southwesters	.40	.75
36		Tin pots	.12	.25
36		Tin pans	.12	.25

OLD SLOPS LEFT OVER FROM THE PREVIOUS VOYAGE

18		Bed comforters	.75	1.50
4 pairs	Blankets	1.92 (pair)	1.50 (each)
1 pound	Yarn	.98	1.50
6		Jack knives	.23	.38
6 pairs	Stockings	.29	.50
20 pairs	Shoes	.93	1.50
4 pairs	Slippers	.75	1.00
1		Monkey jacket	3.60	6.00
4		Vests	.75	1.00
7		Wool shirts	1.00	1.50
40		Calico shirts	.50	1.00
9		Shields caps	.15	.30
4 pairs	Braces	.11	.25
1		Denim frock	.45	.92
3 pairs	Duck trousers	.65	1.00
2½ dozen	Cotton kerchiefs	.75 (dozen)	.17 (each)
10 pairs	Denim pants	.45	.88
5		Striped cotton shirts	.45	.88
8		Spoons	.04	.08
1		Palm	.12	.25

SLOPS PURCHASED DURING THE LAST YEAR OF THE VOYAGE

121 pounds	Tobacco	.25	.50
115 pounds	Tobacco	.20	.40

10		Sheaths and belts	.25	.40
12 pairs		Stockings	.75	1.00
12		Wool shirts	1.75	2.50
24 pairs		Drawers	1.25	1.75
24		Undershirts	1.25	2.00
12		Red shirts	1.50	2.50
40 pairs		Brogans	1.75	2.50
12 pairs		Mittens	.67	1.00
11 pairs		Oil pants	2.50	3.50
10		Oil coats	2.50	3.50
9 pairs		Thick boots	4.50	6.00
18 pairs		Stockings	.34	.50

CONSUMABLES AND TRADE ITEMS CARRIED

100 pairs bleached jean pants
Portland wide bleached cotton cloth
Washington wide bleached cotton cloth
Passaic prints
Atlantic prints
Newburgh prints
Lodi prints
Cohoes prints
Canary prints
Plain shade orange, red, and green print
1 bale brown cottons
Blue drills
2 boxes pipes
24 hatchets
18 axes
1 barrel oil soap
1000 pounds white lead
39½ gallons linseed oil
4 boxes sperm candles
4 cases matches
1 cask saleratus
20 boxes tobacco, "Jones" and "Salmon"
116 pounds olive soap
616 pounds salt water soap
580 pounds No. 1 soap
12 narrow axes

LIST OF IDENTIFIABLE MEMBERS OF THE LAWRENCE AND CHIPMAN FAMILIES MENTIONED IN THE JOURNAL

[This list was compiled from Mary Lawrence's listing of relatives in Captain Samuel Lawrence's slop book and from Amelia Lawrence's genealogical notes in papers of Lewis Lawrence, grandson of Samuel Lawrence's brother, Lewis Henry Lawrence, Falmouth Historical Society, and from information copied from gravestones in the Oak Grove Cemetery in Falmouth, Massachusetts, and several cemeteries in Sandwich, Massachusetts. When known, years of birth and death have been given and also information about these relatives for the period during which Mrs. Lawrence was writing her journal.]

CAPTAIN SAMUEL LAWRENCE'S BROTHERS AND SISTERS AND THEIR FAMILIES

Joseph Lawrence (1812–ca. 1865). Living in Napa, California
  Harriet Taber
    George Willard Lawrence (1844–?)
    Martha D. Lawrence (?–1854)
Celia Dimmick Lawrence (1814–1907). Living in Falmouth
  Samuel P. Bourne (1804–1873). An officer of the Falmouth bank
    Celia Maria Bourne (1835–1858)
    Mary Stuart Bourne (1840–1841)
(Samuel Lawrence [1818–1892])
Augustus Lawrence (1819–1856)
  Sarah Price Robinson (1825–1898). Living in Falmouth
    William ("Willie") Lincoln Lawrence
    Martha Dimmick Lawrence (1855–1889)
Thomas Hanscome Lawrence (1821–1896). Captain of the *Alto*
  Mercy Bassett Dimmick (1828–1886). Aboard the *Alto*
    Fanny Dimmick Lawrence
    Mary Stuart Lawrence (1854–1879)
    Amelia Hanscome Lawrence (1857–1957)
Lewis Henry Lawrence (1823–1901). Captain of the *Commodore Morris*
  Eunice Freeman Davis (1829–1908). Aboard the *Commodore Morris*

Samuel Bourne Lawrence (1854–1882)
Augustus Lawrence (1857–1929)
Charles Grant Lawrence (1859–1860)
George Swift Lawrence (1826–1898). Second mate of the *Harvest*

MARY CHIPMAN LAWRENCE'S BROTHERS AND SISTERS AND THEIR FAMILIES

James Freeman Chipman (1825–?)
  Anna D. Reed
    Anna Abby Chipman (1856–1856)
(Mary Chipman [1827–1906])
Charles Chipman (1829–1864). Living in Sandwich and Taunton
  Elizabeth ("Lizzie") Freeman Gibbs (1829–1920)
    Grace Walter Chipman (1856–1856)
    Edward C. Chipman (1859–1886)
George Nye Chipman (1832–?). Clerk of the U.S. supply steamer
  Guthrie, based in New Bedford
  (Mary?)
Henry Oscar Chipman (1834–1838)
Walter Merrick Chipman (1837–?). Apparently lost at sea
William ("Willie") Nye Chipman. Living in Sandwich
Cynthia Bassett Chipman (1843–1877). Living in Sandwich
Anne ("Annie") Read Chipman (1846–1853)

OTHER RELATIVES

Thomas Lawrence (1779–1856). Samuel's father
  Martha Dimmick (1789–1828). Samuel's mother
Susan Lawrence (1785–1875). Samuel's aunt, living in Falmouth
Jonathan Ellis Chipman (1803–1859). Mary's father, living in Sandwich
  Celia Bassett (1805–1873). Mary's mother

GLOSSARY OF WHALING AND NAUTICAL TERMS

---◆•◄◆►•◆---

[Excerpts from *A Good Catch; or, Mrs. Emerson's Whaling-Cruise* by Mrs. Helen E. Brown (Philadelphia: Presbyterian Board of Publication, 1884) have been used in some of these definitions.]

BARK: A sailing vessel so rigged that her two forward masts carry square sails and her aftermast carries fore-and-aft sails. A bark sails nearly as fast as a comparable SHIP but with the economy of a smaller crew, and for this reason the *Addison* was converted to bark rig immediately upon her return to New Bedford.

BEAT: To tack back and forth across the desired direction of advance to gain distance against an unfavorable wind.

BINNACLE: A case, box, or stand containing a ship's compass and a lamp for use at night.

BLACKFISH: A very small whale related to the dolphin, occasionally taken for its oil in DRY periods.

BLUBBER ROOM: A space below the weather deck for stowing large pieces of blubber ("horse pieces") and mincing them (into "bible leaves") for the TRYWORKS.

BOATSTEERER: A minor ship's officer. Several were "appointed—and, indeed, hired—for the purpose before sailing from home. They must be responsible men, strong, clear-headed and prompt; for the boat-steerer is harpooner as well as steerer, and sits in the bow [of the WHALEBOAT], with his tub at his feet, the harpoon and two or three coils of rope ready to be seized at the right moment."—*A Good Catch*, p. 65.

BOWHEAD: An arctic right whale. It is found in the Bering, Okhotsk, and Arctic waters and has a very large head which yields baleen, or whalebone.

BRIG: A two-masted, square-rigged sailing vessel. A hermaphrodite brig also has two masts: her forward mast is square rigged and her aftermast is rigged fore and aft.

CALIFORNIA GRAY: A small, difficult-to-catch, dangerous whale with wrinkled skin found from Arctic waters to Lower California. Also referred to by Mrs. Lawrence as MUSSEL DIGGER, DEVILFISH, and RIPSACK.

CLEAN: No oil yet taken.

CLIPPER: A vessel with a long, narrow hull, overhanging bow, tall masts, and a large sail area, known for its great speed. Clippers were developed in the 1840's for fast shipment of cargo. A small clipper such as the *Speedwell,* the *Gay Head,* or the *Eliza F. Mason* was sometimes used for whaling and was rigged as a BARK or a SHIP.

COOLER: A kettle in which the hot oil was allowed to cool before being pumped into barrels.

CRUISE: A single sailing to a whaling ground and the subsequent return to port to RECRUIT. A VOYAGE is usually made up of several cruises.

CUT: A successful catch of whales.

—To give up a whale chase by severing the line attached to the IRON embedded in the whale.

CUT IN: To peel the blubber from a whale. "The whole ship was in a commotion now. Every available hand was busy; Minnie and her mother alone were spectators of the scene. The captured whale was towed to the ship, its huge body made fast to the vessel by chains, then the cutting-in process was begun. Some of the men with sharp knives and cutting-spades proceeded to cut through the thick black skin, while others manned the tackles and stripped and hoisted the long strips of blubber to the deck. Here they were cut into smaller pieces and put into the try-pots, and the oil was tried out and strained into barrels."—*A Good Catch,* p. 70.

CUTWATER: The foremost part of a vessel's prow, which projects forward of the bow.

DEADLIGHT: A covering placed over a ship's porthole to protect it in stormy weather.

DEVILFISH: *See* CALIFORNIA GRAY. This is an extraordinary use of the term, which usually denotes an octopus or a kind of ray.

DRY: Without oil.

DRY-SKIN: A whale which yields little or no oil.

DUFF: A pudding frequently served aboard whaleships. It was made of "flour, water, yeast, and raisins or cranberries, steamed in a bag and served with molasses."—Emma Mayhew Whiting and Henry Beetle Hough, *Whaling Wives* (Boston: Houghton Mifflin Co., 1953), p. 210.

FINBACK: A large rorqual whale with a dorsal fin, also known as a finner; a whalebone, or baleen, whale found from Arctic waters to California.

FIN OUT: Of a whale, to roll over after death.

FLUKES: A whale's tailfins.

FLYING COLORS: A flag display signaling success; in whaling it means that a ship's holds are full of casks of oil.

FORECASTLE: The forward part of the ship. Here it means the seamen's quarters under the forward deck. The entire body of seamen were often referred to as "the forecastle." An officer would live in a stateroom or cabin and a BOATSTEERER or other specialist in the STEERAGE. During a long VOYAGE a man might be promoted from forecastle to steerage, or from steerage to stateroom (as was George Bowman upon signing aboard the *Addison*).

GALLY: To frighten a whale.

GAM: " ' "Gamming"?' laughed Minnie. 'What's that, papa?'

" 'That's the sailor's word for "visiting," chicken.'

" 'Why, how can you visit on the water? Will his ship come close up to your ship?'

" 'Dear, no! We'll get into our boat and row over to his ship, and perhaps I'll take you along. Then, if there's time, Captain Halliday will return the call and come to see us.' "—*A Good Catch*, pp. 78–79.

Mutiny was frequent aboard whalers, and prudence dictated that when two captains gathered in one ship, the two mates visited in the other.

GRAMPUS: A member of the blackfish subdivision of the whale family seldom taken because of its speed and paucity of oil.

GREASY: Fortunate; busy processing a whale to obtain its oil.

HUMPBACK: A large whalebone whale with long flippers and a dorsal fin, found from Arctic waters to Lower California.

IRON: A harpoon, or the barbed iron shank of a harpoon to which the line is attached.

LAY: The crew member's fractional share of the proceeds of the VOYAGE, his pay. ". . . all were interested, for on a whaler every man of the crew has a percentage, large or small, of the profit. Therefore every one was ready at his post of duty and bound to do his best in turning the game to good account."—*A Good Catch*, p. 74.

LAY, *or* LIE TO: To lie dead in the water with sails furled or backed.

LINE GALE: A severe storm at the time of the equinox (March 21 or September 23).

LOWER: To send the boats out after whales.

LUFF: To head into the wind, causing the sails to flap ineffectually.

MARLINESPIKE: A seaman's implement resembling an awl.

MASTHEAD: A small platform built around a mast with iron hoops fastened above as railings for the men stationed there to look out for whales.

MATE: The first mate or first officer, next in command after the captain; occasionally, any ship's officer.

—To join another ship in whaling, sharing equally the proceeds and expenses.

MUSSEL DIGGER: *See* CALIFORNIA GRAY.

OFF AND ON: To sail alternately toward and away from a harbor without entering; sometimes, to stand on alternating tacks across a harbor entrance unable to enter against an unfavorable wind.

PACKET: A vessel which travels a scheduled route between destinations carrying passengers, mail, and small cargo.

RAISE: To draw land or another ship into view as the ship approaches: the object in sight appears to "rise" on the horizon.

RECRUIT: To reprovision; to rest.

RECRUITS: The supplies, primarily food, for a cruise.

RIGHT WHALE: A large-headed whale, probably the same species now known as the black right whale, found in the Arctic, Bering, and Okhotsk waters and off Lower California. ". . . when we get up into the Arctic Ocean, we shall get . . . the rorqual, or right whale. He is longer than the other [the SPERM WHALE], but has no teeth. Instead of having teeth, his mouth is an immense sieve, made to catch the little fishes which he likes best. He will gulp them down by the barrelful. This sieve is made of whalebone, three or four hundred layers of it, all fringed with threads. When he is hungry, he rushes through the water with his huge mouth wide open . . . while the little fishes are caught and held in these threads till he gets a chance to swallow them, or till he gets enough to make it an object."—A *Good Catch*, p. 44.

RIPSACK: *See* CALIFORNIA GRAY.

RUN: The bottom part of the stern section of a ship.

—To sail before the wind.

SCHOONER: A vessel with two masts, both rigged fore and aft.

SCRIMSHAW: The whalemen's spare-time occupation of carving toys, implements, and artifacts from SPERM WHALE teeth, walrus tusks, etc.; the product of this work.

SCUPPERS: The drainage holes along the edge of a weather deck.

SHARK: A solicitor of business for the sailors' boardinghouses, outfitters, etc. They met incoming ships in shark boats.

SHIP: A sailing vessel with three square-rigged masts. Also, of course, any large vessel.

—To take on board or arrange for use on board a vessel.

SLOP CASK, SLOPS: The whaler's shipboard store, from which a crewman purchased (at about 25 per cent interest) shoes, clothing, tobacco, and other personal items, charging the amount against his LAY. Overuse of this source of supply sometimes ate up a man's entire share of the profits of the VOYAGE, and a crew member often returned after a long voyage in debt to the owners, as several *Addison* sailors did. See Appendix C for a listing of the *Addison*'s slops.

SLUSH: The cooking grease saved from the galley, which was used at sea to grease the masts. Any remaining grease was sold in port, and the cook was frequently given a share of the proceeds to encourage him to be as economical as possible.

SPEAK: To hail another vessel to exchange information either by voice or flag signals. Whaleship captains tried always to speak and often to GAM when they met another whaler, and they kept accurate records of the information and gossip obtained by this means and reported it to other whalers and to the whalemen's newspapers. Thus an informal but effective communication network was maintained among the widespread units of the industry.

SPERM WHALE: A large and most combative whale found in all warm waters. "The sperm-whale has an enormous head and great teeth. It can whip a boat in two with one flap of its strong tail, or bite it in two with its sharp teeth. In its head, which is square-shaped, very broad and large, there is a reservoir of oil and spermaceti. Ah! that's the sort to get for the money; it is very valuable. We cut a hole in the head and dip it out by the pailful, and sometimes we get ten or twelve barrels."—A Good Catch, pp. 42–44.

STEERAGE: The quarters below deck for a ship's specialists, that is, boatsteerers, coopers, carpenters, and blacksmiths.

STUDDING SAIL: An additional light sail rigged at the yardarm end to take maximum advantage of a fair wind in moderate weather.

SULPHUR-BOTTOM: The blue whale, the largest whale of all, not often taken because of its size, speed, ferociousness, and tendency to sink after being killed.

TRY, or TRY OUT: To boil whale oil out of blubber pieces. "Every part was put to use; even the scraps from which the oil had been strained were gathered for fuel.

"'It is not very pleasant work,' Mrs. Emerson [i.e., Lawrence] and Minnie concluded as they patiently tried to endure the soot, smoke, smell and grease which prevailed for about two days and nights. 'But then it has to be done, and we can bear it . . . .'"—A Good Catch, p. 74.

TRYWORKS: The brick firebed and two iron kettles which form the whaleship's "factory."

TURN FLUKES: To dive, or sound, toward the ocean bottom.

TURN UP: Of a whale, to roll over after death.

VOYAGE: The entire time from leaving home port to the return, usually including more than one CRUISE.

WAIF: A flag left in a temporarily abandoned whale to identify the owner.

WAIST: The middle section of a sailing ship between the foremast and mainmast. Here it is used to indicate the waist area of the side of the ship.

WHALEBOAT: A combination rowing and sailing boat especially designed for attacking whales. ". . . on a well-ordered ship every rope and pulley and hinge [required to lower and man the boats] works to a nicety, and but a minute is required to drop a boat from its davits into the sea and start her on her errand. Her rig and outfit, already in her, are complete; the oars are ready for the rowlocks; the harpoons, lances and knives are in their respective places; the rope is coiled in the tubs so true that it can be paid out like a flash. Should there be a tangle in it, fatal consequences might ensue; for when the iron is thrown and enters the body of the whale, the monster plunges below the surface, and the rope fairly smokes as it runs over the side of the boat. Indeed, water has constantly to be poured upon the line to keep it from setting itself and the boat on fire by friction. With such velocity, we can easily see that a hitch, however trifling, would endanger the boat and the lives of all on board."—*A Good Catch,* p. 64.

GLOSSARY OF OBSCURE
GEOGRAPHICAL TERMS

ARCHANGEL GABRIEL BAY: Guba Gavriila, Siberia.

BOWHEAD BAY: Probably Bukhta Puoten, Siberia.

COMPASS GROUND: The Arctic Ocean area influenced by the North Magnetic Pole, where the magnetic compass becomes nearly useless for navigation, located between East Cape and Cape Lisburne in latitude 68 degrees north, longitude 171 degrees 25 minutes west.

DIEGOS: Diego Ramirez Islands, southwest of Cape Horn.

DOMINICA ISLAND: Hiva Oa, Marquesas Islands.

GORE'S ISLAND: St. Matthew Island in the middle of the Bering Sea.

HAYES ISLAND: Kayak Island, Gulf of Alaska.

HERGEST'S ROCKS: Motuiti, Marquesas Islands.

HOOD'S ISLAND: Fatu Huka, Marquesas Islands.

HOPE, OR FRENCH, ROCK: Esperance Rock in the Kermadec Islands.

INDIAN POINT: Mys Chaplina, Siberia.

ISLANDS, THE: The Sandwich, or Hawaiian, Islands.

KAMCHATKA: Here, the sea area around the Kamchatka Peninsula, Siberia.

KODIAK: Here, the Gulf of Alaska.

LINE, THE: The equator; rarely, the Tropic of Cancer or Capricorn. Two of the great Pacific whale grounds were known as "on the line east" and "on the line west."

MAGDALENA ISLAND: Fatu Hiva, Marquesas Islands.

MARCUS BAY: Iskagan Bay, Siberia.

MARGARITA BAY: Magdalena Bay, Lower California.

MASINKA BAY: Proliv Checkekuyum, Siberia.

MECHIGMEN BAY: Mechigmenskaya Guba, Siberia.

MICHELL'S GROUP OF ISLANDS: Probably Maria Theresa Reef or Ernest Legouve Reef, east of New Zealand.

NEW HOLLAND: Sunda Islands in the East Indies.

NORFOLK SOUND: Sitka Bay, off Sitka, island port on southeastern coast of Alaska.

OKHOTSK: The Okhotsk Sea, but here sometimes used to indicate all of the waters off eastern Siberia.

ONE SEVENTY-TWO PASSAGE: Amukta Passage, Aleutian Islands, located in longitude 172 degrees west.

PARRY: Nuuanu Pali, Oahu, Hawaiian Islands.

PLOVER BAY: Bukhta Provideniya, Siberia.

ROBERT'S ISLANDS: Eiao and several smaller islands of the Marquesas Islands.

ROSE ISLAND: Middleton Island, Gulf of Alaska, south of Prince William Sound.

ST. CHRISTINA ISLAND: Tahuata, Marquesas Islands.

ST. LAWRENCE BAY: Zaliv Lavrentiya, Siberia.

ST. PEDRO ISLAND: Motane, Marquesas Islands.

THADDEUS, CAPE: Mys Faddeya, Siberia.

UGAMAK GROUP: Krenitzen Islands, easternmost of the Fox Islands of the Aleutian chain. Ugamak Island is the easternmost of these, directly across the strait from Unimak Island.

WASHINGTON ISLAND: Ua Huka, Marquesas Islands.

NOTES

NOTES

INTRODUCTION

1. Whalemen's shipping papers for the *Magnolia*, 1842, and the *Lafayette*, 1847, Melville Whaling Room, New Bedford Free Public Library, New Bedford, Massachusetts; Amelia Lawrence's genealogical notes in papers of Lewis Lawrence, grandson of Samuel Lawrence's brother, Lewis Henry Lawrence, Falmouth Historical Society, Falmouth, Massachusetts (Lewis Lawrence Papers); property deed, May 5, 1845, Barnstable County Courthouse, Barnstable, Massachusetts; *The Friend, devoted to Temperance, Seamen, Marine and General Intelligence,* VIII, 69(September 1, 1850); *Whalemen's Shipping List, and Merchant's Transcript,* VIII, 118 (September 24, 1850), 122(October 1, 1850), 130(October 15, 1850).

2. Whalemen's shipping paper for the *Eliza Adams,* 1851, Melville Whaling Room, New Bedford Free Public Library. The captain was Weston J. Swift, of North Falmouth, Massachusetts. There is no evidence to indicate the reason for Captain Swift's withdrawal. Ironically, Captain Swift's record was no better than Captain Lawrence's, for he had wrecked the *Liverpool II* in Bering Strait on July 30, 1853. She limped to St. Lawrence Bay, where she was condemned and sold. Agent's account book and miscellaneous papers in Deacon Isaac Bailey Richmond Papers, property of Carleton R. Richmond, Little Compton, Rhode Island; Alexander Starbuck, *History of the American Whale Fishery from its Earliest Inception to the Year 1876* (2 vols.; Argosy-Antiquarian, Ltd., 1964), II, 480–81; Federal Writers Project of the Works Progress Administration of Massachusetts, *Whaling Masters* (New Bedford: The Old Dartmouth Historical Society, 1938), p. 271. For statistics on the *Addison* see *Ship Registers of New Bedford, Massachusetts,* compiled by The Survey of Federal Archives, Division of Professional and Service Projects, Work Projects Administration, The National Archives, Cooperating Sponsor (3 vols.; Boston: The National Archives Project, 1940), II, 4; also information was supplied by Edouard A. Stackpole, curator of Mystic Seaport, Mystic, Connecticut.

3. The distinction between the "golden age" of whaling and the "age of gold" is made by Edouard A. Stackpole in *The Sea-Hunters: The New England Whalemen During Two Centuries, 1635–1835* (Philadelphia and New York: J. B. Lippincott Co., 1953), p. 470.

4. Excerpt from the diary of Harriet Gifford, entry for August 19, 1854, Lewis Lawrence Papers.

5. *The Friend,* XV, 84(November 8, 1858). For an interesting narrative of the experiences of Martha's Vineyard whaling families who accompanied their men, see Emma Mayhew Whiting and Henry Beetle Hough, *Whaling Wives* (Boston: Houghton Mifflin Co., 1953).

6. Theodate Geoffrey (pseud.), *Suckanesset; wherein may be read a History of Falmouth, Massachusetts* (Falmouth: Falmouth Publishing Co., 1930), p. 84. The Lawrence brothers and their families at sea during the

voyage are mentioned in the following entries of Mrs. Lawrence's journal:
February 19, July 6, October 22, 23, 25, November 4, December 8, 9, 12,
18, 26, 1857; January 12, March 14, August 14, 1858; August 18, 1859;
January 20, 1860; see also Lewis Lawrence Papers. The name Joseph
Lawrence appears on the whalemen's shipping paper for the bark *Leader*,
1840, Melville Whaling Room, New Bedford Free Public Library (this may
be another Joseph Lawrence). Mrs. Lawrence listed all her relatives' names
in Captain Samuel Lawrence's slop book, Falmouth Historical Society,
Falmouth, Massachusetts. The statistics for the ships *Anaconda* and *Alto*
are listed in *Ship Registers of New Bedford*, I, 9; II, 10–11, 15; and the
statistics for the *Commodore Morris* are listed in *Alphabetical List of Ship
Registers, District of Barnstable, Massachusetts, 1814–1913*, prepared by
the National Archives Project, Division of Women's and Professional Projects, Works Progress Administration, The National Archives, Sponsor
(Boston, 1938), p. 19. All three ships are listed in Starbuck, *History of the
American Whale Fishery*, II, 492–93, 508–9, 546–47.

7. Lewis Lawrence Papers; Federal Writers Project, *Whaling Masters*,
pp. 180, 310; Starbuck, *History of the American Whale Fishery*, II, 524–25.
The following dramatization of Mary Lawrence's own decision may have
come from her own lips:

" 'Tell me if you are really going, Mary,' demanded Mr. Will Cumber-
land [i.e., Chipman] as he looked in for a moment at the little white cottage
in Falmouth and espied his sister kneeling before a half-packed trunk.
'Have you decided to bury yourself alive in the Caledonia [i.e., Addison]—
to take three or four of the best years right out of your life? I can't understand it.'

" 'Have you anything further to say?' asked his sister, in her usual de-
liberate tone and looking up with a merry twinkle in her eye.

" 'Yes—volumes,' protested Will. 'It is too bad for a young creature like
you to shut yourself up in that greasy old ark of a whale-ship and deprive
us all of your pleasant society for so long a time. And to take Minnie along,
too! She'll mope herself to death on shipboard.'

" 'I'll risk Minnie with her father and mother,' replied Mrs. Emerson [i.e.,
Lawrence]. 'And, as for myself, my home is henceforth to be with my
husband. Samuel is all the world to me, and why should we live with half
the globe between us? We have been married ten years, and for two-thirds
of that time oceans and continents have separated us, and we have both
decided that it shall be so no longer. From this time, where he goes I shall
go; and my happiness will be in making him a home wherever business
calls him.'

" 'Sentiment!' said Will, with a gesture of dissatisfaction.

" 'Common sense,' rejoined his sister, 'as you will find out yourself, my
dear brother, when you come to have a family. Now, Will, don't say another
word. Of course it is hard to leave the old home and father and mother,
and all the rest, but my mind is as clear as the sunlight as to the right of
the thing; so don't make it any harder for me than you can help. I hope we
may all be spared to meet again.'

" 'What will you do for dry goods?' asked Will, in a mischievous tone.
'There are no shops on the trackless ocean?'

" 'I shall lay in a sufficient supply.'

" 'And medicines?'

" 'We have an ample store.'

" 'Confectionery and knickknacks?'

" 'Are they indispensable?'

" 'I thought so—to women and children.'

" 'We are sensible people.'

" 'Well, books? You must have books and music.'

" 'We shall carry what we can, and do without the rest.'

" 'It will be "do without" many a thing, I reckon. You are launching out on a voyage of self-denial and privation; you'll come home pure and ethereal as an angel, I expect. But if it must be, why we will try to make the best of it.'

"Unmoved by persuasion and argument to the contrary, Mrs. Emerson [i.e., Lawrence] went on with her preparations. She laid in her supplies, packed her sea-chests, big and little, shut up the little white cottage, and on the 25th of November, 1856, commenced her seafaring life."—Mrs. Helen E. Brown, *A Good Catch; or, Mrs. Emerson's Whaling-Cruise* (Philadelphia: Presbyterian Board of Publication, 1884), pp. 1–4.

8. Lewis Lawrence Papers; gravestones in Oak Grove Cemetery, Falmouth, Massachusetts; Barnstable County public records, Barnstable County Courthouse, Barnstable, Massachusetts; obituary notices: Samuel Lawrence, Barnstable (Massachusetts) *Patriot*, September 20, 1892; Mary Lawrence, Falmouth (Massachusetts) *Enterprise*, March 10, 1906; Minnie Lawrence, Herkimer (New York) *Evening Telegram*, April 10, 1923.

9. Entry for October 26, 1857.

10. Entry for February 19, 1857.

11. Entry for January 5, 1857.

12. *One Whaling Family*, ed. Harold Williams (Boston: Houghton Mifflin Co., 1964).

13. *Mrs. Ricketson's Whaling Journal*, ed. Philip F. Purrington (New Bedford: The Old Dartmouth Historical Society, 1958).

14. Entry for July 28, 1859.

15. See Appendix A.

FIRST CRUISE

1. Celia Bassett Chipman. See Appendix D.

2. Psalms 107:23–26.

3. Augustus Lawrence. See the Introduction, p. xvii.

4. ". . . Sunday was a resting-day, if not a day of worship, . . . as it is, indeed, on all well-regulated vessels. Captains usually recognize the fact that six days of work with an intermission on the seventh from all duties not absolutely necessary is better for the health and spirits, for the order and subordination, of a crew than a continuous round of labor without any regular break. But . . . Sunday was more than a break: it was a specialty—a day to be anticipated and recollected with pleasure. A little change in the ordinary table-fare, a cessation of hard work, an opportunity for reading and 'spinning yarns,' with a distribution of papers or books in the morning and singing in the cabin at twilight, marked the day."—Mrs. Helen E. Brown, *A Good Catch; or, Mrs. Emerson's Whaling-Cruise* (Philadelphia: Presbyterian Board of Publication, 1884), pp. 161–62.

5. Susan Lawrence. See Appendix D.

6. This menu would have been served to the officers and perhaps to the boatsteerers and specialists, but it would have been most unusual if the

seamen had received much more than "salt junk and hardtack," which is given as their normal fare in Brown, *A Good Catch*, pp. 150–51. However, the seamen seem to have received particularly good treatment on the *Addison*.

7. Luke 22:42.

8. Above the word "niece" are written, as a correction, in Mrs. Lawrence's handwriting the words: "two nieces." Also there is interlineated in this entry, undoubtedly by Minnie, the following: "Grandpa Lawrence, Uncle Augustus, Aunt Ann Chipman's Annie, 3 mos., Uncle Joseph's Martha D. (?)." Martha D. Lawrence died in 1854, but because the death occurred in California, Mrs. Lawrence may have lost track of the date. See Appendix D.

9. Celia Bassett Chipman, Thomas Hanscome Lawrence, Mercy Dimmick Lawrence, James Freeman Chipman, and Anna Read Chipman. See Appendix D.

10. That is, among the forecastle sailors.

11. "Do they miss me at home—do they miss me?
　　 'Twould be an assurance most dear,
　　 To know that this moment some loved one
　　 Were saying, 'I wish he were here.'"
　　　　 —Caroline Atherton Briggs Mason, "Do They Miss Me at Home?"

12. Deacon Isaac Bailey Richmond (1789–1888), of Little Compton, Rhode Island, agent for the *Addison*.

13. Mrs. Lawrence never mentions being close to land in the Cape Horn area and probably did not see any of the "rude and savage inhabitants," or Fuegians, herself. This description suggests her familiarity with Charles Darwin's *The Voyage of the Beagle*, which appeared a decade earlier.

14. Underwear.

15. George Swift Lawrence, second mate of the *Harvest*. See the entry for October 22, 1857, and Appendix D.

16. "Along the cool sequestered vale of life
　　 They kept the noiseless tenor of their way."
　　　　 —Thomas Gray, "Elegy Written in a Country Churchyard"

17. Job 38:11.

18. Walter Merrick Chipman (see Appendix D). The name of the vessel on which he sailed is unknown.

19. "A life on the ocean wave,
　　 A home on the rolling deep;
　　 Where the scattered waters rave,
　　 And the winds their revels keep!
　　 Like an eagle caged I pine
　　 On this dull, unchanging shore:
　　 Oh, give me the flashing brine,
　　 The spray and the tempest's roar!"
　　　　 —Epes Sargent

20. James Buchanan.

21. Anna Read Chipman. See Appendix D.

22. It was on this island that Captain Lawrence lost the *Lafayette* in June, 1850. The Honolulu whalemen's newspaper reported that "she went ashore in the night; the captain was running in to an anchor when she struck a rock and became a total loss." All of the crew took to the whaleboats;

Captain Lawrence and the second mate were picked up by the *Golconda*, and the first and third mates, who had become separated from the others during the night, were picked up by the *Callao*. Two hundred barrels of sperm oil were saved by the *Nauticon*. *The Friend, devoted to Temperance, Seamen, Marine and General Intelligence*, VIII, 69(September 1, 1850); also *Whalemen's Shipping List, and Merchant's Transcript*, VIII, 118(September 24, 1850), 122(October 1, 1850), 130(October 15, 1850).

23. Cynthia Bassett Chipman. See Appendix D.

24. By this apparent redundancy Mrs. Lawrence may mean the actual number of knots in the taffrail log line paid out during a certain interval after a heave of the log. Modern usage would demand the elimination of the phrase "an hour."

25. See the entry for February 20, 1857.

26. Interlineation: "Gorham, a famous Hawaiian consul at Boston, firm of Gilman Brothers, Druggists."

27. There were two entries with this date, but these have been combined by the editor.

28. "The kitchen and the storerooms were in a little adobe hut at one side and apart from the cottage."—Brown, *A Good Catch*, p. 98.

29. After the abbreviation "Mrs." there is an interlineation "George" and after "Brayton" the interlineation "Middleboro."

30. Matthew 4:20.

31. See the entry for October 19, 1857, and Appendix B concerning this man, William Maxon.

32. James McElwee. Captain Lawrence paid his $5.00 fine and $1.00 detention fee, but McElwee was back in the fort again in November. Upon his release he deserted without repaying the fines. *Addison* account book in Deacon Isaac Bailey Richmond Papers, property of Carleton R. Richmond, Little Compton, Rhode Island.

33. This is one of the few errors of fact in Mary Lawrence's journal. Captain Cleaveland commanded the *Julian*. Elsewhere in her journal Mrs. Lawrence associates the captain correctly with the *Julian*.

34. "Praise God, from whom all blessings flow!
Praise Him, all creatures here below!
Praise Him above, ye heavenly host!
Praise Father, Son, and Holy Ghost!"
—Bishop Thomas Ken, "Morning and Evening Hymn"

35. Matthew 7:24-27.

36. " 'Now, this is the reason why we left home in the winter—that we might sail down here and round Cape Horn and get through these southern seas when it was warm weather. I intend to cruise in these seas for a while, and hope to catch plenty of whales. Then we shall sail up north on the other side of the American continent . . . through the Pacific Ocean. We shall perhaps stop at some of these little islands to get water and fruit, and then we shall come to the Sandwich Islands . . . There we shall stay a few weeks. You and mamma will go on shore, and we shall clean house on the Caledonia [i.e., *Addison*]. If we catch a good many whales, as I hope to, we shall have a sufficient cargo of oil and whalebone on board, and this I shall then transfer to another ship and send it home to be sold. Then we shall get in a fresh stock of provisions . . . and sail up through Behring's Strait . . . into the Arctic Ocean, perhaps to catch whales in its waters. We shall get summer again by that time. When we have stayed there a

while, we shall come back to the Sandwich Islands to send our catch home, and by that time it will be summer weather down here, and we shall come south again. . . . We'll swing about up and down for a few years, keeping summer with us all the time, until we have laid in a little fortune, and then we'll go home and enjoy it . . .

.   .   .   .   .

" 'The whale doesn't now frequent the seas in the warm regions of the earth; he likes the cold, icy seas best. . . . so many ships sail . . . along the European coasts of the Atlantic . . . that the whales don't go there so much. They have been hunted away. We have to go farther south and away up north for them.' "—Brown, *A Good Catch*, pp. 37–38, 41–42.

37. Joseph C. Avery. This and other personnel changes are listed in Appendix B.

38. "Those were not the days of quick transit. A railroad across the continent was then but a fancy in some enterprising brain, and Chinese and Australian steamers, which now touch every week or two at these islands of the sea to bring and carry the welcome mail, were hardly yet a dream. The only way of postal communication was by way of the Isthmus of Panama to San Francisco, and from thence across the sea by sailing-packets. So our friend was fain to wait for news from home till her next visit to the island. A whole year in uncertainty about friends! How could she bear it? But it was one of the privations which she had anticipated when she decided to accompany her husband . . . "—Brown, *A Good Catch*, pp. 118–19.

SECOND CRUISE

1. Captain Samuel Lawrence's slop book in the archives of the Falmouth Historical Society, Falmouth, Massachusetts, shows that Mrs. Lawrence and Minnie also played various writing games for amusement and instruction. They listed all of Minnie's grandparents and great-aunts and uncles and all of the children of Minnie's generation of the Chipman and Lawrence families. Then they listed all of the family of Mrs. Lawrence's generation and their husbands or wives, coupling with the name of each unmarried member the phrase, "Who, deponent saieth not." Tiring of this, they would write down all of the words or Christian names they could think of beginning with A, then all beginning with B, and so forth. Then they would construct a riddle around the spelling of a word to be guessed, writing, "My first is . . . , my second is . . . ," until each letter of the word was suggested by a separate question.

2. Deuteronomy 33:25.

3. Little could be done at sea about dental trouble except to dull the pain. The *Addison* carried a medicine chest, containing laudanum, which was replenished whenever possible by a doctor. In his journal (February 4, 1860) George Bowman describes using creosote to dull toothache pain. Visits to the Sandwich Islands usually meant a session of tooth-pulling for the crew. Miscellaneous invoices in Deacon Isaac Bailey Richmond Papers, property of Carleton R. Richmond, Little Compton, Rhode Island; also George Bowman, Journal, Nicholson Collection, Providence Public Library, Providence, Rhode Island.

4. He gave Captain Heath fourteen assorted irons in exchange for four bomb lances. Slop book.

5. Probably at the Sandwich Academy, which early in the nineteenth century provided a special room for the education of girls.

6. Lewis Henry Lawrence and Eunice Davis Lawrence (see Appendix D) at this time sperm whaling out of New Zealand.

7. Forty-four bomb lances. *Addison* account book in Richmond Papers.

8. Captain Lawrence bought a whaling gun from Captain Wing during this visit for cash and some oars. The cash was paid through a chandler in the Sandwich Islands, which was the usual practice. *Addison* account book and miscellaneous invoices in Richmond Papers.

9. The *Pele* was locally built from imported plans by James Munroe, who had no experience in this kind of construction. She was named for the Hawaiian goddess of the volcano, who lived in the Kilauea crater of Mauna Loa on the island of Hawaii, and was launched by Queen Emma on July 31, 1856. The *Pele*'s towing fee at this time was $45.00. *The Friend, devoted to Temperance, Seamen, Marine and General Intelligence,* V, 61 (August 19, 1856); miscellaneous invoices in Richmond Papers.

10. Of this the owners of the *Addison* paid $15.00 per week captain's expenses. *Addison* account book in Richmond Papers.

11. The Reverend Samuel C. Damon, the "Seamen's Chaplain" and editor and publisher of the weekly whalemen's newspaper, *The Friend.* The Lawrences occasionally contributed money for the distribution of this evangelical publication among the seamen. But note the entry for July 25, 1858, which records a later quarrel between Mrs. Lawrence and Mr. Damon.

12. Celia Lawrence Bourne. See Appendix D.

13. On this date the *Addison* shipped home 8,867 pounds of whalebone on the *John Land,* W. H. Bearse, master. Bills of lading in Richmond Papers.

14.   "SANDWICH, August 1st, 1857
"DEAR BROTHER AND SISTER,
"I will write you a few lines this evening and perhaps tomorrow I may add a little more. We were very glad indeed to hear from you and that you were all well—Mother had been worrying ever since a few weeks after you sailed because you were not spoken. I guess that she would have been more so if she had heard of that gale after you had been out a short time. A ship sailed about the time that you did, reported a very heavy gale, and did not expect to live through it but finally rode it out. I was a little anxious about you, but Thomas said that the old *Addison* was good for it. We are well at home. Father's health is much better than it was when you went away. I should think from what you write that Minnie was getting to be 'some pumpkins.' I think that you will have to give her a lay after you have been out awhile. Isaac is at home now but will leave again in a week or two; is going in the same ship, the *Ceylon,* but is not going to Honolulu this time, so he will not have quite so long a voyage. That trout breeding affair was a total failure; couldn't make it work.

"Blackberries are quite plenty this summer. Father, Mother, and Cynthia went yesterday. They got between four and five quarts in a short time. You, Mary, did wonders writing so many letters. I hope you will hold out so throughout the voyage. Samuel, you didn't do quite so well. I hope that you will improve. But as you didn't get those valuable letters that we sent to Paita, I guess that I will excuse you; all is, the next time you must make up for it. Don't forget to give my letter to George Lawrence when you see him, for I promised to write him soon after he sailed but neglected it until you sailed. We miss Old Dick and his driver very much about this time. I suppose that you would enjoy it very much if you could go aberrying with us once. I hope that you have got 15,000 barrels of sperm oil by this time but feel rather doubtful about it. We are going to have our meeting house lit up by gas next week. We shall take the shine all off the other churches, I guess. Plenty of peeps now, Sam. You ought to have your double-barrel shooter here now with Sam Lawrence at the other end of it. They are about as wild though as those ducks that we went after one morning. If you was at home now, I would go fishing with you off those big rocks where I used to lose so many lines for you. I think I like that kind of fishing better than any other.

"I am still at work at the same old place where I always shall be probably, if nothing takes place to prevent.

"This letter looks rather short beside your letters, but it is one of the longest letters that I ever wrote. Lizzie thinks that she will wait and write by the next steamer, as she is very busy now helping to fix Isaac off. She sends a great deal of love to all. So does Sarah and Mother Gibbs. Lizzie and I wrote twice to Paita, but my letters won't be any great loss, but I presume that Lizzie's would have made up for mine. I must close now. Give Minnie fifty kisses from me and (as I wrote in the letter that I sent to Paita) one kiss for you, and slap Sam for me.

"From your affectionate brother,
"CHARLES CHIPMAN"

This letter is the property of Francis Freeman Jones, Palo Alto, California, grandson of Charles Chipman.

15. Probably George Nye Chipman. See Appendix D.

16. Evidently a sister of Augustus Lawrence's widow, Sarah.

17. King Kamehameha IV. His queen was Emma Rooke, a much-admired Sandwich Islands belle.

18. On this date the *Addison* shipped home 125 barrels of whale oil and 12 barrels of sperm oil on the *Harriet and Jessie,* Dennis Janvrin, master. Bills of lading in Richmond Papers.

19. Bernard Fallon, James McElwee, and Thomas C. Weeks. Fallon was in the fort again in November. Fort bills in Richmond Papers.

20. The Falmouth Ladies' Seamen's Friend Society. A letter from the secretary of the Society concerning the furnishing of this room was published in *The Friend,* V, 68(September 17, 1856):

"MR. SPAULDING, SIR:

"You have probably received, ere this, a box in your care, for the room 'Falmouth,' in the Sailor's Home at Honolulu.

"It was the intention of our Society to furnish a room, the cost of which would be about fifty dollars.

"The contents of that box were a sufficient quantity of bedding (sheets, pillow cases, blankets and spreads) and toweling of different kinds, the amount of which articles, exclusive of the labor, was nearly twenty-six dollars. It also contained an ambrotype of our pastor, the Rev. Mr. Hooker, in a frame, to be hung in the room, and a Bible from Mrs. Hooker. Enclosed you will find thirty dollars, which we wish to have sent for the purchase of such other articles as may be needed for the full furnishing of the room. We send these things in your care, according to the direction of Mr. Damon.

"Respectfully,
"MRS. HARRIET H. GIFFORD
"*Secretary of Ladies' Seamen's Friend Society*

"FALMOUTH, MASSACHUSETTS, June 27, 1856"

21. On leaving port shortly after this visit, the *John Gilpin* raced the *Eliza F. Mason* to New Bedford. Although the latter was a conventional, ship-rigged whaler, Captain Jernegan made the fastest passage between the two ports in the history of whaling, beating the clipper by sixteen days. Captain Ring was relieved of command of the *John Gilpin* as a result. Emma Mayhew Whiting and Henry Beetle Hough, *Whaling Wives* (Boston: Houghton Mifflin Co., 1953), p. 54.

22. Her officers were Commander Charles Henry Davis, captain, J. S. Maury, T. T. Houston, and William H. Ward, lieutenants. *The Friend*, VI, 70 (September 26, 1857).

THIRD CRUISE

1. Altogether the ship received 3 cords of wood, 20 bunches of bananas, 9 turkeys, eggs, and refreshments in exchange for 2 pieces of brown cotton, 3 pieces of bleached cotton, 2 pieces of calico, and 6 striped shirts. For a list of slops and trade items carried on the *Addison* see Appendix C. *Addison* account book in Deacon Isaac Bailey Richmond Papers, property of Carleton R. Richmond, Little Compton, Rhode Island.

2. Most likely an error. Macauley Island (sighted December 14) is in longitude 178 degrees west.

3. At this time all three surviving whaling captains among the Lawrences, along with their unmarried brother George, were in the Pacific with their wives and children.

4. Several facts give this entry special significance. Just before the ship sailed from New Bedford several young men with Anglo-Saxon names and foreign accents (if, indeed, they spoke English at all) signed on for the voyage. An audit of available crew lists shows that they were actually Portuguese "Western Islanders" who had used pseudonyms to conceal their alien status, a common practice in the whaling industry (see Appendix B). Although Azoreans were quite common at this time in the larger whaling ports, these swarthy foreign-speaking Roman Catholics must have seemed strange to Mary Lawrence, of Falmouth.

One of them, "Francis Finley," was given the job of cabin boy, which brought him into intimate contact with the family. He was actually one of two crew members named Antone Jacinto (the other was an experienced boatsteerer) and was often referred to as "Boy Antone" in the records of the voyage. He was the youth who was lost when the whaleboat capsized.

Aside from her explicit statement that she "had become quite attached to him," there are other indications of a special relationship between the foreign boy and the New England lady. Her proposal to take home one individual out of the thousands of young men of the whaling fleet, many of whom would have benefited from some education, is quite surprising. Captain Lawrence would hardly have considered it independently. But even more revealing is a unique error in the entry which strongly suggests that she was momentarily disoriented by the accident. In the following sentence she had written, "I had proposed to the," clearly intending to add the word "captain," a title which she never applied to her husband except when she was in a playful mood. Then she recovered her balance, crossed out the word "the," and corrected the phrase to read, "I had proposed to Samuel." The deep undercurrent of her innermost feelings, having in this small slip of the pen come momentarily into the open, then disappeared beneath the surface of her nineteenth-century rhetoric.

After Antone's death the whaling routine aboard the *Addison* continued as before, and his clothing was sold at reduced prices to the other crew members, according to Captain Lawrence's slop book, Falmouth Historical Society, Falmouth, Massachusetts. And in later years other Francis Finleys sailed from New Bedford.

5. *Precept upon Precept* was written by Mrs. Favell Lee Mortimer and published in 1847, and *The Peep of Day*, also by Mrs. Mortimer, was published in 1849, both by Baker and Scribner, of New York. *Line upon Line* may have been written by the same author.

6. Mark 4:39.

7. Elizabeth Gibbs Chipman. See Appendix D.

8. This and the following entry were incorrectly dated by Mrs. Lawrence and have been corrected by the editor.

9. That is, the "on the line" whaling ground.

10. No book with this title has been found. Mrs. Lawrence may have been referring in this instance to [Sir John Barrow], *A Description of Pitcairn's Island and its Inhabitants, with an authentic account of the mutiny of the ship Bounty, and of the subsequent fortunes of the mutineers* (New York: J. and J. Harper, 1832), which was published in England under the title *The Eventful History of the Mutiny and Piratical Seizure of H.M.S. Bounty* (1835). This book, made up from accounts of survivors, including Admiral Bligh, was reprinted as late as 1914 in the "World's Classics" series.

11. The pseudonym of Alexander Smith.

12. Island natives occasionally attacked the poorly armed whalers despite the false gunports which were usually painted on their sides. The most famous incident of this sort occurred abroad a Falmouth ship later commanded by Augustus Lawrence. The *Awashonks* was captured by natives of Namorik Island, who were visiting on board on October 5, 1835. The captain, mate, second mate, and four seamen were killed, and others were wounded. Then in a daring maneuver the third mate, Silas Jones, retook the ship, driving off the natives and killing several. Alexander Starbuck, *History of the American Whale Fishery from its Earliest Inception to the Year 1876* (2 vols.; New York: Argosy-Antiquarian, Ltd., 1964), I, 129–31.

13. Captain Lawrence bought 22 boatloads of wood, 26 hogs, 50 fowls, 2,500 coconuts, 23 bunches of bananas, breadfruit, and other fruits in exchange for 25 pounds of tobacco, 5 axes, 2 muskets, 3 hatchets, 8 flints, 12 belts, 5 old oars, 3 kegs of powder, 9 sheath knives, 48 boxes of matches, 7 handkerchiefs, 1 monkey jacket, 8 shirts, and 5 hanks of thread. *Addison* account book in Richmond Papers.

14. " 'Our ship is filled with them [natives] every day but Sunday; then Samuel tells them the ship is tabu . . . for the day. . . . They like powder, and we had made some little bags containing about three-quarters of a pound, and for one of these we could buy a pig. . . . A woman may not eat from a fish from which a man has eaten, or share a cocoanut or a banana he has tasted; she must have her articles of food quite separate. When they were on board, Minnie or I would sometimes be eating fruit, and would offer them some; but they would always say, "Tabu! tabu!" ' "—Mrs. Helen E. Brown, *A Good Catch; or, Mrs. Emerson's Whaling-Cruise* (Philadelphia: Presbyterian Board of Publication, 1884), pp. 210–11.

" 'I must tell you of a purchase Minnie made a few days ago, one which highly pleases the little maiden. A native came on board with four fine fowls, and asked if my daughter had any beads; he wanted to buy a string. She had plenty that had been given her at the Sandwich Islands for her amusement; so she gave him a string and took the fowls. She is quite proud to call them hers, and has tied a bit of ribbon on their legs, that they may be recognized as hers, and so not be killed.' "—Brown, *A Good Catch*, p. 213.

15. Kekela furnished the *Addison* with 4 barrels of potatoes. Captain Lawrence sold the missionaries 28 gallons of whale oil, 28 gallons of molasses, 5 gallons of paint oil, 11 pounds of green paint, 4 gross of matches, 12 hatchets, 18 striped shirts, 2 axes, and about 950 yards of assorted calico. *Addison* account book in Richmond Papers.

16. The manuscript is unclear at this point. The reading of the word "here" especially is uncertain.

17. "Many were the hours of pleasant play they [Minnie and Mary White] enjoyed together during the stay of the Caledonia [i.e., *Addison*] in the harbor, renewed at subsequent visits of Minnie on this foreign shore, and years afterward in their American homes."—Brown, *A Good Catch*, p. 175.

18. " 'God tempers the wind,' said Maria, 'to the shorn lamb.' "—Laurence Sterne, *A Sentimental Journey Through France and Italy*, Introduction by Wilbur L. Cross (New York: J. F. Taylor and Co., 1904), p. 386.

19. The *Addison* shipped 1,383 pounds of bone home on March 23 abroad the *Polynesia*, J. Warren Perkins, master. Bills of lading in Richmond Papers.

20. During this period in port Bernard Fallon was sick and in the fort. Captain Lawrence paid the fine of John Scott so that he could ship him for the coming cruise. Fort and miscellaneous bills in Richmond Papers.

FOURTH CRUISE

1. Anna Read Chipman. See Appendix D.

2. Interlineation: "over the wash tub!"

3. The *America* carried an experimental steam whaleboat, which proved to be impractical and later became a harbor boat at Honolulu. *The Friend, devoted to Temperance, Seamen, Marine and General Intelligence*, VIII 78 (October 13, 1858).

4. That is, German.

5. Pronounced by whalemen and spelled by Mary Lawrence "Rosseau," apparently as an expression of their distaste for the philosopher's supposed impiety. Conversation with Reginald Hegarty, curator, Melville Whaling Room, New Bedford Free Public Library, New Bedford, Massachusetts.

6. " 'The days seem very long to me sometimes,' said Mrs. Skinner. 'I get so tired and homesick! If I had a little companion, as you have, it would be different.'

" 'The days are not long to me,' replied Mrs. Emerson [i.e., Lawrence]— 'unless,' laughing, 'when it is sunlight for sixteen or twenty hours. I have a variety of occupations. My housework—which includes washing and ironing, sewing and reading, schoolkeeping and play—furnishes all I need. I never have to complain of *ennui* or seek diversion to pass away the time.'

" 'Reading? What do you read? I get so tired of books!'

" 'I get a complete file of papers every time we stop at the islands, and then I make it a point to post myself up in all the news; if I did not, I should be a veritable Rip Van Winkle when I got back. I should not like to lose four years right out of life as it regards the history of our country or the events of our native town and State. Then I always find good and improving books among my friends at the islands. I couldn't live on stories all the time, I assure you; it would be like feeding on sweetmeats. I must have solid food for mind as well as for body. And I find having my little girl with me quite a stimulus for study, she asks so many questions, and often such as I cannot answer without thought and research. . . . I think that this long cruise will prove one of the most profitable seasons of my life. And there is another object ever before me—the benefit of our crew.'

" 'Do you mingle much with them?' asked her friend, in evident surprise, and with a marked emphasis on 'them.'

" 'No; often I do not speak to one of them—excepting the officers, who come to our table, and the steward—from one week's end to another. My husband does not think it well for me to have much to say to them. But there are many ways in which I can ease their life of hardship and privation, and by example I can teach them many a good lesson. We have aboard some lads in whom I feel deeply interested. But Minnie runs about among them freely.'

" 'How do you dare let her? I could not bear the thought of bringing my two little girls, who are rather older than Minnie. They wanted to come, but we placed them in a good boarding-school instead. We thought they were safer there.'

" 'On the contrary, I feel that Minnie is far safer with her parents than she could be elsewhere. She is a favorite with the men—I might say, a pet. Not one has ever offered her the slightest disrespect. They all seem to love her—really to love her, to count her as something very precious; and I do not believe there is one who would not risk his life to save hers in case of accident. And I think the calling forth of this feeling among men who are, as a class, hard and morally degraded benefits them.' "—Mrs. Helen E. Brown, *A Good Catch; or, Mrs. Emerson's Whaling-Cruise* (Philadelphia: Presbyterian Board of Publication, 1884), pp. 230–33.

7. On his return to New Bedford on the *John and Edward* on December 10, 1858, Captain Francis C. Smith was tried for beating crewman Warren Epps, wounding him, and forcing him ashore. He received a light sentence because of mitigating circumstances. Captain Smith was stoutly defended by other whaling captains. *The Friend*, VIII, 46(June 15, 1859).

8. On such an occasion a group of captains boarded a stricken vessel to survey its condition. This procedure had a legal aspect: if the ship were damaged badly enough, it could be condemned and sold on the spot for salvage. In this case the inspecting captains signed a "protest," which the owners accepted without question. Ships were usually insured for northern cruises, but because the policies ran until September 15, whalemen made every effort to clear dangerous seas by that date. Conversation with Reginald Hegarty.

9. This entry and the three following were incorrectly dated by Mrs. Lawrence and have been corrected by the editor.

10. This Eskimo word has been transcribed "ma-sink-er," and the group of natives who lived here were consequently known as Masinkers. Herbert L. Aldrich, *Arctic Alaska and Siberia; or, Eight Months with the Arctic Whalemen* (Chicago and New York: Rand, McNally and Co., 1889), p. 42.

11. Broke free of it, leaving a buoy to mark its location.

12. "'. . . I was very anxious. I wonder if at times this is not right? It certainly seems unavoidable. So I passed the night watching with my husband. A strangely short night it was.'"—Brown, *A Good Catch*, p. 226.

13. Interlineation: "Captain Benjamin Gibbs."

14. "Almost daily do we meet persons whose minds are full of wrong opinions and foolish prejudices, because they expected too much. Persons arriving here, fresh from Old or New England, bringing with them their own standard of civilization, refinement and Christianity feel sadly disappointed when they look around them and contemplate the striking contrasts which everywhere abound between scenes in Polynesia and other parts of the world. After a few months residence and more extensive observation, they learn to take juster views and form more correct opinions. Some months since, we met Mrs. ———, wife of Captain ———, from ———, Massachusetts. On arriving at the Sandwich Islands, she expressed herself as sadly disappointed. The missionary enterprise was not what she had supposed. The natives were not what the missionaries had represented in the *Herald*. We heard her expressions of disappointment, but having listened to so many who harped upon a similar chord, our nerves were not greatly shocked, or mind quite thrown off its balance. We inwardly reasoned, it is not strange that persons should feel disappointed, if they have expected too much; and so the matter was forgotten. The ship ——— sailed for a cruise in the South Pacific, and on its return touched at the Marquesas. There our good lady friend found a state of things so much worse than at the Sandwich Islands, that she was willing to conclude, well, after all, this missionary enterprise is not exactly a failure. At Marquesas she saw some of Melville's interesting sons and daughters of nature, uncontaminated by missionary training! There she saw a few Sandwich Island missionaries, toiling and praying to evangelize those who were ready, if possible, to steal anything they could lay their hands upon, when they visited her husband's ship, and, alas! they were but too successful, for they even stole a bound volume of the *Friend!* Among the visitors there was one Natua, a convert, whose character beautifully and strangely contrasted with that of his fellow islanders. He was invited to sit at the cabin table, but no food would he eat until, like the Divine Master, a blessing was implored. The following is the exact English phraseology that the converted Marquesan employed, and being among those speaking English, the poor man did his best to address God in the language once spoken by Milton and Bacon:

" 'O Great Fadder! got no fadder, got no modder, got no brodder, got no sister;—make first the sea, make first the dry land, make first the moon and stars, make first the trees, then He make man; and now, Great Fadder, give man his belly full. Amen!'

"We wrote down the foregoing just as repeated to us by the lady, who was quite willing to acknowledge that the missionary cause had done good. Reader, do not expect too much, and the reality will not disappoint reasonable expectations."—[Rev. Samuel C. Damon], "Do Not Expect too Much, and You Will Not be Disappointed," *The Friend*, XV, 28–29 (April 1, 1858). The captain's wife referred to is, of course, Mary Lawrence. Although Mr. Damon pretended to conceal her identity, he printed a note elsewhere on the same page, which began: "Marquesas Islands—From Captains Murdoch, of the *Nassau*, and Lawrence, of the *Addison*, late intelligence has been received from the Hawaiian Missionaries." And of course the *Nassau* had no lady on board. The conversation which led to this article must have occurred during the visit to Mr. Damon mentioned in the entry for March 23, 1858.

15. *The Friend*, XI, 80 (November 1, 1853), describes the incident as follows:

"Killed by a whale in August, 1853, Mr. Freeman R. Eldridge, of Falmouth, 1st officer of the bark *Awashonks*. After the boat was capsized, he was struck and so severely injured as to survive but two hours after being taken on board the ship. . . . The remains of Mr. Eldridge were interred on the south side of Cape East. He leaves a wife and child to mourn his loss." Starbuck erroneously gives his name as Jones.

16. Adapted from Shakespeare, *Richard III*, V, iv.

17. An error. The child was a son born on Norfolk Island on December 31, 1857. He was named Augustus after his deceased uncle. Amelia Lawrence's genealogical notes in papers of Lewis Lawrence, grandson of Samuel Lawrence's brother, Lewis Henry Lawrence, Falmouth Historical Society, Falmouth, Massachusetts.

18. Captain Childs named one of his Honolulu-born children Minnie Lawrence Childs. Theodate Geoffrey (pseud.), *Suckanesset; wherein may be read a History of Falmouth, Massachusetts* (Falmouth: Falmouth Publishing Co., 1930), p. 127.

19. See "Burial of the Dead" in *The Book of Common Prayer*.

20. Identified by *The Friend*, VIII, 78 (October 13, 1858), as Donati's comet.

21. "Rocked in the cradle of the deep,
      I lay me down in peace to sleep."
         —EMMA WILLARD, "The Cradle of the Deep"

22. Mrs. Lawrence misdated this entry October 3; this entry and those following through October 7 have been corrected by the editor.

23. ". . . William Kalama . . . had been with them a year. . . . It was at sunset when all hands were called on deck to the funeral service, never so solemn as at sea. The body was wrapped in its coarse winding-sheet, laid upon a plank and heavy weights attached. Mrs. Emerson [i.e., Lawrence] and Minnie sat in their camp-chairs at the head; the men, with uncovered heads, stood in a circle about their comrade; while the captain read the burial service. Then the remains were lifted to the railing and in silence committed to the deep."—Brown, *A Good Catch*, pp. 255–56.

24. Trade winds.

25. It was necessary to wait for the *Pele* to bring the *Addison* alongside a wharf for repairs. Part of Captain Lawrence's business ashore was to arrange twenty days of shore berthing at the Seamen's Home for the crew so that the ship could be hove down. He also visited Consul Abner Pratt this same day to protest the damages to the ship for insurance purposes, taking with him as witnesses Heughan, Manuel, Conroy, and Leighton. The consul appointed an inspection board of two ship captains and a shipwright to board the *Addison* the following day. There they found that eight square feet of the larboard bow were broken in; then they delayed the amplification of the report until the area was out of water. When this occurred, they estimated damages at $3,000.00. The ship was hove down for two weeks while repairs were made. Damages recovered from four insurance companies in the New Bedford area totaled $3,324.47. During

this period Mrs. Lawrence's cabin was painted and varnished, and new tableware and a new brass lamp for the cabin were purchased. Protest, inspection reports, miscellaneous invoices, *Addison* account book, agent's account book in Deacon Isaac Bailey Richmond Papers, property of Carleton R. Richmond, Little Compton, Rhode Island.

26. The following day the *Addison* shipped 11,317 pounds of bone home aboard the *Sky Lark*, Benjamin A. Follansbee, master. On October 29, 34,432 gallons of whale oil and 105 gallons of sperm oil were shipped home aboard the *West Wind*, Allen Baxter, master. Bills of lading in Richmond Papers.

FIFTH CRUISE

1. But George Bowman states that she leaked quite badly on her cruise home. See Seventh Cruise, n. 21.

2. Presumably Mrs. Lawrence's differences with Mr. Damon were resolved at this time.

3. Also during this period Paul Joseph da Sylveira, or "Joe Portuguee," was in quite serious trouble and had a fort bill of $20.00. Boatsteerer Antone Jacinto was ill, apparently with a venereal disease, and on the return of the *Addison* from Mexico the doctor's bill included "clap mixture, $3.50." It was also necessary to buy a truss for boatsteerer Heughan and to have a number of teeth extracted among the crewmen. Miscellaneous bills and invoices in Deacon Isaac Bailey Richmond Papers, property of Carleton R. Richmond, Little Compton, Rhode Island.

4. The *Rajah* was wrecked on the northwest end of Big Shantar Island because of a navigational error. She broke up in less than five minutes. *The Friend, devoted to Temperance, Seamen, Marine and General Intelligence*, VIII, 93 (December 4, 1858).

5. That is, on the New Zealand sperm whaling ground.

6. Here Mrs. Lawrence uses a local New England name for the hard-shelled round clam.

7. During January and February the *Addison* received 1,661 pounds of beef, 128 pounds of cheese, 60 pounds of raisins, and 3 sacks of figs, for which she traded 6 gallons of turpentine, 1 whaleboat, 29 assorted shirts, 2 pounds of tobacco, 38 pounds of coffee, 65 pounds of sugar, 1 pound of thread, 2 gallons of paint oil, 4 sheath knives, 556 yards of bleached cotton, 410 yards of blue drill, and 727 yards of assorted calico. *Addison* account book in Richmond Papers.

8. Careful accounts were kept of this mating, which seems to have included the *Scotland*. Oil taken and equipment expended were accounted for exactly. Captain Samuel Lawrence's slop book, Falmouth Historical Society, Falmouth, Massachusetts.

9. Edward Leighton and John Jones, who were paid $10.00 extra wages for this service. Agent's account book in Richmond Papers.

10. "Many were the good times the children had together. They played with their dolls and kittens, the little pigs and chickens, washed, ironed, made pies and kept house generally, just as children do on the land; only they could not go and come to one another so readily: they had to time their visits back and forth by the convenience of each 'captain-papa.' When whales were around, they must content themselves with hoisting flags and shaking handkerchiefs; but when a leisure day occurred, they

were ready for a meeting."—Mrs. Helen E. Brown, *A Good Catch; or, Mrs. Emerson's Whaling-Cruise* (Philadelphia: Presbyterian Board of Publication, 1884), p. 259.

11. Steward Henry Drew was fined $2.00 on February 20, according to Captain Lawrence's slop book. Since this does not correspond with the dates of his later offense (see the entries for February 28–March 2, 1859), it seems likely that Captain Lawrence meant January 20.

12. " 'These trees are a species of mangrove growing down almost under water or where they can be covered at high water. The oysters cling to the branches.' "—Brown, *A Good Catch*, p. 262.

13. "After dinner the little people had a merry time scampering about, playing tag, picking up shells and making mounds of sand and pebbles, which they adorned with the pretty flowers that luxuriantly grew all about them; the ladies strolled along the beach and talked: a promenade was pleasant after being limited for a walk to a ship's length for months . . ." —Brown, *A Good Catch*, p. 264.

14. "But he [Captain May] knew that the island [*sic*] was infested with savage little coyotes—animals resembling the prairie-wolf—and that in all probability they would be drawn shoreward by the scent of food. A bright fire, however, would keep them at a safe distance; so they piled on the brush and sat down to tell stories."—Brown, *A Good Catch*, p. 270.

15. Five bomb lances each were used on this and the next whale. Slop book.

16. The wives were usually swung up on deck by a chair rigged to the cutting tackle. But the ladies here clamber up and down the ship's rope ladder in their bulky clothing to avoid interfering with the whaling work.

17. Note in Captain Lawrence's slop book: "Used nine bombs in the whale that run out of the passage. Used four in the whale that Mr. Higgins struck that come to the *Addison* January 26."

18. Captain Lawrence bought a bottle of sarsaparilla from the *Scotland* for seventy-five cents. Slop book.

19. " 'These trunks of trees are thrown down by the wind where the tide washes over them every day; the little fishes are lodged in the hollow, decayed centres, and there grow. They are under water half the time, so they can live and flourish. I know of no other explanation.' "—Brown, *A Good Catch*, p. 264.

20. To rid it of vermin.

21. In addition to whatever compassion Captain Jernegan may have felt, there was a practical reason for this. A whaler carried a minimum number of men, and every hand was needed. The loss of these deserters would be felt severely aboard ship.

SIXTH CRUISE

1. Hominy.

2. Mrs. Lawrence wrote May 1, but it has been corrected to June by the editor.

3. James 1:4.

4. From this date until July 28 Mrs. Lawrence's figures are in error. They have been corrected by the editor.

5. Mrs. Lawrence dated this entry August 1. In the following entry she corrects herself and then redates this entry July 31.

6. Each whaling captain had a set of signal flags that was used to give

instructions and information to the whaleboat crews from the masthead lookouts of his ship. The signal flags of the *Addison* were of red calico. The code for the signals was kept secret to avoid passing valuable information to nearby competitors. The following code, originally written on blue paper in Mary Lawrence's handwriting, was found tucked separately into Captain Samuel Lawrence's slop book, Falmouth Historical Society, Falmouth, Massachusetts, by the editor. Separate documents of secret signal codes such as this one of Captain Lawrence's are rarities in whaling collections:

"Fore—Whales are up.
Main—Whales to windward.
Mizen—Whales to leeward.
Peak—Come to, or towards, the ship.
Fore and Peak—More whales in sight.
Fore and Main—Whales ahead.
Fore and Mizen—A boat fast.
Main and Mizen—Whales astern.
Mizen and Peak—Boats far enough.
Main and Peak—More to the right.
Main, Mizen, and Peak—More to the left.
1/2 Mast Peak—One boat come on board.
All three Mastheads—All come on board."

7. Interlineation: "Bakers."

8. In a calm whales gallied easily. Also when there was a suitable breeze, the whaleboats often boated their oars and sailed in for the kill. The *Addison's* boats might be recognized by their blue sails. Slop book.

9. See entry for November 27, 1856.

10. Captain Benjamin B. Lamphier of the *Lagoda*. His death is recorded in Alexander Starbuck, *History of the American Whale Fishery from its Earliest Inception to the Year 1876* (2 vols.; New York: Argosy-Antiquarian, Ltd., 1964), II, 502–3.

11. See Appendix A for the *Addison's* take.

12. The *Addison* shipped home 5,620 pounds of bone aboard the *Black Sea*, David Cate, master, on November 5, 1859. Bills of lading in Richmond Papers.

13. The king was Kamehameha IV (Alexander Liholiho), the governor was Kekuanoa, and the princess was Victoria Kamamalu Kaahumanu.

14. Mr. Damon printed the following report of his death in *The Friend, devoted to Temperance, Seamen, Marine and General Intelligence*, VIII, 88 (November 1, 1859):

"Drowned, May 20th, in the Okhotsk Sea, off Jones Island, Capt. Palmer, master of the ship *Kingfisher*. He was taken out of the boat by the line while making efforts to save a man who was swimming nearby, but supposed to be in danger. Capt. Palmer leaves a wife and two children. Having been intimately acquainted with Capt. Palmer and his estimable wife, we do most deeply sympathize with her, in view of this most unlooked for providence. They were inmates of our family a few months since, Capt. Palmer leaving his wife with us when he sailed for the Okhotsk. She subsequently left for Hilo. He was an able and efficient master, and a most worthy man." Captain Tallman, whose death is also noted in this entry of Mrs. Lawrence's journal, was buried at Ayan on August 5, 1859, by an Orthodox priest, as noted in the same issue of *The Friend*.

15. See entry for March 12, 1858.

16. A memorial to him was placed in the Oak Grove Cemetery in Falmouth, Massachusetts, where it may still be seen.

17. The Swiss bell ringers performed at the Royal School on October 22, 1859, and *The Friend*, VIII, 85 (November 1, 1859), took a benign attitude toward the entertainment, "although somewhat Puritanic in our notions." However, Professor Anderson's performance was quite another matter. The following article entitled, "Deception Highly Prized," voiced the displeasure of *The Friend*, VIII, 92 (December 1, 1859):

"A certain writer has remarked that there is nothing so gratifying, and for which people will more readily pay their money, than for being deceived. The late visit of Mr. Anderson, the Magician, is a good illustration of this remark. Our people, from the merchant to the porter, are complaining of the hard times and little money in circulation, which is doubtless true; now just see what the good people of Honolulu did a few days ago. A vessel arrives from Australia *en route* for San Francisco. Professor Anderson comes on shore and announces himself a great deceiver. He frankly tells the people so; still the poor people, complaining of the hard times, club together, pay the Master demurrage on his vessel, say $1000—pay Professor Anderson, above all expenses, say $1000—pay all expenses, say another $1000. At the very lowest estimate, the poor and simple people of Honolulu, *these hard times*, pay $3000 for being cleverly deceived one week!"

SEVENTH CRUISE

1. George Bowman disagrees on the sailing date, claiming that on the second of December the wind was unfavorable, delaying the *Addison* until the fifth. George Bowman, Journal, December 2, 6, 1859, Nicholson Collection, Providence Public Library, Providence, Rhode Island.

2. The *Lagoda* was one of the most famous whalers, primarily because her cruises were consistently profitable. A one-half scale model of her can be seen at the Old Dartmouth Historical Society whaling museum at New Bedford, Massachusetts.

3. "This day we are keeping as a Sabbath, no unnecessary work being done. The object of keeping this day for Sunday is this: at Aitutake they are one day ahead of the right time; and as we shall be there by night and we intend to recruit some here, and if we keep our Sabbath too, we shall have here one day more (but I think that it is a very wrong thing to shift the days so as to suit our convenience). At 10:30 A.M. Aitutake, one of the Friendly [Cook] Islands group, about seventeen miles distant." —Bowman, Journal, December 31, 1859.

4. The transcription of this sentence is uncertain. The *Addison* received wood, hogs, refreshments, and the services of 3 boats and crews, for which they traded 700 or 800 yards of cloth, 3 boxes of soap, 1 old chest, 8 buckets, 1 lot of thread and needles, and 2 pairs of shoes. *Addison* account book in Deacon Isaac Bailey Richmond Papers, property of Carleton R. Richmond, Little Compton, Rhode Island.

5. See entry for February 20, 1857.

6. ". . . felt quite a shock of a earthquake; the effect which it had upon the ship was like a vessel going over a sunken shoal, but strange to relate the shock was not felt aloft by those that were aloft."—Bowman, Journal, January 19, 1860.

7. Anna Read Chipman. See Appendix D.

8. This circumstance gave rise to a family legend that the three brothers had met aboard the *James Arnold*. Amelia Lawrence's genealogical notes in papers of Lewis Lawrence, grandson of Samuel Lawrence's brother, Lewis Henry Lawrence, Falmouth Historical Society, Falmouth, Massachusetts.

9. "The air beginning to grow quite chilly. We all get along together first rate; everything appears to go along smooth."—Bowman, Journal, January 29, 1860. But see also Seventh Cruise, nn. 14 and 23, which give contrary evidence.

10. That is, the ship in sight bore the signal flag of Jonathan Bourne, Jr. He was the agent for both the *Marengo* and the *Washington*. Each whaling agent required his ships to bear an identifying flag, which was listed with those flags of other whaling agents in books carried by the whaling captains. The signal flag for Jonathan Bourne can be found in William C. Taber, Jr., *New Bedford, Fairhaven, and Dartmouth Signal Book* (New Bedford: William C. Taber, Jr., 1855) and in other versions of this book published near the time of the Civil War.

11. "I went on board and there found an old shipmate (John Green), where I took a watch and writing desk to carry home for him."—Bowman, Journal, February 22, 1860.

John Green and Bowman were shipmates on the *Hobomuk*, of Falmouth. During an attack on a whale Bowman's boat was upset, and he was being dragged under to his death, caught around the feet by a line, when John Green rescued him. Bowman made God a "promise" on the spot, but on April 7, 1860, he wrote in his journal, ". . . it being just five years today since . . . I formed a resolution, but alas, alas, I have broken it." Theodate Geoffrey (pseud.), *Suckanesset; wherein may be read a History of Falmouth, Massachusetts* (Falmouth: Falmouth Publishing Co., 1930), p. 126.

12. Interlineation: "The *Rambler* brought them all home to New Bedford and sent them to Minnie." The following account of the episode appeared in *The Friend, devoted to Temperance, Seamen, Marine and General Intelligence*, IX, 17 (March 1, 1861), entitled "Minnie's Pigeons":

"About eighteen months ago, Capt. Lawrence, of the whaleship *Addison*, touched at Honolulu on his homeward passage. Capt. L. was accompanied by his wife and little daughter, Minnie. The latter took away some pigeons but we never expected to hear they had reached the United States. The following paragraph from a letter written by Mrs. L., and dated Falmouth, Mass., Dec. 3d, 1860, will be read with interest:

" 'I will give Frank an account of Minnie's pigeons now, as I have nearly filled my sheet. After we had kept them confined in their house nearly a month, we let them out. They were very tame, and would fly all around the ship aloft; by and by they flew off quite a distance, and then returned. Afterwards, whenever we spoke a ship, they would all go on board to make a call, then fly back again. Well, one day, when we were off New Zealand, we spoke the *Rambler*, they all flew aboard, and about that time a strong breeze sprung up; we watched for a long time, they did not come back, and we thought they were lost. Minnie mourned for them very much! On the arrival of the *Rambler* in New Bedford several weeks after our arrival, judge of our surprise to receive a box containing two of them. One had died on the passage. Capt. Lawrence made a house for them, where we kept them some time. In the course of the summer we let them out again, but we saw nothing of them for nearly a week, until one morning Cousin Willie came with one in a basket which he said flew around his grandmother's house in search of food. We told him to keep a good look out, for perhaps the other one might come too—and sure enough that night he came with the other. We confined them again for a few days, then let them go. Now they come and go at their own free will, sleeping in their own house every night—and a few days ago they brought another one home with them. Minnie thinks one of them has taken a wife!' "

13. "[It was] quite a treat for them to come on board of a ship, as there has not been one here for twelve months. Peaches and apples is quite plenty, but very high price for them. The land around here is quite mountainous. The anchorage is about five miles from the entrance of the bay, the bay being (I should judge) from one to one and a half miles wide. The town is quite small; I was informed [that it] contained about four or five hundred whites, mostly English, although it was first settled by the French. The white people live mostly on one side of the bay and the Maoris on the other side of the bay, the English government allowing them a certain tract of land, but are subjects to the English government."— Bowman, Journal, February 26, 1860.

14. "At 8 A.M. made a bone pen between decks and commenced to break out a few barrels of oil in order to see if we could not find a cask that leaked, but the men forward (the cruisers) refused to break it out (and one boatsteerer). They were all called, or rather sent, aft, where they, the captain and first officer, undertook to seize a man's hands behind him; but as he made some resistance, he fell to the deck, and then the men forward interfered, crying out 'fair play.' One or two of them had an engagement with the first officer. A few blows were exchanged but without much effect. But when told that a few hours work would finish the job, and after a short time they were called to the main hatch that were going to work (they having gone forward a few moments previous to this), and they all immediately turned to and went to work. But it is my firm opinion that if the case had been properly stated to them and asked to go to work, and after five minutes considering that, every man would have gone to work.

"The first mix commenced around the forehatch between an officer and one of the men, when the man immediately seized an axe and the officer took a stick of wood out of the deck pot, and then the captain came forward. The second mate and two boatsteerers (William Heughan and Edward Leighton) were called out of the lower hold, I being on deck at the time. At 10 A.M. finished stowing back the oil, finding no leak."— Bowman, Journal, February 26, 1860.

15. Probably one of the French settlers who arrived in Akaroa in 1840 to colonize the area. But the British claimed it a few days before their arrival.

16. A Turkish sea and island. Probably here the name of the French lady's estate.

17. Interlineation: "pair."

18. "This day commenced with fine breezes. Employed the fore part in sailing about the harbor with Mr. Green, fourth officer of the ship *Marengo*. At 8 A.M. opened the slop cask and sold one boat from overhead to the Maoris and received two ton of potatoes for it. At 9 the Captain and Mrs. Captain Lawrence went ashore."—Bowman, Journal, February 29, 1860.

19. For 2 tons of potatoes and various other items from A. White & Co.

and J. Poinker Co. Captain Lawrence traded 192 pounds of towline, 2 old boats, 2 frocks, 2 thick pants, 4 assorted shirts, and 2 pairs of shoes. *Addison* account book in Richmond Papers.

20. L. N. R. (Ellen Henrietta [White] Ranyard), *The Book and Its Story: A Narrative for the Young on Occasion of the Jubilee of the British and Foreign Bible Society,* Introductory Preface by T. Phillips (London: Kent, 1853); and Charlotte Elizabeth (Mrs. Charlotte Elizabeth [Browne] Phelan Tonna), *Judah's Lion* (New York: John S. Taylor and Co., 1843). The first, the nature of which is self-explanatory, sold tens of thousands of copies and went through many editions. The second is a typical tractarian novel which builds on a picaresque plot of a voyage from England to Palestine, an extended theological dispute leading to the conversion of the protagonist from Judaism to Christianity.

21. "Ship leaking about twenty-five strokes per hour [of the hand-operated bilge pump] with a fresh breeze when before the wind, but when on the wind and carrying sail, she increases the leak all of one half."– Bowman, Journal, March 29, 1860.

22. "Note: at the commencement of this day Miss Minnie presented me with a pair of garters which she has been to work on for about one month." –Bowman, Journal, March 31, 1860.

23. "I begin to feel quite dissatisfied on account of there being so little discipline on board of this ship. I find it is useless for one officer to try. A single cord may be broken, but twist several of them together and it will be hard to part them. I am now reading a book called *The Voices of the Dead* by the Rev. John Cumming, D.D., from whence I derive sweet consolation." –Bowman, Journal, April 4, 1860.

24. Whalemen thought that dogs had fits from staying on board ship too long without going ashore.

25. Mrs. Lawrence repeated the date of the preceding entry here; this and the following dates through May 10 have been corrected by the editor.

26. See entry for May 25, 1857.

27. Mark 7:37.

28. Following this entry Mrs. Lawrence wrote a brief entry, "Made 100 miles in twenty-four hours," which she dated May 10. The editor believes it to be a duplication of this entry and has omitted it.

29. In the entry in his journal for May 14, 1860, George Bowman writes of crossing the equator, but because he dates his journal from noon to noon, he is always twelve hours ahead of Mrs. Lawrence. Thus May 14 of his journal, for example, begins with events told in the afternoon and evening of May 13 in Mrs. Lawrence's journal.

30. "Employed the fore part in cleaning the mincing machine, and at 4 P.M. put the machine and deck pot down in the forehold. Latter part, employed cleaning the spades and trypots.

"At 3 P.M. scraped down the foretopmast. . . . Employed the latter part breaking out ship's stores and painting ship outside."–Bowman, Journal, May 15, 17, 1860.

31. "We shall not be able to paint the ship all over inside, on account of being short of paint oil to mix the paints with."–Bowman, Journal, May 21, 1860.

32. "Painting the monkey rail white, the waterway lead color, and the bulwarks kind of a yellowish color."–Bowman, Journal, May 22, 1860.

33. "At 4 P.M. the sailors went in swimming, having ropes over the ship's sides to prevent getting astern of the ship."—Bowman, Journal, May 23, 1860.

34. "Finished painting this afternoon, having mixed all the oil."—Bowman, Journal, May 25, 1860.

35. "A needless Alexandrine ends the song,
    That, like a wounded snake, drags its slow length along."
    —ALEXANDER POPE, Essay on Criticism, Part II, l. 142

36. Perhaps pale flounder.

37. "At 9 A.M. the pilot came on board, Mr. Allen (a Vineyard pilot), from the schooner Hornet. This night I had eight hours in, but slept but little. I appeared to be very restless when I came to realize the nearness of my native home after an absence of forty-two and a half months. All hands appear to be very lively; all hardships and toils is soon forgotten. The latter part of this day is my watch below, but sleep appears to have deserted my eyes. 10 A.M. With a good breeze eight hours will take us up to the wharf, but it is now but a light air."—Bowman, Journal, June 13, 1860.

38. Added to the end of the journal, probably by Minnie: "Journal of Mrs. Samuel Lawrence. Confirmation. She arrived to hear in New Bedford of the death of her father, Jonathan E. Chipman, of consumption several months before, which the papers had given her before. His death is recorded on page 28 [of the second volume of the manuscript journal in the entry for November 1 through 30, 1859]. She first heard of it on reading a paper in November."

EPILOGUE

1. See Appendix A.

2. George Bowman, Journal, July 7, 1861, Nicholson Collection, Providence Public Library, Providence, Rhode Island. Bowman apparently did not set down the events of the last day of the voyage in his journal until more than a year later. George Chipman's residence in New Bedford is recorded in the New Bedford directories from 1856 to 1860 in the New Bedford Free Public Library, New Bedford, Massachusetts. Mrs. Lawrence mentions his residence there in her journal in the entries for January 12, March 12, 1858, and August 20, 1859. See also Mrs. Helen E. Brown, A Good Catch; or, Mrs. Emerson's Whaling-Cruise (Philadephia: Presbyterian Board of Publication, 1884), p. 288.

3. Brown, A Good Catch, p. 289.

4. Barnstable (Massachusetts) Patriot, July 10, 1860.

5. The Friend, devoted to Temperance, Seamen, Marine and General Intelligence, IX, 22(March 1, 1860). The article, written by "J. F. B. Marshall, Esq.," from Boston and dated December 2, 1859, was quoted from the Pacific Coast Advertiser, San Francisco.

6. Information about the Lawrences' wartime activities comes from references in letters from Charles Chipman to his wife, Elizabeth Gibbs Chipman, written during the Civil War, especially those of August 22, September 7, 11, November 6, 7, 1861; February 6, April 18, 24, 1862; and October 17, 1863. Also among the letters is a half-finished one intended for his wife and dated August 8, 1864, the day he was killed in

battle at Petersburg. All the letters are property of Francis Freeman Jones, Palo Alto, California. Samuel Lawrence's will, dated September 11, 1862, is in the public records of Barnstable County, Barnstable County Courthouse, Barnstable, Massachusetts. Captain Lawrence's new ship command is recorded in Amelia Lawrence's genealogical notes in papers of Lewis Lawrence, grandson of Samuel Lawrence's brother, Lewis Henry Lawrence, Falmouth Historical Society, Falmouth, Massachusetts (Lewis Lawrence Papers).

7. The events leading to the demise of the whaling era are generally known. However, the editor relied, primarily, on the material in the Introduction to Alexander Starbuck, *History of the American Whale Fishery from its Earliest Inception to the Year 1876* (2 vols.; Argosy-Antiquarian, Ltd., 1964), I, 100–9, in particular.

8. The historical statistics for the *Addison* are given in *Ship Registers of New Bedford, Massachusetts,* compiled by The Survey of Federal Archives, Division of Professional and Service Projects, Work Projects Administration (3 vols.; Boston: The National Archives Project, 1940), II, 4; also information was supplied by Edouard A. Stackpole, curator of Mystic Seaport, Mystic, Connecticut.

9. Journal entries for December 26, 1857; January 12, 1858; March 14, 1858; August 18, 1859; and January 20, 1860; obituary for Thomas Lawrence, Falmouth (Massachusetts) *Enterprise,* September 26, 1896; whalemen's shipping paper for the *Ohio,* Melville Whaling Room, New Bedford Free Public Library, New Bedford, Massachusetts; obituary for Lewis Henry Lawrence, Falmouth *Enterprise,* December 7, 1901; Lewis Lawrence Papers, including also two deeds, one dated August 20, 1880, the other April 14, 1896; Brooklyn directories from 1882 to 1908 in the Brooklyn Public Library, Brooklyn, New York.

10. The following obituaries for Samuel and Mary Lawrence appeared in local Massachusetts papers:

"Capt. Samuel Lawrence, aged 74, died of asthma at Brooklyn, on Sunday night. He was born in Falmouth, Mass., and was one of the best known shipmasters in New York. When quite young he commanded a New Bedford whaling ship. He entered the employ of the Old Dominion Steamship Company many years ago, and at various times had command of many of their vessels. Of later years Capt. Lawrence did shore duty for the company, and was one of the oldest shipmasters in that line. He leaves a widow and one daughter. The body will be taken to Falmouth for interment."—Barnstable *Patriot,* September 20, 1892.

"Mrs. Mary (Chipman), widow of the late Capt. Samuel Lawrence, formerly of this town, died at her home in Brooklyn, N.Y., March 3, age 78 years. Interment was in Oak Grove cemetery, this town, Mar. 6. Prayer was offered at the grave by Rev. M. S. Stocking of the M. E. church. Mrs. Lawrence is remembered by many in Falmouth as a lady of strong Christian character and by her deeds of love and charity endeared herself to all who knew her.

"Mrs. Lawrence is survived by one daughter, Miss Minnie C. Lawrence of Brooklyn, and one brother, William Chipman of Middleboro. Mr. and Mrs. Thomas H. Lawrence of Brooklyn, and and [sic] William Chipman accompanied the remains to this town."—"Death of Mrs. Samuel Lawrence," Falmouth *Enterprise,* March 10, 1906.

11. Theodate Geoffrey (pseud.), *Suckanesset; wherein may be read a*

History of Falmouth, Massachusetts (Falmouth: Falmouth Publishing Co., 1930), p. 126.

12. The description of Minnie Lawrence and some facts of her life come from conversations with Francis Freeman Jones and from the following obituary. The editor considers the obituary unreliable in several instances in which the newspaper editor apparently relied on hearsay reports and perhaps information from Brown, *A Good Catch:*

"A lovable character was summoned to the Great Beyond in the death yesterday afternoon of Miss Minnie Chippendale Lawrence. The end came after a long illness from heart trouble. She had reached the advanced age of 72 years. A native of Massachusetts, she was born at Sandwich, that state, July 8, 1851, being the daughter of Captain and Mrs. Samuel Lawrence.

"After many years spent in Brooklyn Miss Lawrence had for 12 years been a resident of Mohawk, where she had endeared herself to a large circle of friends by her fine character and charming personality. Possessed of knowledge of a wide scope, much of which she had attained through personal contact and observation, she was an excellent raconteur and highly interesting in relating her personal experiences and observations.

"Miss Lawrence's father was the captain of a whaling vessel in the days before the leviathan of the deep was pursued by a steam driven vessel and dispatched with a bomb harpoon shot from a gun.

"Miss Lawrence made many voyages with her father, both to the Arctic and the Sandwich Islands in pursuit of whales. Of these voyages she still had most vivid recollections of the lookout from the crow's nest awaking the calm of the prosaic everyday life on shipboard with his "There she blows," followed by the direction from the ship in which he had seen the whale break from the deep and spout.

"Almost simultaneous with the lookout's alarm came the slap of the lowered boats striking the water, for in those days there was a prize to the crew of the first boat launched, as well as for the first "iron" (harpoon) driven into the unsuspecting whale. Then followed the excitement of the chase continued until the boat crews had to abandon the whale to save their own lives after having been towed for miles and lost overnight to be picked up next day; or the final killing of the exhausted monster, which sometimes in its death struggles wrecked the boats, injuring and maiming the crews.

"More cheerful were her stories of the nights aboard ship when the skies were lighted by the fires under the kettles, rendering the blubber, at which the men as they worked recounted tales of their daring exploits on other whaling trips to which she was a thrilled and breathless listener.

"Miss Lawrence on her father's ship organized a Sunday school class among the crew, which gained for the ship a unique distinction.

"Miss Lawrence was a poetess and author of note and cherished her personal acquaintance with the author Joseph C. Lincoln.

"The nearest surviving relatives were cousins, one Mrs. F. F. Jones of New Bedford, Mass., being with her at the end.

"The funeral is held privately from the home tomorrow. Rev. A. B. Boynton will officiate. Burial will be made at Falmouth, Mass."—"Mohawk Woman as Child Made Whaling Trips: Lovable Character Lost In Passing of Miss Minnie Lawrence—Poetess and Author Had Wide Circle of Friends," Herkimer (New York) *Evening Telegram*, April 10, 1923.

INDEX

INDEX OF WHALESHIPS AND
THEIR CAPTAINS MENTIONED
IN THE JOURNAL

Abraham Barker, ship, New Bedford (Mass.), George W. Slocum, 130, 131

Adeline, ship, New Bedford (Mass.), Asa Taber, 135

Alto, bark, New Bedford (Mass.), Thomas H. Lawrence, 78, 183, 214

America, ship, New Bedford (Mass.), Charles R. Bryant, 89, 92, 107, 114, 116, 117, 186–87, 193–94

Amethyst, ship, New Bedford (Mass.), William F. Jones, 52(?), 60

Anderson, Matthew. See *Fortune*

Andrews. See *Francis*

Antilla, brig, Bremen (Germany), Molde, 93, 145, 147, 155

Arab, ship, Fairhaven (Mass.), Edwin Grinnell, 165, 175, 189

Arnolda, ship, New Bedford (Mass.), Andrew S. Sarvent, 107

Ashley, Edward R. See *Reindeer*

Athearn, George. See *Hercules*

Augusta, bark, Sag Harbor (N.Y.), James M. Taber, 165, 166

Austin. See *Goethe*

Austin. See *Harmony*

Austin, James L. See *William Tell*

Awashonks, ship, Falmouth (Mass.), Augustus Lawrence, 115

Baker, Daniel. See *Ohio*

Baker, Hiram. See *Ocean Wave*

Baker, Nehemiah P. See *William Gifford*

Baltic, bark, New Bedford (Mass.), L. B. Brownson, 29, 100, 113, 115, 120, 124

Barber, Albert D. See *Benjamin Tucker*

Barker, Henry P. See *Pioneer*

Barnstable, ship, New Bedford (Mass.), Nehemiah C. Fisher, 51

Bartholomew Gosnold, ship, New Bedford (Mass.), George H. Clark, 179, 182, 188

Belle, bark, Fairhaven (Mass.), Roswell Brown, 213

Benjamin Morgan, ship, New London (Conn.), Sisson, 47, 195

Benjamin Rush, ship, Warren (R.I.), Wyatt, 35, 150

Benjamin Tucker, ship, New Bedford (Mass.), Albert D. Barber, 44, 45, 79, 85, 100, 102, 103, 104, 105, 106, 107, 108, 109, 111, 123, 128, 129

Black Eagle, bark, Sag Harbor (N.Y.), Edwards, 51, 54

Black Warrior, bark, Honolulu (S.I.), Robert Brown, 124–25, 146

Booker, William. See *Hibernia*

Braganza, ship, New Bedford (Mass.), Andrew Jackson, 102, 115

Bragg, James G. See *Caravan*

Brown, John. See *Enterprise*

Brown, Robert. See *Black Warrior*

Brown, Roswell. See *Belle*

Brownson, L. B. See *Baltic*

Bryant, Charles R. See *America*

Caravan, ship, New Bedford (Mass.), James G. Bragg, 90, 92, 104, 105, 106, 176, 177

Carib, bark, San Francisco (Calif.), Reynolds, 141, 155

Caroline, bark, Greenport (N.Y.), Pontus, 165

Caulaincourt, Le Havre (France), Labaste, 101, 112, 113, 115, 128

Champion, ship, Edgartown (Mass.), Coffin, 87, 88–89, 91, 112, 113, 175, 176, 177

Chapel, Edward A. See *Northern Light*

Charles Caroll, ship, New London (Conn.), William J. Parsons, 38, 39–40

Chatfield, Thomas. See *Massachusetts*

Chester, A. C. See *Majestic*

Childs, Peter E. See *William Thompson*

Christopher Mitchell, ship, New Bedford (Mass.), Edward Manchester, 95, 96, 99, 113, 175, 192

Cincinnati, ship, Stonington (Conn.), F. Stanton Williams, 24, 35

Clark, George H. See *Bartholomew Gosnold*

Cleaveland, Jacob L. See *Julian*

Cleone, bark, New Bedford (Mass.), John E. Simmons, 40, 175, 182, 189, 191, 192

Coffin. See *Champion*

Coggeshall, Edward. See *Silver Cloud*

INDEX

INDEX

INDEX

INDEX